A Section of Now

I0811680

A Section of Now: Social Norms and Rituals as Sites for Architectural Intervention

Canadian Centre for Architecture
Spector Books

TABLE OF CONTENTS

Ownership: Do you own, rent, or subscribe to your housing? How many people are you willing to share a kitchen with?

Life Cycles: What will you do if you live to 100? Do you know how you were conceived?

Family: Does your family fit into the standard single-family home? When was the last time you received a hug?

Giovanna Borasi
Attention to New Sites for Architecture

The relation between society and architecture has always existed. Societal transformations have inspired architectural interventions to house our rituals, norms, and cultural patterns—architecture mirrors our collective values. However, the rates of transformation undergone by society and architecture respectively are no longer in sync, and parts of contemporary life are misaligned with the spaces they occupy. As architecture is also at times instrumental in perpetuating and embedding inequalities in our built environment, we could end up living in spaces framed by societal values that no longer represent a shared vision of who we are.

The built environment conditions the ways we live. So how could we imagine ways for architecture to become a more attuned platform for society to exist upon? A real act of listening and a continuous search for sites to intervene could allow architecture and the built environment to respond more aptly to, and at times anticipate, our changing set of needs. To do so, it is crucial for all the actors—not just architects—to constantly observe how society evolves, not in an opportunistic way, to satiate the latest market trends, but instead as an act of care.

Many shifts occurred in the last decades that radically modified the way we understand what living is, and how to organize and ultimately support it. Taken all together, these shifts continue to change the very way we live. We are now more than ever in control (or so we perceive) of our ability to design and influence the nature of our life cycle. Thanks to advancements in medical treatments, and to healthier routines organized around better food and exercise, we have generally doubled our life span. And more people than ever live alone—one reason being that, as we tend to live longer, we may lose our life companion on the path and face more years of dwelling alone. We also divorce more, and economic development is allowing women to enter the labour market and provide for themselves sooner, instead of going straight into wedding and family-creation as *the* way to get out from their parents' houses. The traditional family itself, as the most recurrent bonding "network," is becoming less and less the relevant and referential model, at least in Western society.

Science is supporting family creation beyond the conventional limits of age and gender, and regardless of whether there are one, two, or more parents. As an answer to environmental threats associated with global overpopulation, as well as to perceived positive existential outcomes of not procreating, some societies and individuals are committing to a child-free lifestyle, while others are still embracing families with many kids. Further, the idea of love has become a more complex set of layered and fluid sentiments and forms that range from sexual love, to romance, to friendship, to kinship. It is not that love was ever simple or uniform, but certain modes of love—take "free love" for instance—that used to manifest as cultural movements distinct from the mainstream ethos have now become a commonplace way of life. On top of that transition, there are, in technologies like dating apps, entirely new ways to bring about and mediate love relationships.

These desires for new forms of living and potential new forms of aggregation—together with other radical changes that touch our societal, economic, environmental, and technological paradigms—constitute a call from society at large to architects and designers to devise spatial arrangements and strategies that could support these new and diverse conceptions of living. For instance, in the last decade, we have witnessed an exponential growth of shared living models (which are certainly also pressured by economic forces), such as multi-generational housing, social or co-housing for groups of elderly people or various other socio-economic groups, and alternative housing models that aim to mitigate debt. Overall, society is asking for a more equitable distribution of wealth and resources—for a less hierarchized and more transparent world.

Giovanna Borasi

Dafydd Jones, *Screen Time*, 2010

These societal shifts have led to such variations and proliferations of ways of life that they have by necessity led also to polarities. As the many desires and questions posed by society cannot be characterized as unidirectional, it is certain that a set of general and univocal answers will neither be possible nor desired. It is a lot for architects to grapple with. And these considerations are ultimately added to all the other technical, ecological, financial, legal, pedagogical, and cultural preoccupations architecture has already to figure out inside its own discipline and practice. Yet, in a sense, such considerations are *inherent* to architecture's own discipline and practice, and it is better for architecture not to see them as extraneous.

Royal mail postwoman at the front door of a house, delivering mail to a customer. Photograph: Peter Titmuss

The best architectural approach is indeed the one that tries to understand these issues (this could be called an expanded idea of "context") without responding literally to them. We have seen[1] when it comes to health issues, for example, that it is in fact very dangerous if architecture tries to play a role similar to that of the medical discipline in attempting to be part of the cure. Simply put, staircases could not be *the* solution to the obesity epidemic—fighting one illness might create a societal divide with those who experience others. Architecture should be cautious not to adopt a similarly bellicose approach, and endeavour to care, and not cure. This means being aware of the context, understood as the sum of the forces at play, both immediately on a site and in our broader and ever-changing cultural, social, and economic conditions. Architecture should suggest, as best it can, spatial organizations that support life, whatever it means now.

Solitude

In January 2018, British Prime Minister Theresa May created a new position in her cabinet: the Minister of Loneliness. Symbolic in nature, it pointed to a growing concern over chronic loneliness embedding itself into our societal fabric, with public health experts deeming it a looming epidemic.[2] Unlike gauging the claimed health of our economy, no metrics exist to measure the strength of our social bonds; an exact picture of our current moment remains murky. Countries globally have begun examining loneliness, as our present iteration of cultural patterns—aided by architecture—have created the conditions for us to grow apart.

One of the first acts from the British Loneliness Minister was partnering with the Royal Mail and asking postal workers to check up, during their usual delivery rounds, on those who may be lonely. Mail carriers speak with individuals and offer information on how to access support networks, but this new practice immediately raises spatial questions: where will they talk? Is there a comfortable space in front of their door that would be conducive for

1 Giovanna Borasi and Mirko Zardini, "Demedicalize Architecture," in *Imperfect Health*, eds. Giovanna Borasi and Mirko Zardini (Montreal: Canadian Centre for Architecture, 2012; Zurich: Lars Müller Publishers, 2012), 15–37.

2 Sarah Marsh, "Combat Loneliness with 'social prescribing', says Theresa May," *The Guardian*, October 14, 2018, https://www.theguardian.com/society/2018/oct/14/loneliness-social-prescribing-theresa-may.

this and similarly supportive social encounters to take place? Is there, in general, enough space outside of our homes to comfortably socialize?

It seems that scarce in our daily social lives is the element of chance encounters. Perhaps it is real estate's demand for spatial efficiency; or the increasing desire for more privatized spaces versus shared amenities; or a want for more safety in our physical environment; or the intensification of digital space in our daily lives; or the current generation of emerging architects' obsession with "rooms" (particularly as geometric and conceptual centres that temper the spatial hierarchy, and collapse the circulation in dwellings);[3] but some combination of forces has caused the gradual disappearance of transitional, neutral, thematically social spaces from architectural plans. Such spaces are some instances of what sociologist Ray Oldenburg deems the "third place" in his 1989 book, *The Great Good Place*. In contrast to home, the "first place," and work, "the second place," "third places," which along with intermediate and transitional spaces would include restaurants, cafés, book and video stores, and hair salons, provide space for neutral and democratic interaction. Oldenburg—and this was several decades ago—drew attention to a deficiency in deliberately designed third places in the modern world, particularly urban and suburban America, as compared to what we know of earlier historical periods and of other places in the world.[4]

Perhaps the only transitional zones that haven't been subject to diminishment are those that are functionally needed, such as elevators, or waiting rooms in doctors' offices and hospitals. In these spaces, conversations are now marred with suspicion and discomfort. The experience of shared space, when we do go there, is undeniably changed by the ubiquity of smartphones; portals into digital space. It seems natural that the places built to accommodate the diverse trajectories of myriads of individuals—subways, buses, platforms, lobbies, elevators, corridors, and galleries—should be teeming with conversation. But what we see now is a self-feeding loop that mitigates that potential: with more people in shared space only semi-present because they are also in digital space, it becomes less appealing and socially fruitful for one to be fully present oneself, in turn making digital space appear as a somewhat more entertaining or productive environment.

The thematization of liminal and intermediate spaces in big-tech architectures is a notable exception to the evidence of a slow and general erasure of such spaces in other typologies. The ever more common omission of spaces for interaction in housing complexes has corresponded, whether directly or indirectly, to a societal drifting-apart, a fraying of our social bonds. But the companies in

3 Giovanna Borasi, "Reframing How We Live," *Architecture and Urbanism* (July, 2021).

4 Ray Oldenburg, *The Great Good Place: Cafés, Coffee Shops, Bookstores, Bars, Hair Salons, and Other Hangouts at the Heart of a Community* (New York: Avalon, 1999), 17–18.

Silicon Valley that have retained and amplified these informal spaces—from a soaring open space for thousands of employees, to communal "garden floors" (entire floors devoted to verdant, open-air social space) between divisional floors, to replacing copious localized office coffee stations with several large cafés for company-wide use—are guided not by creating a sense of community, but by trying to increase the "collisions" that generate profitable ideas.[5]

Architecture is often complicit in the social draining of shared space. In most cities, the ground floors and lobbies of housing complexes have become efficient spaces for distribution. If there is a concierge, the lobby may be transformed into a terminal for receiving and holding packages purchased online. Some condominiums in cities like New York and Milan have installed technologies in their lobbies to notify homeowners of parcels and have equipped rooms with fridges for holding food deliveries.[6] Once a site to welcome, talk, and check in on each other, the lobby has become more overtly a security and logistics station, where the furniture is primarily decorative and social engagement is shaded with feelings of uneasiness. Reflecting on earlier examples of liminal space, the grand lobbies and mail rooms of Mies van der Rohe's towers, which once read as spaces of luxury, could now be read as having been conducive to building stronger social bonds. The ambiguity and undefined nature of these spaces fashioned an appropriate setting to nurture new relationships and entertain casual conversations, which are important facets to our social health. Comparing the spatial ambiguity of Mies van der Rohe's lobbies to the spatial (and increasingly technical) specificity of many new lobbies and vestibules, it becomes clear that architecture's support of rich social rituals is sometimes about spatially determining activity and other times about simply making space. Regular interactions with those on the periphery of our social network make us feel part of a larger community, but the gradual erasure of unprescribed spaces from our architectural lexicon has left us with less fertile ground. Architecture is the mise-en-scène in which our social lives unfold, discretely but actively shaping our social interactions. So, how can architecture care for its inhabitants, social animals that they are, in spatial terms?

More and more we witness the birth of new forms of improvised spaces to cope with isolation and loneliness, with makeshift flexible structures holding open a space to re-socialize architecture. Cuddling rooms—soft, horizontal architectures filled with couches, covered in cushions, and draped with blankets—welcome strangers who are there to be held or cuddled [Jamie Diamond, *Skin Hunger*, p. 320 and opposite]. Research on cuddling shows that it releases endorphins, dopamine, and oxytocin, which helps

5 Ben Waber, Jennifer Magnolfi, and Greg Lindsay, "Workspaces That Move People," *The Harvard Business Report*, October, 2014, https://hbr.org/2014/10/workspaces-that-move-people.

6 Paola Dezza, "La casa ai tempi di Amazon con il custode digitale," *Il Sole 24 ore*, February 20, 2019, https://www.ilsole24ore.com/art/la-casa-tempi-amazon-il-custode-digitale-ABnBicTB.

Jamie Diamond, *Skin Hunger (Cuddler Jackie, Queens, NY, $80)*, 2019

reduce stress and blood pressure, enables better sleep, improves communication between couples, and increases overall happiness and well-being.[7] As our lives take place more and more in the digital realm and our physical selves consequently become increasingly siloed off, our society heads deeper into in the midst of what Lucy McRae, sci-fi artist and body architect, posits is a "crisis of touch."[8] Her *Compression Carpet* [p. 326], a pinkish contraption requiring two people to operate, mechanically simulates a full-body embrace, and is conceived as an antidote to symptoms of this crisis. It is part of what McRae calls the *Future Survival Kit*, a larger collection of low-fi mechanical experiences she designed in response to our trajectory into greater submission to (and isolation in) the digital realm.

McRae's work identifies and runs in contradistinction to a pervasive irony: never more than now has our reliance on digital technology to fight physical isolation been as high. This tendency

7 India Morrison, "Keep Calm and Cuddle on: Social Touch as a Stress Buffer," *Adaptive Human Behavior and Physiology* 2 (2016): 344–362, https://doi.org/10.1007/s40750-016-0052-x.

8 Lucy McRae, "Future Survival Kit," https://www.lucymcrae.net/future-survival-kit.

opens up a receptivity to new forms of digital intervention into the most personal aspects of our lives. Taking a section of our contemporary moment, we see the emergence of "smart-homes" that emulate behaviours of companionship by being able to talk with their inhabitants, or by becoming an interface for families living apart to check in on one another. While there is a push for new spaces where touch is deemed acceptable, there is a growing offloading of care and contact to machines. As baby boomers enter elderhood, the healthcare system will require a larger number of workers to meet an increased demand of care; robots are being developed to help meet those needs. Technologies promise simple and "cheap" solutions, providing new robotic caretakers and technical devices to monitor health constantly and remotely, as well as animatronic pets and therapeutic robots to serve as companions. *Buddy*, *Elli-Q*, *Paro*, *Care-O-Bot*, *Zenbo*, *Stevie*—these are just some of the caretaking robots in the continuously growing industry whose primary function is to swap human with robotic care and reduce feelings of isolation at old age. However, with increased capabilities, will these new technologies be applied in our most intimate and vulnerable moments? Will they be used as a way to entertain, to medicate with bedside manner, to console you while you die alone?

The *End of Life Care Machine* [p. 274] by artist and designer Dan Chen takes an extreme vision of how robotic intimacy technology could be deployed to comfort and care for people at the end of life. Composed of a padded appendage that caresses the dying person's arm back and forth, and a customized recording offering "soothing words," the device aims to simulate human comfort and care as one goes alone through their final rites of passage. The project challenges the application and capabilities of technology to replace humanity and acts of intimacy in our most sensitive states.

Loneliness is a salient condition in our present. We have seen architecture's complicit and active roles in worsening this condition, but we have also seen its inherent ability to allow for contact between people. Designers have recently made attempts to ameliorate contemporary solitude by critically extrapolating on the same technological principles that have possibly been that solitude's primary catalyst. We are beginning to witness the spatial manifestations of new gestures toward supporting the diverse bonds that are so important to us and to a healthy society.

Love

Questions around love, relationships, and family have predominantly circled around the image and narrative of the nuclear family: man meets woman, man and woman get married, man and

9 Statistics Canada, "Private households by household type, % distribution 2016, Canada, provinces and territories, 2016 Census – 100% Data," Families, Households and Marital Status Highlight Tables, accessed February 23, 2021, https://www12.statcan.gc.ca/census-recensement/2016/dp-pd/hlt-fst/fam/Table.cfm?Lang=E&T=21&Geo=00&SP=1&view=5#shr-pg0.

woman have children, and so the story went. But on the fringes of these images have been non-traditional families that have, over time, slowly moved their way into mainstream consciousness: open relationships, ethical non-monogamy, polyamory, same-sex marriage, three-parent families, single parenthood, co-parenting, singletons, child-free adults, chosen family, etc. Today we could consider the traditional family as just one of the many possible permutations: approximately only one in four households in Canada are made up of married couples with children.[9] Yet our institutions, laws, policies, and especially the way we build have lagged in recognizing newly expanded definitions of family and companionship. Policies, or more to say the biases behind policies, might in fact prevent some newly-formed or atypical communities from using certain housing typologies. Such barriers may even manifest in the zoning of cities by family organization type. In many municipalities across North America,[10] a single-family dwelling may only be inhabited by a group that conforms to the traditional definition of what a family is—even if extended, the family needs always to be bonded by blood or contract.[11] Thankfully, as a result of society becoming more open to changing ideas around love, and about what constitutes a family, exclusionary definitions of family in zoning laws are starting to be revised. What once were taboo subjects are now gaining more mainstream acceptance: the younger generation, for example, is more open to a polyamorous life, or to one in which they live with their friends and call them their family. How will zoning processes interpret these newly salient relationships? Further, will zoning and architecture be able to anticipate and design for forms of community and family that have yet to manifest?

For our housing stock to best meet changing societal conceptions of family, there needs to be an openness and acceptance to build for non-traditional families and relationships. We can start to understand how we could design spaces for non-normative family types by trying to perceive the traits common to architectures that were created specifically to accommodate *nuclear* families. In a suburb just outside of Berlin, a group of nine young professionals (and one toddler) purchased a traditional house to accommodate their sense of kinship and their strategies around issues of affordability [Anais Langlais-Schmidt, *Traumhaus Royal*, p. 334]. Though the spatial organization of the house suggests a familial structure at odds with their own, a simple redefinition of spaces combined with a renegotiation of domestic, social, and romantic roles render this former single-family home a testing ground for new ways of forming a family. From the basement to the attic, spaces formerly accommodating a luxurious version of nuclear family life now house the gradient of intimacies and varying work arrangements at play within this close group of friends. No

10 The *New York Times* estimated in 2019 that 75% of residentially zoned land in the United States was specifically zoned for single-family. See Emily Badger and Quoctrung Bui, "Cities Start to Question an American Ideal: A House With a Yard on Every Lot," *The New York Times*, June 18, 2019, https://www.nytimes.com/interactive/2019/06/18/upshot/cities-across-america-question-single-family-zoning.html.

11 For example, the Town of North Hampstead in New York had the following definition of "single family" in their municipal zoning legislature: "[o]ne (1) or more persons related by blood, marriage or legal adoption residing or cooking or warming food as a single housekeeping unit; with whom there may not be more than two (2) boarders, roomers or lodgers who must live together in a common household." In *Group House of Port Washington v. Board of Zoning and Appeals of the Town of North Hempstead, 45 N.Y. 2d 266, at 272 (1978)* this definition was challenged in the Court of Appeals and deemed to be exclusionary. See "Legal Memorandum LU05: Definition of "Family" in Zoning Law and Building Codes," dos.ny.gov, March, 2021, https://dos.ny.gov/legal-memorandum-lu05-definition-family-zoning-law-and-building-codes.

walls were removed, no walls were added—nonetheless, this case demonstrates both a certain friction experienced by non-traditional families in traditional architectures, as well as approaches to critically and fruitfully inhabiting those architectures.

Indeed, aside from adapting new human arrangements to existing architectures, ideas of how to share space have also moved toward *formal* spatial reconsideration. In a new housing block in Berlin designed by June14 Meyer-Grohbrügge & Chermayeff [*Kurfürstenstrasse*, p. 236], for example, two units are no longer divided by a wall but by a room. The idea of transforming a dividing wall into an inhabitable volume in order to accommodate a multi-family unit and co-living contrasts with the notion of a space being structurally flexible simply by the removal, addition, or shifting of walls. The intermediary space's use is open to different functions, which are discussed between the inhabitants of adjoining units and are contingent on their relationship with each other—whether a communal space of gathering, a mutable space responding to the changing needs of each occupant, or a porous hall between the two units. Living there, one may need to accept the fact that a toddler or a cat living in such a framework might not perceive the boundaries of its apartment, and roam as freely in space as smells from a kitchen.

The unaffordability of housing, the cost of living, and the widespread inability to independently build equity through real estate have created a growing receptibility to non-traditional forms of cohabitation. As a result, new digital tools are emerging to bring unlikely groups of people together. For instance, the website Nesterly [p. 332], through an algorithm similar to ones used by dating apps, helps initiate living arrangements between students and the elderly. Many older adults have spare spaces to rent out, and like anyone—but perhaps more crucially as they age—have a need for a certain amount of companionship. Each person in the arrangement lives their life independently but shares moments of connection and household work; this allows many older adults to age in place. The concept is something like a mix between student housing and a retirement community. As a student, one may have a hard time deciding to move in with their grandparent, as some emotional dynamic, precarious self-image, and forced commitment will be at stake. However, this new kind of "deal" facilitated by Nesterly can be seen as mutually voluntary and based on both parties' economic benefits, somehow making it the "new acceptable"—and maybe a new form of multi-generational friendship would be an unexpected result. Physical and digital environments that coordinate multi-generational relationships may become more and more prevalent as populations around the world are aging, and we are already seeing design and social gestures that specifically

Samantha Friend, *Table for One*, 2017

foster the collaborative use and stewardship of space by non-nuclear groups. In Japan, for instance, where the elderly represent a particularly large percentage of the population,[12] Airbnb and Go Hasegawa have collaborated on the project *Yoshino Cedar House*, a guest house and communal facility maintained and administrated by thirty one "community hosts" from multiple generations.

Meanwhile in Baltimore, *Carehaus*, designed by Rafi Segal Architecture and Urbanism with activist and artist Marisa Morán Jahn, uses space as a catalyst for the development of care-based communities. Independent living units for disabled and older adults, and for their caregivers and caregivers' families, are clustered around shared spaces and amenities.[13] In addition to housing, caregivers at *Carehaus* receive fair wages and childcare, all factors that allow for greater stability in their community. Economic and social justice issues around domestic labour, along with the many new problems posed to an aging population and the communities that support them, are tackled together in one building, as one spatial and community form.

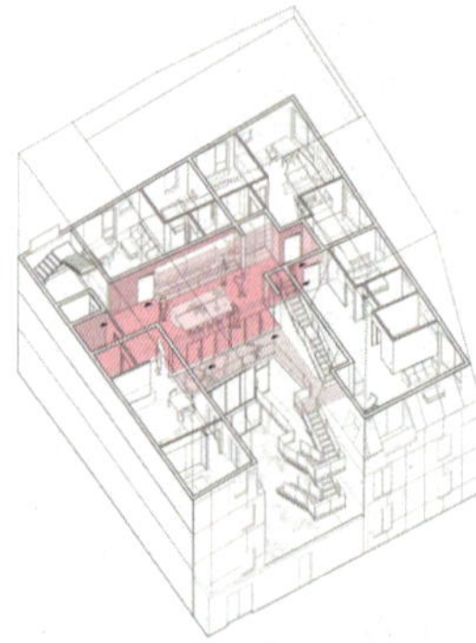

Marisa Morán Jahn and Rafi Segal, axonometric drawing of Carehaus by Rafi Segal A+U, 2021

Sociologist Eric Klinenberg, in his book *Going Solo: The Extraordinary Rise and Surprising Appeal of Living Alone,* argues that another demographic change we are witnessing, with singletons becoming the most diffuse urban dweller globally, will bring with it not so much a society disconnected, individualized, or lonely, but rather a society based on intentional connection, positive ecological habits, and creative or mixed-use living.[14] Looking for contact, those who live alone tend to participate much more in social activities; to live in dense urban areas and therefore take advantage of public transportation or shared services; and to consider the home just one of the loci of life, with the city itself offering all the other venues and supports for life's many aspects. However, as the inhabitants of the city of the future play out their lives less and less in their homes, the city may transform itself more and more into a series of housing complexes composed, on one hand, of identical, hotel-like rooms, and on the other hand, of complete sets of amenities and venues in the complex's communal spaces—the consequence being the reduction of communities to the trait of mere proximity.

Typical ideas around contemporary living in the city have centred on having less personal space and more shared amenities, whether in the building complex or throughout the city itself. For his 2018 project *Apartment House in Tokyo* [p. 316], Takahashi Ippei divided the house into eight spaces, each a singleton home with a sink, a toilet, and a place to sleep, and each defined otherwise by a different domestic function—one is for bathing in, one is for working in, one is for cooking in, one is for relaxing in, and

12 Since the 1960s, Japan's government had honoured its citizens who reached 100 years of age by giving them a solid silver sake cup. They gave out 153 cups in 1963. But in recent years the centenarian sector of the population had grown so large, and the cost of the tradition so expensive—¥260 million in 2014—that the government had to change the material of the cup to a silver-plated nickel alloy. "Japan to Downgrade Gift to Centenarian as Population Ages," *Kyodo*, August 19, 2015, https://www.japantimes.co.jp/news/2015/08/19/national/japan-downgrade-gift-centenarians-population-ages/#.VdYYwPlViko.

13 "About," Carehaus, https://www.carehaus.net.

14 Eric Klinenberg, *Going Solo: The Extraordinary Rise and Surprising Appeal of Living Alone* (New York: Penguin Press, January 29, 2013).

so on. Each resident chooses their space based on how they envision spending their time alone at home, and they need to reach out to the others if they are interested in utilizing the functions missing from their own room. The city itself fills in remaining moments and fulfills all the functions that were not included in the home, encouraging the inhabitants to seek social interactions in the urban sphere. The idea is also that if societal needs will change again in the future, the house that now holds all the functions in different rooms can be easily inhabited as one large home rather than eight interconnected small homes.

Age

The defining features of the phases of life—infancy, childhood, adolescence, adulthood, parenthood, retirement, elderhood, death—are far from stable across time and place, and these changes are accelerating under the current forms of late capitalism. Often the duration and quality of these life phases are contingent upon a complexion of economics, expected familial structures, and ideas of one's societal role as informed by some of the variables of identity (those being, among others, gender, class, race, sexuality, religion, vocation). Life will always begin with birth and end with death, but how we go through the stages between is increasingly open-ended. And despite the ultimate unnegotiability of birth and death as biological facts, even the processes by which they are mediated are far from immune to the influences of historical change; though manners of conception (not to mention contraception) and delivery, and manners of dying and of handling the dead, have never been uniform, we are beginning to see a profusion of new alternatives for how we negotiate the boundaries of life, no less than we are seeing a profusion of new alternatives for how we exist in life's basic stages and in the transitions between them. These alternatives are a matter of design, and often manifest spatially.

It may be useful to begin the overview of these shifts by looking at work, a sphere of activity that typically spans several life stages, almost invariably beginning with adolescence. Traditionally, work life has been framed by a positive correlation between age and acquired expertise, until eventually dissipating in old age. But this relationship is coming undone. The peak of one's relevance and influence at work, of one's authority—particularly in the tech industry—has become increasingly young and brief. In Tad Friend's article "Why Ageism Never Gets Old," he observes that "this sharp shift in the age of authority derives from increasingly rapid technological change," and undergirding this phenomenon is a belief held by Silicon Valley "that bold ideas are the province of the young."[15] By the time those working in the digital economy have moved into their thirties, they are perceived as being old:

15 Tad Friend, "Why Ageism Never Gets Old," *The New Yorker*, November 13, 2017, https://www.newyorker.com/magazine/2017/11/20/why-ageism-never-gets-old.

the feeling of obsolescence is creeping downward. In response, luxury resorts and retreats like the Modern Elder Academy located in El Pescadero, Mexico, aim to support those going through midlife transitions, including workers in the digital economy who feel, in their mere thirties, that they are no longer able to keep up with its pace of change as an industry, and that they are losing professional and cultural relevance.[16] The space and programming of the Modern Elder Academy are designed to provide emotional support and a sense of community to guests, and to be a place where they can each share, among other aspects of transitioning into mid-life, their respective encounters with ageism in their workplace.[17]

OMMX Architects, Interior perspective of Naked House, 2017

But the phenomenon of certain traits typical to old age descending into earlier life stages may in some cases be desirable. The new plausibility of concentrating the arc of one's career to the early years of life has reignited an interest in early retirement: FIRE (financial independence, retire early) is a growing movement among millennials where the tenets of aggressively working, saving, and investing are observed in order to accrue enough wealth to retire in one's thirties or forties. The principles associated with FIRE may represent not only a financial leap toward assets, but also a shifting of assets toward lower tiers of wealth. Though the techniques for early retirement are grounded in financial strategy, the concept of prosperity moves away from generic symbols of material wealth to the experiential wealth found in the expansion of one's time. By working and generating income in a more compressed timeframe, we may supposedly free ourselves from the obligations of indefinite years of labour. Images of retirement have often evoked tropes of watery leisure and relaxation—fishing, cruises, and beaches come to mind—but what will the young retiree's space of life look like?

The project *Naked House*, desgined by the architecture office OMMX in 2017, is an example of an effort to create a new housing type that provides a financially accessible threshold to home ownership. The model brings down initial cost by outfitting the home with only the bare necessities: it is something of a domestic shell, with no internal walls, floors, or finishes. Over time, the space is materially added to by the residents, giving them the freedom to respond architecturally in proportion to their changing needs, desires, and financial circumstances. This helps them avoid amassing crippling amounts of debt. Designing new models of home that are essentially informed by the concept of affordability frees up home, as an attainable asset, from its place near the middle of the rigid itinerary of life phases—not only younger people, but elderly people who have not hitherto been able to afford their own homes, would now be able to.

Giovanna Borasi

16 Nellie Bowles, "A New Luxury Retreat Caters to Elderly Workers in Tech (Ages 30 and Up)," *The New York Times*, March 4, 2019, https://www.nytimes.com/2019/03/04/technology/modern-elder-resort-silicon-valley-ageism.html.

17 Bowles, "A New Luxury Retreat."

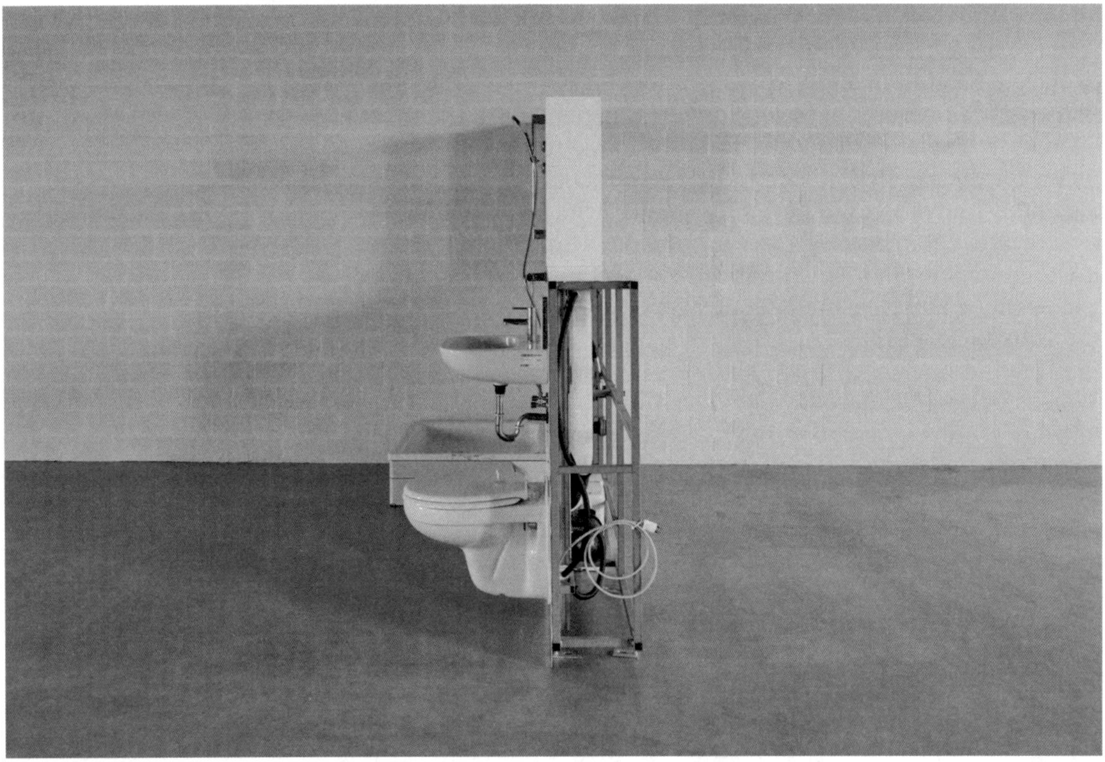

Degelo Architekten, *Sanitary element, artists and studio house Erlenmatt*, 2018–2019

A more extreme example of such a model is Heinrich Degelo's and Homebase Cooperative's *Artists' Studios* in Basel, which offers a dwelling radically reduced to the provision of basic bodily requirements. Citing converted factory lofts in New York City as a precedent,[18] each unit in the cooperative is an empty, unsegmented space equipped with nothing more than a sanitary block and a technical wall that includes both bathroom and kitchen facilities. No heating system is even integrated in the building. Instead, human bodies and appliances are estimated to produce enough warmth year-round. The technical and spatial minimalism of the units in the building mean that their predominant form is an "emptiness that gives freedom and possibilities."[19] This freedom is to be understood in two ways: as an extreme flexibility of program, and as an extreme affordability of access. The two are fundamentally connected, and can be seen clearly through the lens of age. Though the thematic demographic of the building is artists, the spatial and financial flexibility that characterizes many artists' lifestyles is certainly at play in broader societal spheres. With minimal interior elements, the inhabitants can, first of all, very easily shape their space to their requirements, which are often determined by parameters correlated to age, at the outset of cooperative

18 Heinrich Degelo, "Heinrich Degelo: "It's about the emptiness that gives freedom and possibilities."," interview by Architektur Basel, November 26, 2018, https://architekturbasel.ch/heinrich-degelo-es-geht-um-die-leere-die-freiheiten-und-moeglichkeiten-gibt.

19 Degelo, interview.

tenancy, and then gradually invest their time, labour, and finances when feasible to make their space more livable and responsive to their changing needs and values. As Degelo says: "Different phases of life require different living concepts. Shared flats are becoming single apartments, family rooms and finally apartments for the elderly."[20] The physical minimality also guarantees a monthly rent of 10 CHF per square metre, which is less than half the average rent in Basel. Thus, the architecture of *Homebase* both invites people from a greater spectrum of age through financial accessibility, and is spatially malleable enough to be liveable for the same spectrum.

Work can be considered an overarching engagement that ties together life phases and to some extent determines their characteristics and even durations, but it can also be considered a changing physical environment of life. Each generation forms new notions around work. Gen Z (born between 1997 and 2012), the first generation of true digital natives, are entering the workforce having grown up sharing themselves online. "The self," that amalgam of image, relationships, tastes, and personality, has become commodified, and for some, the broadcasting of oneself has become a viable profession. One architectural phenomenon to emerge from this new field, particularly in Los Angeles, is the "content house" or "collab house," where social media influencers live together. The explosive growth and popularity of the social media platform TikTok has spurred the latest iteration of content houses, the most notable being "Hype House," a McMansion-type home where some of the platform's most prominent young stars have formed a content creator cohabitation group [Michelle Groskopf, *Hype House*, p. 118]. As noted by reporter Taylor Lorenz, the draw for living together "allows for more teamwork, which means faster growth, and creators can provide emotional support for what can be a grueling career."[21] And even if the settings seem to imply a constant party house, strict rules tuned to productivity are in place to make sure everyone is doing their job—producing videos. Home and work have here fully coalesced.

This coalescence has enjoyed its most intense development thus far in the paring down of the workspace, in many industries, to employee and their computer or phone. What was, for a number of years, theoretically possible became for many an involuntary global experiment during the COVID-19 pandemic. But the reordering of values provoked by this technological paradigm shift is ambiguous. On one hand, many people whose jobs can be practically executed remotely have experienced a revaluation of work-life balance, such that they do not want to let go of their newfound abundance of domestic time, suffused with professional duties and video conferences as it may be. Certainly, this has the

20 Degelo, interview.

21 Taylor Lorenz, "Hype House and the Los Angeles Tiktok Mansion Gold Rush," *The New York Times*, January 3, 2020, https://www.nytimes.com/2020/01/03/style/hype-house-los-angeles-tik-tok.html?.

potential for interesting cultural, familial, and infrastructural outcomes, but no less could it produce a precarious model of employment that aggravates prevalent inequity and exploits new degrees of flexibility in one's work-life dichotomy, afforded by teleworking, to gain greater capital.

Meanwhile, just as some of the conventional signifiers of old age are extending into earlier life, "youth" is simultaneously extending into later life phases. Technological and scientific developments contribute to changing the parameters of the traditional life cycle, especially as it relates to the body, to aging, and to fertility. Having a baby or creating a family was normally understood to take place in a specific timeframe in a woman's life. But new forms of fertility treatments—egg freezing, in vitro fertilization (IVF), egg donation, surrogacy, etc.—along with women's increased autonomy in the Western world, have challenged those assumptions, giving those who have access to treatment new flexibility in family planning. In the United States, about one-third of adults have said they or someone they know required some form of fertility treatment, with millions more around the world.[22] Meanwhile, globally, more than eight million babies have been born via IVF since 1978.[23] As fertility treatments have become more commonplace, a need for architecture to thoughtfully reconsider the spaces where these procedures take place has emerged. Currently, they often exist as independent clinics, siloed off spaces imbued with an atmosphere of secrecy or shame. But could they become sites for a new social infrastructure? As architect Hilary Sample has imagined:

> The new clinic could be recalibrated to focus on the well-being of those needing reproductive assistance. A space we could imagine linking reproductive health to environmental health—clinics that are in neighborhoods of poor health could bring awareness to those within them. Children should be allowed in the reproductive clinic; often children are forbidden, yet in poor and less served neighborhoods, bringing a child would be an opportunity for additional support and care. The clinic can be the doula for the neighborhood.[24]

Other kinds of facilities directly involved in the growing business of the health and performance of our tissues could be subject to architectural reconsideration. The twentieth century saw the rise of repositories, or banks, for human fluids—blood, sperm, and breast milk—but biotechnology is making it increasingly feasible to procure other material aspects of the body, like body parts, genes, cell lines, and, in special circumstances, even faces.[25] Over the past century, we have been able to stretch the average human life expectancy by thirty years.[26] Now, biotechnology

22 Gretchen Livingston, "A third of U.S. adults say they have used fertility treatments or know someone who has," *Pew Research Center*, July 17, 2018, https://www.pewresearch.org/fact-tank/2018/07/17/a-third-of-u-s-adults-say-they-have-used-fertilty-treatments-or-know-someone-who-has.

23 European Society of Human Reproduction and Embryology, "More than 8 million babies born from IVF since the world's first in 1978: European IVF pregnancy rates now steady at around 36 percent, according to ESHRE monitoring," *ScienceDaily*, www.sciencedaily.

24 Hilary Sample, interview with author, June 2020.

25 Kara W. Swanson, "Banks of Blood and Sperm," Interview by Rebecca J. Rosen, *The Atlantic*, July 31, 2014, https://www.theatlantic.com/business/archive/2014/07/banks-of-blood-and-sperm/375341. See also: Kara W. Swanson, *Banking on the Body: The Market in Blood, Milk, and Sperm in Modern America* (Cambridge: Harvard University Press, May 19, 2014).

26 Adam Gopnik, "Can We Live Longer But Stay Younger," *The New Yorker*, May 13, 2019, https://www.newyorker.com/magazine/2019/05/20/can-we-live-longer-but-stay-younger.

may offer a way to further increase our quality of life in those years, marking these body banks as sites with greater community importance. Could they become more widespread as structures integrated in our urban settings? And would they, in their new degree of presence, need a special architectural interface to engage with the public? Would they be designed as hyper-discreet alcoves tucked away behind almost secret entrances, and internally geared toward privacy and emotional well-being? Or would they be just as decisively visible and mundane as our financial banks and walk-in clinics?

Common Accounts, Perspective of memorial garden and liquified body in Three Ordinary Funerals, 2017

We can extend our lives, but death is still inevitable. Yet just as the rituals around birth are being reconsidered, funerary practices and the rituals surrounding death are also subject to redesign. By basing designs for new death-oriented rituals on novel technologies, Common Accounts' project *Three Ordinary Funerals*, an installation at the Seoul Biennale of Architecture in 2017–2020, has challenged the fact that technological progress has generally distanced the material business of death from everyday life:

> Sanitized and disease-controlled, the funeral industry has kept [death] neat, tidy, out of sight. The contemporary city has modified and restricted many of the urban typologies that once played host to societal activities around death. Death is visible in home décor, in fitness programs, and in virtual space, and yet architecture today has failed to acknowledge the potential posed by the accidental situations and infrastructural networks built around death. Architecture has failed to recognize these entities as a site for action. Further, cities can no longer afford to keep the material business of death at arm's length.[27]

Common Accounts is referring to the fact that traditional body disposal is threatened by diminishing land availability, environmental concerns, and the prospect of a digital afterlife. *Three Ordinary Funerals* explores how material, ceremonial, virtual, and ecological values surrounding death can be produced by novel technologies—including the application of alkaline hydrolysis, or "water cremation," which reduces human or pet remains to a small amount of dust and fluid in a stainless steel capsule. If the practice of alkaline hydrolysis becomes the basis of common ritual, will we see a new architecture materialize around it?

Technologies can change our values, values are frequently articulated through rituals, and rituals have a way of finding support in specific architectural form. This interrelationship is also articulated in the *Crematorium* by Office KGDVS [p. 270]. This project puts the fire cremators and a place for the family of the deceased

27 Igor Bragado and Miles Gertler, "Three Ordinary Funerals," in *Imminent Commons*, ed. Hyungmin Pai (Barcelona: ACTAR, 2017), 105.

to observe the treatment in the most capacious and climactic point in the architecture, and demonstrates an insistence on changing the typology of the places where post-death treatments are performed. The new crematorium is, as Kersten Geers explains in a lecture he gave at the Lisbon Triennale of Architecture in 2019,[28] a kind of replacement both for the traditional function of a church and for the standard technical function of a crematorium,[29] and responds to the new rituals that emerge with shifts in attitudes vis-à-vis the visibility of death. The project intends to give the emotional states arising from the ceremony a connection to the outside landscape, to balance the whole operation through obscuring the machine-like anatomy of the building. And it is a technical building: it contains ovens that produce black smoke (a smoke that, as Geers says, no one should see), and so contains other ovens called "afterburners" that burn that black smoke into a fainter, less detectable one.

A specific proximity to death—close enough to properly integrate it as a fact but not so close as to be traumatic—is an architectural matter. Whether architecture focuses the user's senses on technologies necessary for the program (in this case, post-mortem treatments and rituals), or conceals those technologies, to one degree or another it will be shaped by the requirement of those technologies and how human beings interpret them. A project by Norwegian architect Carl-Viggo Hølmebakk from 2000, the *Mortuary at Asker Crematorium*, includes a preparation room that was designed to accommodate not only the undertaker, but also family members of the deceased who wish to participate in the pre-cremation treatment of the body—a ritual that must have had a decisive influence on the atmosphere Hølmebakk materially crafted. And we see other architectural maneuvers effecting our proximity to death at the urban scale: Columbia GSAPP's DeathLab, for instance, has been working to imagine memorial shrines as integrated pieces of urban infrastructure and public amenity, while also providing a space in which to publicly grieve [DeathLAB, *Constellation Park*, p. 272].

And what about the afterlife, that especially other life phase? Our relation as the deceased to the spaces in which we lived, particularly in which we had significant experiences, is for many a subject of great fascination: if technological change has opened up new "spaces" for life, then what becomes of those spaces when we die? For instance, what becomes of our social media space after we die? The possibility of digital legacy and digital memory creates a new set of considerations when making end-of-life decisions—this will only become more apparent as our digital and physical lives become increasingly intertwined.

28 Kersten Geers, "Economy of Means – Conference. Part 1/3. Éric Lapierre, Kersten Geers, Robin Collyer," Lisbon Architecture Triennale, November 30, 2019, video, 13:04–13:50, https://vimeo.com/399875768.

29 In Belgium, currently 60% of the deceased are cremated. Crematoria have become one of the most 'desired' post death treatments. See Geers, "Economy of Means," 13:15–13:20.

Debt

In his lucid reading of today's society, sociologist Maurizio Lazzarato argues that, as never before, our society is now mainly governed by debt. He cites American universities as *the* example of a society of debt. Lazzarato says that while being the "temple for transmission and production of Western knowledge," the university "is also a model of the financial institution and, with it, of debt economy," and adds, "... the American student perfectly embodies the condition of the indebted man by serving as paradigm for the conditions of subjectivation of debt economy that one finds throughout society."[30] In reporting data, Lazzarato adds that in 2012 the total amount borrowed by students (and still owed) in order to finance their education had reached 904 billion USD. This number surpasses half of the total public debt of countries like Italy and France. Ten years later, students in the US remain "indebted before entering the job market and stay indebted for life ... many young graduates struggle to find a job as repaying their debt becomes less and less likely."[31]

British architect Jack Self, citing Jean Baudrillard's *A System of Objects*, argues that it is indeed principally the credit card that has changed the relationship between ownership, capital, space, and time:

> Baudrillard says you think you have bought something, but actually you haven't bought it. What you have done you have taken possession of it, but it belongs to your bank ... What it is going to do is to create on the one hand a complete disconnect between your relationship with the objects around you, on the other hand it's going to rapidly accelerate the way in which the transactions are made because there is no longer any barrier to your acquisitions of objects. We are going to shift from an economy based on production to an economy based on debt.[32]

Furthermore, as writer Eula Biss notes, "Credit is a form of optimism: it depends on the belief that the future will be more prosperous than the present. Credit creates the illusion of equality, in that we can all buy the same things on credit, but we can't all pay the debt back."[33] This being the baseline condition of Western society, why do we continue to project a future where individual ownership is the main framework?

Traditionally, home ownership was considered a significant life milestone that represented stability, a component of social order, and a means to build generational wealth. However, as people and capital became increasingly mobile, housing in turn underwent financialization. Today, property is associated with unbridled

30 Maurizio Lazzarato, *Governing by Debt* (Los Angeles: Semiotext(e), 2015), 64.

31 Lazzarato, *Governing by Debt*, 65.

32 Jack Self, "Jack Self Shares With Francis Aguillard," interview by Francis Aguillard, *Plat* 7.0 (Spring-Summer 2018): 20.

33 Eula Biss, *Having and Being Had* (New York: Riverhead, 2020), 73.

speculation, class division, and social inequity. We may think we own a home, but most probably we own a mortgage. The mortgage is a means through which homes become embedded in global flows of financial capital.

The fact that so many people have accrued significant debt has radically changed ideas around ownership—it might no longer be possible for most people to own property. When housing becomes a commodity, constructed for profit rather than community, it is urgent for architects to contribute not only to the building of houses but also to the conception of new forms of ownership. Some architects have been working on imagining new models of ownership with the aim of reducing financial pressure, especially for young people entering the labour market or for elderly people exiting it. Other more aggressive models are offered by companies that understand they can leverage this moment and its needs, transforming housing into a product and a form of service provider.

With music streaming services, auto-sharing, and other new models of access, we are already moving past the idea of owning many of the things that we use and enjoy on a daily basis. Will these new conceptions of membership filter into how we think about housing? Might we not own a house, but instead subscribe to one? It is indeed already the case: subscription-based rental platforms claim to offer solutions to ubiquitous urban deficiencies—such as the shortage of affordable housing, or the difficulty in securing temporary office space—through short-term co-living and co-working arrangements.

Almost one third of New Yorkers fall into an income category that is high enough to make them ineligible for affordable housing, but too low to allow them to meet their rent.[34] Claire Flurin, co-founder of Co-Liv Lab in New York City, characterizes the rationale of co-living as an "unbundling" of the elements of a home, such that one could pay only for the amenities they really need.[35] As urban policy specialist Diana Lind asks, "Why not pare your square footage to the bone and get additional amenities in exchange? One of those amenities is, allegedly, an authentic experience of a community ..."[36] Certainly, the rise of co-living or cooperative models is not only due to the fascination with a new lifestyle and diverse forms of living, but is to be understood also, as Jack Self puts it, as "a highly pragmatic response when you have highly polarized wealth inequality in society."[37]

Access to co-living spaces is typically attainable without the financial commitments of a standard lease agreement, and with the flexibility to relocate to other properties within a given platform's network. While these platforms have relatively similar target mar-

34 Diana Lind, *Brave New Home* (New York: Bold Type Books, 2020), 103.
35 Lind, *Brave New Home*, 103.
36 Lind, *Brave New Home*, 97.
37 Jack Self, interview, 21.

Vincent Fournier, *The Man-Machine, Reem B #5 [Pal]*, 2010

kets, each one caters to a particular niche of young professionals. Los Angeles-based PodShare taps into the backpacker lifestyle, providing bunk beds, branded as "pods," in an open environment designed to maximize "social collision" [p. 219]; OYO offers generically furnished homes and hotels rooms, alongside a full range of domestic services consolidated into a single platform; while ROAM boasts deluxe co-living and co-working options for digital nomads in many locations globally. In each case, housing is reduced to a service—alongside music streaming or meal kits—to be consumed according to a daily, weekly, or monthly subscription plan—a pay-as-you-go-housing.

It is worth considering the transformations connected to this model with regard to what writer Nick Srnicek defines "platform capitalism."[38] Multi-billion dollar companies like Uber have little in terms of fixed assets but are "platforms," operating as intermediaries enabling two or more groups to interact. With Airbnb or other similar companies, real estate is undergoing a similar transformation, as the companies act as platform intermediaries

38 Nick Srnicek, *Platform Capitalism* (Cambridge: Polity Press, 2017).

between physical space and potential users. Rebranding what are essentially real estate activities as a "platform" has generated immense speculative value, and therewith transformations of the physical and demographic complexions of the built environment.

But alongside these service models that manifest as digital interfaces, still based on intentions for limitless profit and not yet on a real effort to enhance affordability, many architects are working to create new, more inclusive frameworks and typologies. Jack Self, with the creation of the cultural institute Real, intends to promote democracy, inclusivity, and spatial equality with alternative models of ownership.

> We are always working backwards from the economic conditions that we find ourselves in. We start from a particular financial condition and a particular financial objective, and we design entirely inside those parameters to create something that the system didn't want to create. It's a way of trying to pervert or overturn current systems of capitalism by forcing capitalism to be consistent at times when it doesn't want to be.[39]

The many projects Self and Real have worked on in the past decade are built on the understanding that democracy and all types of equality are based on the precondition of secure and stable housing. With the latest chapter of Real Homes, Self intends to offer "a first ethical housing product"[40] that aims to concentrate in one place environmental investments (carbon neutral) and social investments (using a pay-what-you-can model, effectively meaning that everyone pays a maximum of between 28–33% of their income), all managed by a different governance. The new position of Real Homes is that it will provide a scenario for the architecture to be effective, but grounded in the first action of designing its financial system. This model will allow not only for an always-affordable rent, but also for the dwellers to be able to buy shares of the building that will ultimately pay an annual dividend, such that after a certain amount of time they will own a percentage of the building (with the other 50% staying with Real Homes in order to invest in more housing properties).

In Self's conceptual project the *Ingot* [p. 222], the tower—often seen as a symbol of capitalist speculation—becomes a way to democratize the high-rise building. The project imagines a long-term bond financing structure (50 years); this is a very low-pressure model compared to others typically used in real estate development, and it would allow the developer to charge tenants extraordinarily reduced rent, thereby offering them a highly secure home. Meanwhile, French architect Édouard Francois has written about and

39 Jack Self, "An Ethical Real Estate Project," interview by Kim Courrèges and Felipe de Ferrari, *Canadian Centre for Architecture*, June 14, 2021, https://www.cca.qc.ca/en/articles/issues/28/with-and-within/79973/an-ethical-real-estate-project.

40 Jack Self, interview.

realized several projects in France that aim to rethink the tower typology itself, designing against its typical vertically embedded inequality. In his model, elaborated upon in his book *La hauteur pour tous,* an apartment in the tower is composed of different rooms vertically dispersed through the building—one at the lower level near the street, with no view, is coupled with a terrace at the top of the building, and so on [p. 220]. In this way, a new form of equality—of exposure to natural light, views, and other conditions contingent on vertical position—is achieved.

In fact, besides the work that an architect can do, it is really at the macro level—at the scale of urbanism and policy—that the opportunity to create greater volumes of affordable housing exists. The City of Minneapolis serves as a great case study of what a local government can do to offer more housing options.[41] Jacob Frey, running for mayoral election in 2017, emphasized the impact of zoning on affordability. 70% of the city was zoned for single-families, and that meant that homes were unaffordable for a large part of the population. Furthermore, this paradigm was keeping the city racially segregated. In response to this condition, Frey proposed that each area should allow the construction of triplexes. In 2019, the plan was approved by city council. The implementation of the simple decision to take exclusionary zoning off the table is expected to create density, allowing for multifamily dwelling, ADU (accessory dwelling units), multigenerational dwelling, and, as a consequence, affordable housing city-wide. As the case in Minneapolis has come to illustrate, zoning can serve as an integral way to tackle intertwined issues of affordability, equity, segregation, and climate change.

Pier Vittorio Aureli of the architectural practice Dogma insists that the task of architects is "not to create new typologies or smarter homes, but to connect in a strategic manner alternative forms of ownership with specific typological arrangements that aim to reinforce a sense of trust and solidarity among dwellers."[42] Initiatives such as housing cooperatives, in which residents do not own their dwellings directly but own shares of the corporation that owns the set of dwellings to which theirs belongs, present alternatives to private home ownership by limiting the speculative value of housing. Furthermore, in certain co-op equity models, such as "limited equity" and "group equity," there are mechanisms in place that immunize individual co-op shares against market value fluctuations, thus disincentivizing speculative investment and keeping the financial barrier to co-op access very low. [43] According to Aureli:

> When addressing contemporary housing crises, it is common for architects, planners, and the public to refer to

41 Lind, *Brave New Home*, 205–210.

42 Pier Vittorio Aureli et al., "Promised Land: From Commodification to Cooperation," *e-flux*, December, 2019, https://www.e-flux.com/architecture/collectivity/304772/promised-land-housing-from-commodification-to-cooperation.

43 "Housing Co-op Equity Models," Nasco, https://www.nasco.coop/development/handbook/equity.

terra0, *Can an augmented forest own and utilize itself?*, 2016

a shortage of affordable housing and social housing. What often goes missing in this assessment is the very origin of this crisis, which coincides with the long and controversial process of the privatization of land. To put it bluntly: there is no housing affordability without access to land.[44]

Models like the Community Land Trust (where the property of the land and of the building are kept separate, with the land retained by the CLT in perpetuity) become extremely productive in developing new housing in urban areas, as they prevent land speculation. In an effort to rethink the privatization of land and the notion of housing as a commodity, Dogma's CLT project *Promised Land* [p. 224] uses various sites (London, Brussels, and Helsinki) and the unique opportunities offered by each particular context and governance to bring about a different housing model. Each project considers policy, labour, and real estate as integral elements of the design process, rather than as impingements or extraneous influences.

Other examples of how different frameworks and governances around ownership may produce alternative paradigms of access and land occupation are revealed when we open ourselves to new ways of understanding land sovereignty. In Humboldt, California, the Wiyot tribe and a series of settler organizations are currently working together to create a legal framework to give the land back to First Nations. It is a project at the intersection of land justice, language justice, and ecological restoration. They will create a community land trust to be sure the Wiyot tribe will maintain decision-making power on the land forever.[45]

Further toward the extreme, there are others who think land should not be owned by humans at all, but by nature itself. *terra0* is a project started by theorists, developers, and researchers at Berlin University of the Arts that aims to create hybrid and economically autonomous ecosystems in our new digital era. In this project a piece of forested land would be bought by the project initiators, who then, through a "smart contract," sign over ownership of the land to the forest itself, defined in the contract as a Non-Human Actor (NHA), in exchange for debentures called "terra0 tokens."[46] Though owner of itself in title, the forest is still indebted to the project initiators and thus financially tethered to human interest. However, the forest is also synthesized with automated cybernetic systems which constantly register its own body of resources and health, and in turn allow it to sell these resources (in the form of logging licenses, camping permits, and so on) back to human consumers. Through these cybernetic systems, the forest is ultimately able to accumulate money to buy back terra0 tokens from the project initiators, thereby becoming its own sole stakeholder and an

44 Aureli, "Promised Land."

45 Aaron Fernando, "How To Give The Land Back," shareable.net, September 7, 2021, https://www.shareable.net/how-to-give-the-land-back.

46 Paul Seidler, Paul Kolling, and Max Hampshire, "Terra0: Can an augmented forest own and utilize itself?," terra0, May 2016, https://www.terra0.org/assets/pdf/terra0_white_paper_2016.pdf.

independent entity on the market. It could also use income to buy adjacent land, and thus expand itself. This release of the land from human ownership would free it from the decisions of individual people and groups, interested as they often are in protecting and managing land not for the sake of its own immanence but for the sake of what it can yield for them personally.

Accountability

In November 2018 in France, far from the country's global metropolises, people gathered in roundabouts outside small and medium cities and in rural areas, all wearing the bright yellow safety vests that European drivers have been obligated since 2008 to keep in their cars. This moment, organized in response to the economic, cultural, and geographic divide between peripheral populations and the urban centres where labour and wealth is created, was the root of what has since become known as the *gilets jaunes* movement [p. 177]. As the French geographer Christophe Guilluy states:

> This movement does not resemble any traditional social movement ... Supported by the majority of French opinion, it united very different categories: workers, employees, independent people, farmers, women, men, retirees, and youth. These ordinary people, mostly from the working classes, but without class consciousness, nevertheless share a common feeling: that of being culturally relegated. ... It illustrates the fundamental cultural, social, and geographical divide of today: that which opposes a new "popular block," that of the peripheries, to a new "bourgeois block," that of the globalized metropolis. It raises the question on which the future of Western democracies depends: what is the place of the working classes in a globalized model marked by deindustrialization?[47]

The *gilets jaunes* protests made evident this opposition in France, while in the UK it was Brexit, and in the Unites States it was the increasingly striking divergence of urban and rural voters' beliefs. The protested model is one which concentrates wealth in large cities, where public transportation is robust enough to eliminate many citizens' need for cars, and subjects those who do depend on cars—inhabitants of peri-urban and rural areas—to fuel taxes (and speed-limit reductions) burdensome at their typically lower income levels. It is significant that though challenging policy and inequality forged in urban settings, the *gilets jaunes* protests took place largely in the peripheral and infrastructural spaces where the majority of protesters lived, commuted, worked, and felt the weight of the new laws.[48] This siting shows an important element in the message being communicated; that they did not all travel to urban centres to protest can be read as emphasizing their point.

47 Christophe Guilluy, *No Society : La fin de la classe moyenne occidentale* (Paris: Champs-Actuel, Flammarion, 2019), Preface, I-II.

48 Paris did see very intense demonstrations, but the movement as a whole was broad and generally more active outside of cities. One study showed that in Occitania, for example, the movement involved 4% of inhabitants of larger cities, and 12% of inhabitants of medium-sized cities and small towns. Jean-Yves Dormagen and Geoffrey Pion, "« Gilets Jaunes », combien de divisions?," *Le Monde diplomatique*, February 2021, https://www.monde-diplomatique.fr/2021/02/DORMAGEN/62755.

But it can also be read as a result of the decentralized way the movement emerged and spread—through social media. A petition on Change.org posted in May 2018 accrued one million signatures within a month, and within about a year, three million French citizens, by one estimate,[49] had participated in *gilets jaunes* protests in one way or another. Though coherent movements being actuated through multiple sites across large geographical areas is not new, social media can make the process much swifter, more expansive, and potentially more horizontal. It can introduce a new level of visibility not only of the movement's message but also of the mechanisms of its growth, and a democratization, decentralization, or even suppression of governance within it. These qualities may have supported the *gilets jaunes* movement's consistency across its geographic range.

Movements concerned with environmental issues, equity for gender and race, labour equality and rights, students' rights, and so on all use public space to signify their opinion and to ask for change. This is not new, but what is new (arguably with the launch of Twitter in 2006) is that these movements in physical public space also exist within a parallel *digital* public space. Digital space is no longer simply a technology of documentation for an event and the ideas it brings up, but a new place for gathering, debating, and informing. The hashtag has become a new congregating space, and one particularly conducive to a form of activism. Indeed, "hashtag activism" is not only a way to show support for a cause, but also, as it concentrates activity around a subject, to spread the discussion, to advance counter-narratives, and to build dissent more widely and quickly.

But the hashtag could be thought of as just one place in a growing digital landscape of intervention. Besides hashtags, formats like collaborative spreadsheets and lists could become regular sites of collective vocalization. It was the infamous "Shitty Architecture Men" list[50] that appeared in 2017 that was most probably the first time a spreadsheet, the typical tool for accounting, was transformed into an open tool of accountability in the design field. As Jia Yi Gu, Laida Aguirre, Gary Riichirō Fox, and Cyrus Peñarroyo argue in a conversation around digital vigilantism and what it means for architecture, "Open letters and spreadsheets share the same motivations—they are systems of accountability that have emerged on the Internet in the past few years that attempt to hold architecture accountable for invisible or unspoken transgressions."[51] This act of listing and enumerating through crowdsourcing information has become a way to describe an environment. It contains an embedded narrative that is not always explicit (the spreadsheets are sometimes compiled by anonymous creators and contributors), but that is used for

49 Dormagen and Pion, "« Gilets Jaunes »."

50 This spreadsheet is no longer accessible to the public, but its creator has spoken about its origins. See: Anonymous as told to Suzanne Labarre, "Exclusive: Why I Started a Shitty Architecture Men List," *Fast Company*, March 15, 2018, https://www.fastcompany.com/90164300/exclusive-why-i-started-a-shitty-architecture-men-list.

51 Laida Aguirre, Gary Riicherō Fox, Jia Yi Gu, and Cyrus Peñarroyo, "The Open Letter and the Spreadsheet: Digital Vigilante Practices in Architecture," *MAS Context* 33 (June 2020), 281.

empowerment and hopefully to render the identified or referenced parties accountable.

While the intention of the "Shitty Architecture Men" list was intended to denounce harmful practices or individuals in architecture, a more recent spreadsheet, "Art/Museum Salary Transparency 2019," exposes salaries of staff across art galleries and fine arts institutions, hoping to raise the question of pay inequality. This spreadsheet suffered accidental deletion of information, then accordingly switched to a form submission method of accruing data, then was closed to new additions. But it remains viewable, and with just over 3,300 entries from 2019 it serves as a document of historical value. Another example, the "BIPOC Studios" spreadsheet [p. 188] initiated by a group comprised of individuals from art, design, architecture, and criticism[52] registers design practices founded and lead by BIPOC architects and designers. Created in June 2020, and at the time of writing this essay entailing entries for 430 practices around the world, the BIPOC Studios spreadsheet demonstrates the plurality of voices already existing in architecture and aims to catalyze society's engagement with them.

These digitally mediated endeavours offer a new way to make accountability a top priority—accountability not only for people working, teaching, or employing in design disciplines, but also for the ones creating and using the spreadsheets. Ensuring that these tools are used and interpreted responsibly has been a salient part of the discourse surrounding them. The "BIPOC Studios" spreadsheet, for example, includes an "Asshole Disclaimer" that states: "This list isn't meant to validate the working conditions, antiracism, or general human kindness of any of the studios below. BIPOC can certainly be assholes too."[53] A disclaimer is of course a commonplace notational feature of many kinds of documents; it protects the document's users, its authors, and anyone or thing implicated in it. It is instructional. But when a document transforms into a real space, then the disclaimer can be seen as a part of that space's design. How can we further design these spaces to support a healthy society?

The questions incumbent on designing our physical environment so that it is conducive to individual, social, economic, and biological health are no less applicable to digital space, particularly because the latter creates or radically cultivates a potentially inextricable dynamic between the individual and the collective. For the first time in history, the role of the consumer or the user becomes, through the use of digital platforms and their capabilities, simultaneously a role of critique: of voicing, gathering, and multiplying effects of individual dissent to a critical mass, thereby

52 The "BIPOC Studios" spreadsheet was initiated by Virgil Abloh, Dong-Ping Wong, Tei Carpenter, Dominic Leong, Preeti Sriritana, Oana Stănescu, Joey Swerdlin, Naïla Opiangah, Esther Choi, Hassan Rahim, and Mahfuz Sultan. See: Eleanor Gibson, "Architects and designers create Google Docs spreadsheet listing black-owned studios," *Dezeen*, June 10, 2020, https://www.dezeen.com/2020/06/10/bipoc-google-docs-spreadsheet.

53 "BIPOC Studios," Google Docs, https://docs.google.com/spreadsheets/d/1ZiWjlfqc02OeWL4hTNZymVT_kyNnO42xG-hucO3rC0E/edit#gid=636314262.

actively fighting against economic, racial, social, environmental, and spatial injustices.

A New Society

We are able to construct a frank picture of how our society has changed and is still changing. Architecture is in this picture, but not in the same way that it used to be. We have focused here on recent phenomena, but it can be said that it was in the 1980s and the beginning of the 1990s that some of the qualities we now find typical of our sense of society first began to really show themselves. In that period, socioeconomic, cultural, and biological changes owing largely to advances in technology—such as the expansion of the internet into public hands, the proliferation of home videogames, the emergence of reproductive manipulations that would lead to the first "designer babies," and the intensification of a worldwide *laissez-faire* capitalism—would establish a new rate of change. Is this when architecture started to find itself misaligned with society more often? Transformations in the way we live have since become so fast, complex, and varied that society and its reflection in the built environment have become out of step. Architecture struggles more than ever to cope with or reflect this speed, complexity, and diversity. But this current misalignment also poses an opportunity for the discipline.

Inquiries into how architecture can realign with society should not be bound by our particular present—they should attend to the present as something which has always changed and will always change. It is therefore more than an inquiry into how a particular spatial form can be achieved; it is an inquiry into how we can achieve modes of attention to emerging sites for architecture. These sites can make fertile space for new norms and rituals. Architecture should actively listen for the pulses of societal transformation to engage with these sites, to better support and encourage, and to more carefully frame each moment of life.

LIFE STAGES
CHILDHOOD
ADOLESCENCE
EMERGING ADULTHOOD
YOUNG ADULTHOOD
MIDDLE ADULTHOOD
LATE MI
PERSONAL GROWTH
GROWTH
IDENTITY/ CONFUSION
FRIENDSHIP/ ISOLATION
SOCIAL INTEGRATION
CONSOLIDATION
REPRODUCTION
PUBERTY/ MENSTRUATION
REPRODUCTION/CHILDFREE
OCCUPATION
PRE-SCHOOL AND PRIMARY SCHOOL
RECEPTIVENESS
INVENTION, CREATIVITY
OUT-OF-THE-BOX THINKING
CRITICAL THINKING/ FIRE (FINANCIAL INDEPENDENCE, RETIRE EARLY)
EXPE
RESIDENCE
FAMILY HOME
HOUSE SHARING
NEW NOMADISM
URBAN LIVING, CO-HOUSING
URBAN LIVIN
0
5
10
15
20
25
30
35
40
45
50

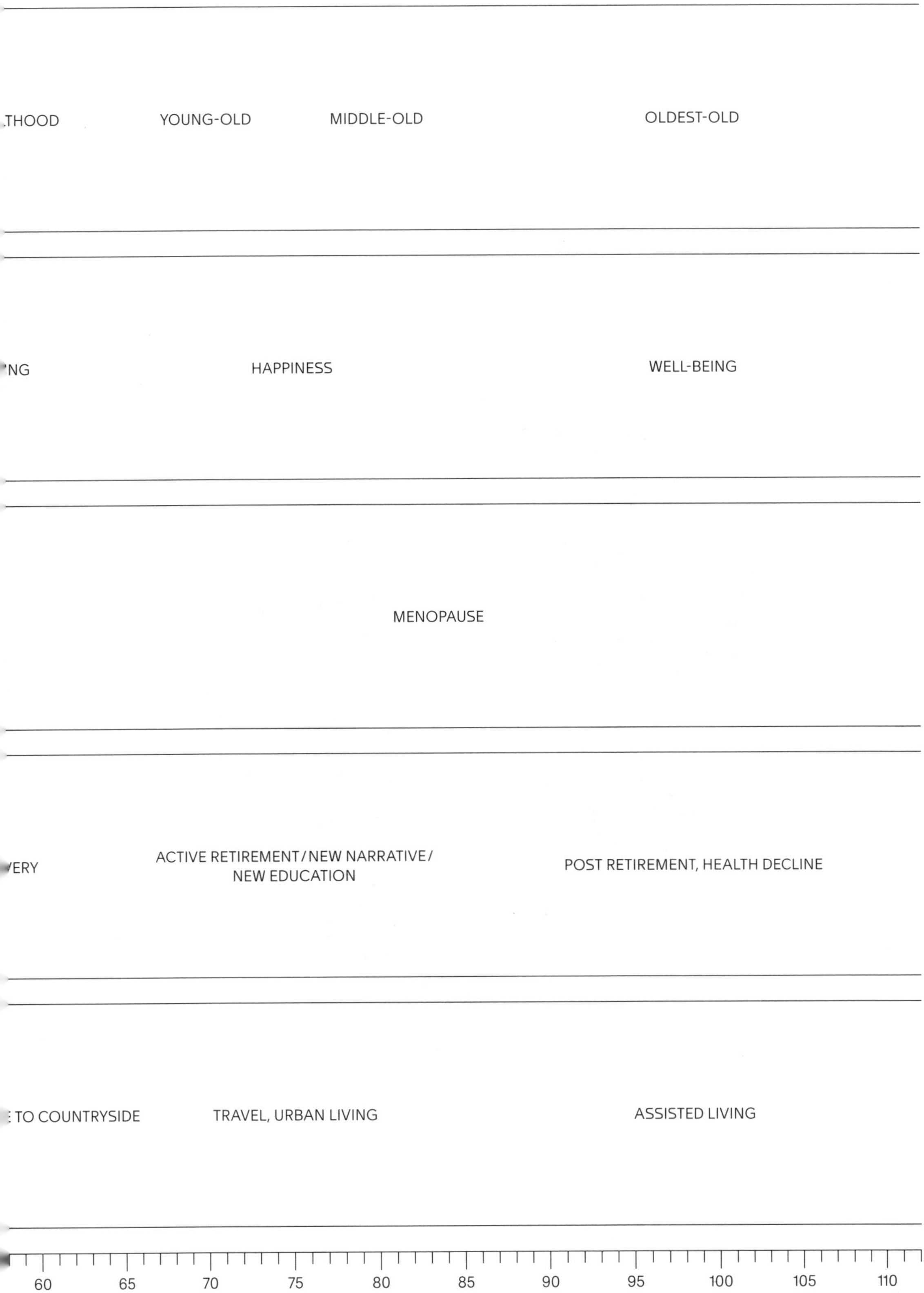

Section sketch of contemporary life cycles and expectations

Labour

Do you need a side hustle to make a living wage? Are you prepared to share your workplace with a robot, or to be replaced by one?

chair
table
NYPD

Alice Proujansky, *24-Hour Daycare*, 2018

Alice Proujansky, *24-Hour Daycare*, 2018

chair
table
EOS 60D

Alice Proujansky, *24-Hour Daycare*, 2018

While short-term gigs tend to offer workers flexibility and autonomy (such as setting one's own schedule and working remotely), they also serve to make flexible work precarious work and create unreasonably competitive working conditions through which work itself is devalued. Fiverr is one of several online marketplaces through which people offer and seek freelance gigs in a broad range of categories—from video editing to graphic design—all while working and hiring from anywhere in the world. As its name suggests, Fiverr was founded on the premise that skilled labour should be available for as little as five dollars per gig—an idea that garnered criticism from gig workers, criticism that only intensified when the company ran an advertisement in 2014 that read: "You're paying too much for design." This assertion—which centres the point of view of the buyer rather than the seller—characterizes the gig economy more broadly.

A contract gig worker places charged-up Lime scooters on a street corner in downtown Austin, Texas, 2020. Photograph: Bob Daemmrich

Following the success of public bike shares, American start-ups such as Lime and Bird have expanded the scope of the sharing economy in recent years by scattering dockless electronic scooters across the sidewalks of numerous cities around the globe. As a result of their unavoidable presence in so many locations, these scooters have gained notoriety as both a hyper-convenient form of transportation and a public nuisance to sidestep. Less visible, however, is the workforce that supports their operation, because it is largely distributed as a "side hustle" that reduces the need for actual employees—along with the obligation to offer minimum wage, insurance, and paid leave. Apart from a few exceptions—such as in California where law AB5 was put in place in 2020 and set new rules for employment within the gig economy—scooters are typically collected *en masse* by workers at the end of each day. These independent contractors, deftly branded by Lime as its "juicers" and Bird as its "bird hunters," make a few dollars apiece to charge the scooters overnight using personal equipment in their own homes.

SAMANTHA INGALLINA AND BENSON CHIEN
TORRE DOMESTIKAH, 2019

There are currently an estimated 2.4 million domestic workers in Mexico—90% of whom are women—who have historically operated within an informal economy characterized by a lack of employment standards and social services. Reflective of these social conditions, the spaces of domestic labour and for domestic labourers have been systematically designed to remain unseen, resulting in architectural configurations that reproduce sexism, classicism, and racism. In 2018, however, the Mexican government passed a law entitling domestic workers to social security benefits such as healthcare and labour rights. In response to this shift, Torre Domestikah investigates the spatial configurations of Mexico City's residential towers and reimagines them such that domestic labour is rendered visible. Focusing on Torre Mitikah, a prominent Mexico City skyscraper, the project—conceived of during a studio run by Frida Escobedo—proposes a scheme that consolidates spaces associated with domestic labour, maximizing daylight and visibility, and providing amenity spaces for both domestic workers and tenants.

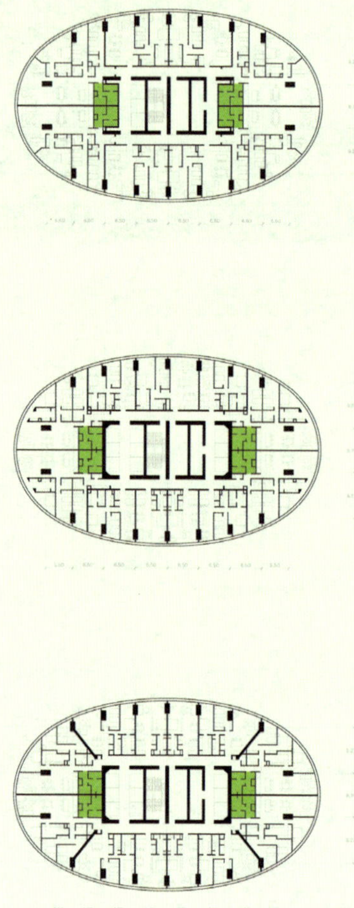

Spaces of domestic labour

Left: Existing floor plan of Torre Mitikah, Mexico City, Mexico
Centre, right: Consolidation and redistribution of domestic space

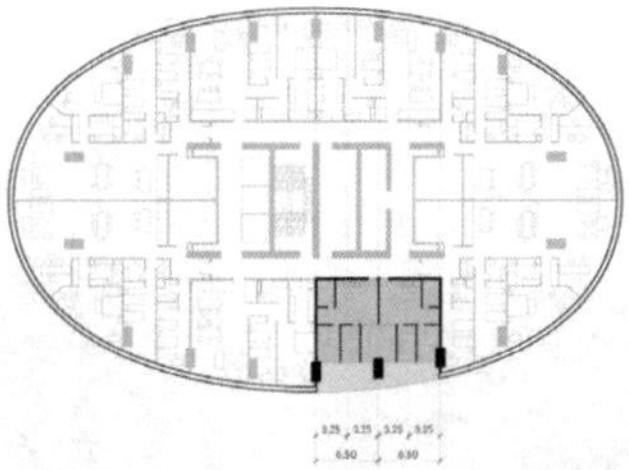
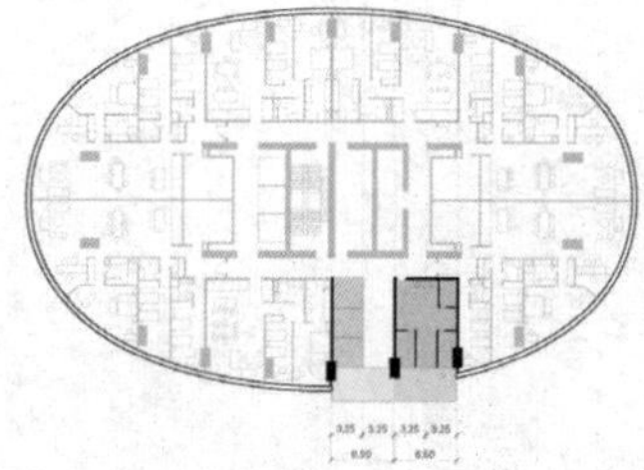
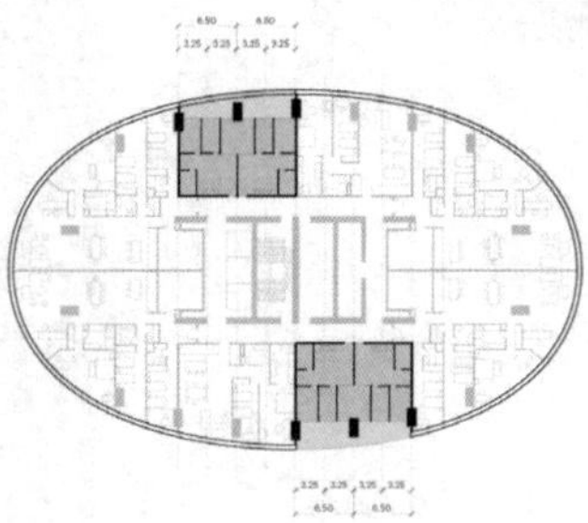
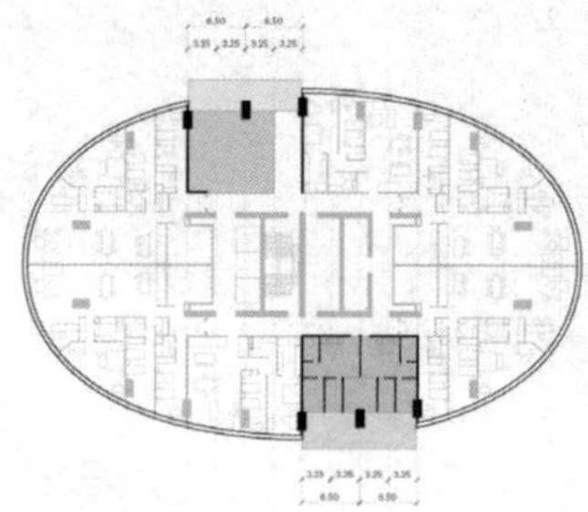
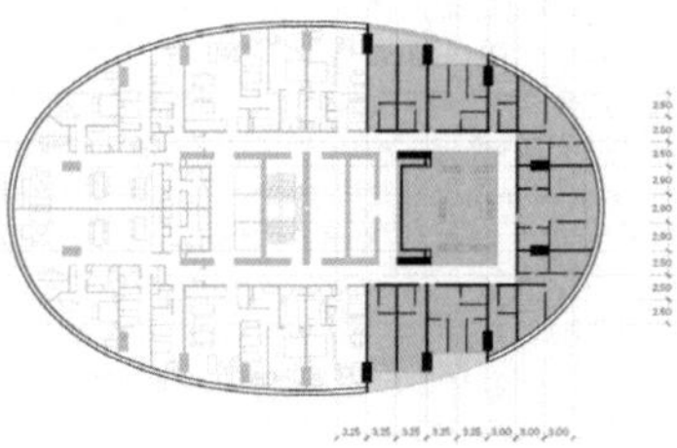
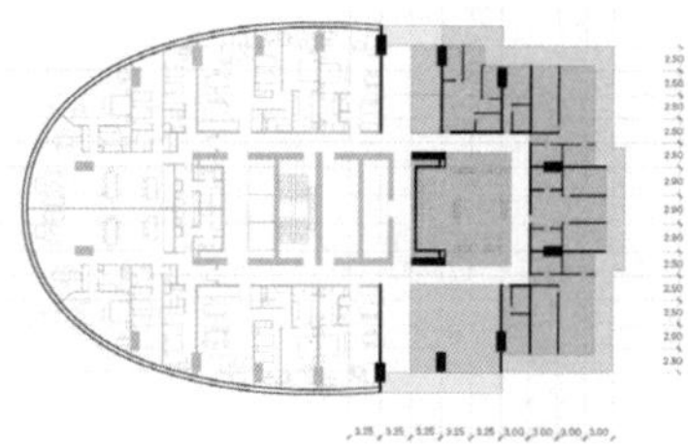
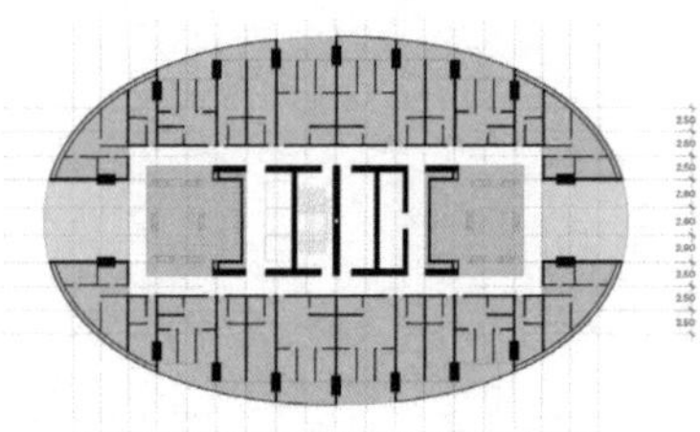
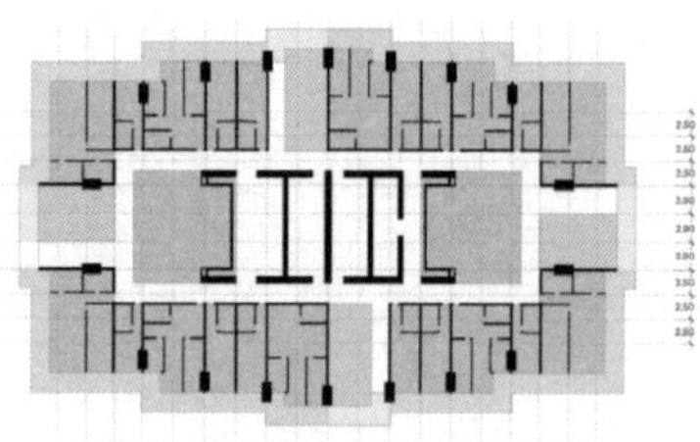

A ghost kitchen in Los Angeles, 2020.
Photograph: Mariah Tauger, *Los Angeles Times*

The demand for food delivery services rapidly increased in the mid-2010s, prompting the creation of an adaptive typology referred to as a dark, ghost, or cloud kitchen. Existing restaurants offering delivery and pickup through apps such as DoorDash and Deliveroo began scaling their services, not through the opening of new locations of their restaurants but through the proliferation of satellite kitchen operations, typically housed in shipping containers and retrofitted buildings located in proximity to potential customers. These dark kitchens subsequently enabled restaurateurs to reduce their overhead even further by creating virtual restaurants, whose offerings are available only through delivery apps and for which no physical dining location exists. Typically, several virtual restaurants operate out of one kitchen space, with staff preparing different types of cuisines in response to incoming orders. While this logistical framework creates a frictionless ordering experience for the consumer, dark kitchens, as their name suggests, render the labour invested in meal preparation as invisible as possible.

2050+ AND -ORAMA
RIDERS NOT HEROES, 2020

Contemporary cities enable the proliferation of sharing and delivery platforms that bring services and goods directly to one's doorstep. This industry relies on an immense number of precarious workers, who are hired for increasingly smaller jobs and salaries. The short documentary *Riders Not Heroes* follows the everyday reality of people who deliver food as they bike the streets of Milan during the COVID-19 pandemic. When the entire city was under an enforced stay-at-home order, these workers were suddenly considered "essential," a status that brought public attention to the precarious and, in this case, dangerous conditions inherent to this app-organized world of individualized labour. The pandemic catalyzed protests for better working conditions for these individuals and shed light on the particular precarity of the work for undocumented migrants, who represent a significant number of food delivery riders not only in Milan, but in many cities around the world.

JESSE LECAVALIER
BROOKLYN AMENITY UTILITY, 2021

In response to food exclusion zones in New York City, Brooklyn Amenity Utility imagines the transformational potentials of food as an urban right and civic utility, similar to potable water, electricity, or waste management. The project strategically integrates food production and distribution points into empty parcels of land managed by municipal agencies, creating a public network of "amenity utilities" that provide food staples to residents at no direct cost. The industrial dimensions of food production are grounded through close attention to their spatial and technological requirements (in this case grain milling), leading to a wide range of locally-determined applications that ultimately improve food equity and encourage a sense of community. In a multi-step process—involving the identification of suitable sites, the development of site-specific prototypes, and the democratic selection of the use of each prototype by the local community—the project aims to improve local living and working conditions without increasing land prices or displacing residents.

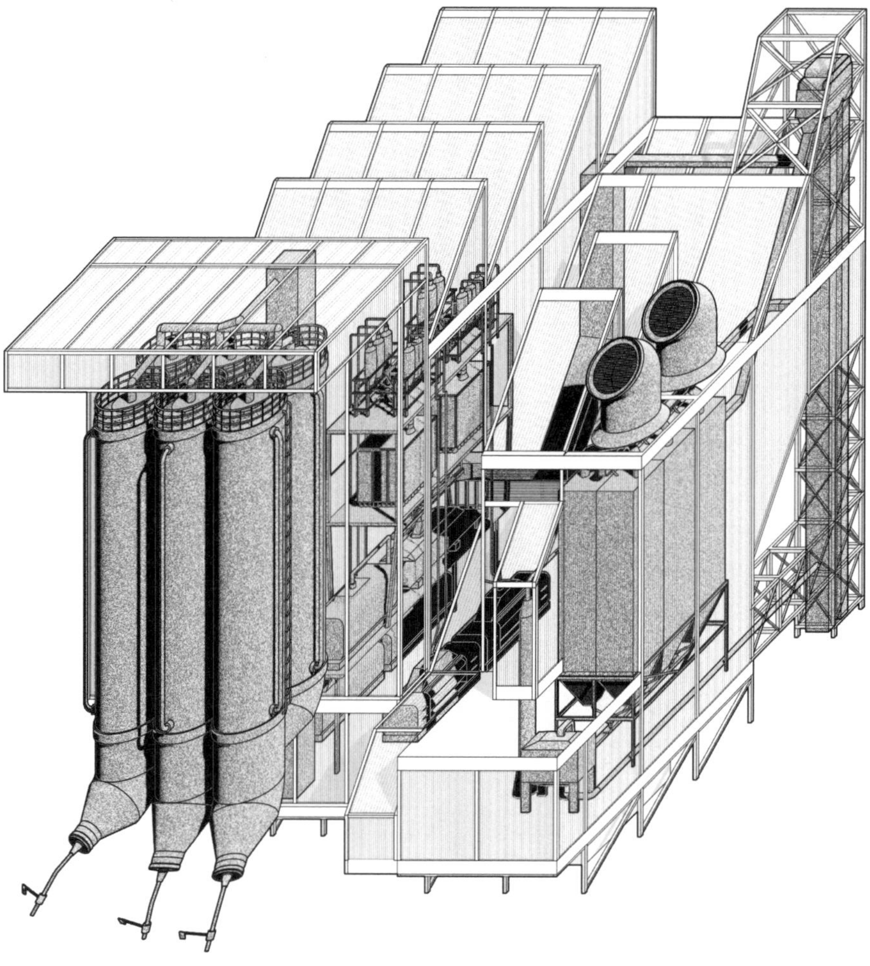

A Storage/Processing

B Public Commons

C Mill/Treatment

D Local Dispensary

E Neighbourhood Hub

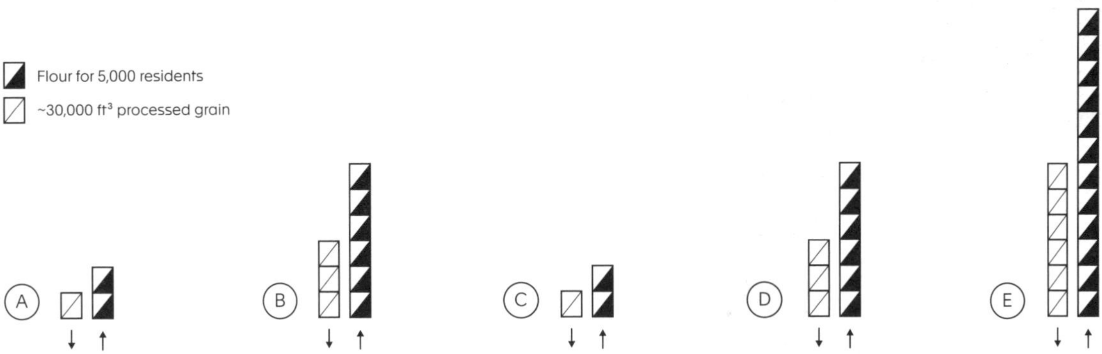

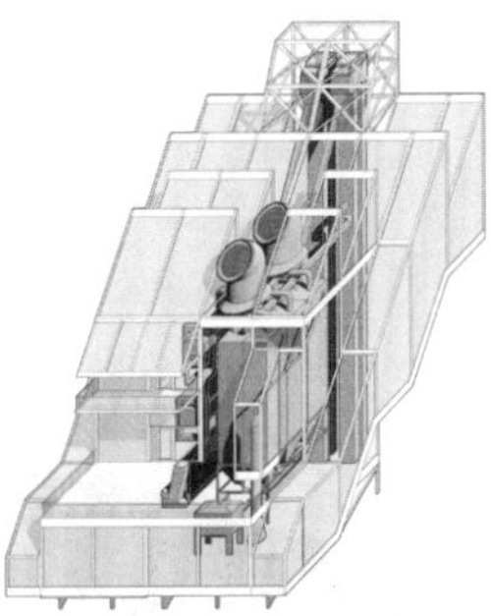

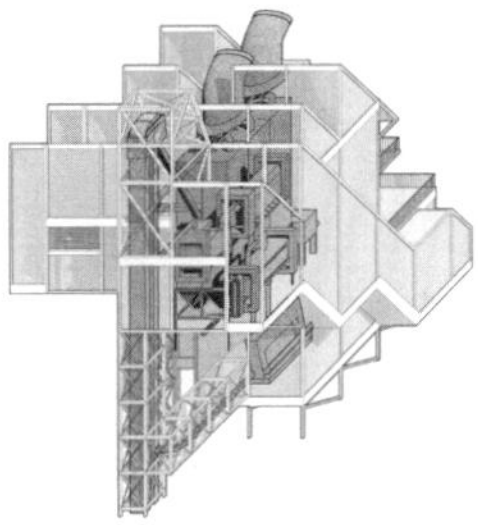

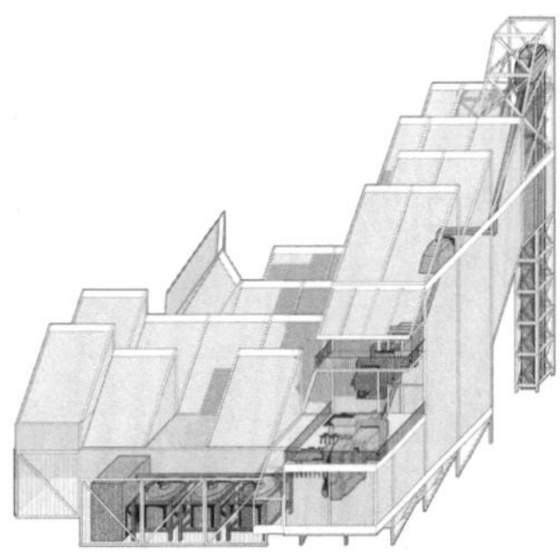

Title: Broad City
Season/Episode: S03E07
Year: 2016
Network: Comedy Central
Country: USA

From *Sex and the City* to gig economy in the city, Ilana and Abbi are fun and carefree women in their twenties, both of whom are self-starters. They are independent, but for them, everything is fleeting and available on-call, from work to sex, love, and certainty. In "B&B-NYC," they rent out their apartments for one night via an online service and find themselves out in the street. There are a lot of laughs, but that is only because a sitcom, unlike life, is written in three acts, and in the last one, a solution always materializes.

ARE YOU PREPARED TO SHARE YOUR WORKPLACE WITH A ROBOT, OR TO BE REPLACED BY ONE?

Helen Hester

Material Hegemony Now: Domestic Realism and Financial Capitalism

Introduction: Resisting Domestic Realism

The domestic sphere has, for too long, been denuded of a sense of political opportunity. Despite a rich heritage of domestic design and community planning, contemporary feminists in the Anglosphere have largely come to accept the "spatial design of the home ... as an inevitable part of domestic life."[1] More generally, the single-family residence is not only something to which people feel resigned, but an aspirational norm—an achievement to be celebrated and strived for. Beyond localized pockets of determined experimentation, this version of the home dominates the cultural imagination. Indeed, whether one embraces it wholeheartedly or attempts to resist it, the conventional family home still shapes the possible spaces of our intimate lives. Elsewhere, I describe this state of affairs as "domestic realism."[2] Domestic realism names the phenomenon whereby the isolated dwelling (and the concomitant privatization of household labour) becomes so accepted and commonplace that it is almost impossible to imagine life being organized through any other form. That this should be the case, despite many people's lived experiences of the pressures and difficulties attendant upon home-based reproductive labour (not to mention domestic violence and abuse), makes such an attitude all the more remarkable.

1 Dolores Hayden, *Grand Domestic Revolution: History of Feminist Designs for American Homes, Neighbourhoods and Cities* (Cambridge: The MIT Press, 1996), 294.

2 This is a riff on Mark Fisher's concept of capitalist realism, which he describes as "the widespread sense that not only is capitalism the only viable political and economic system, but also that it is now impossible even to imagine a coherent alternative to it." See Mark Fisher, *Capitalist Realism: Is There No Alternative?* (Winchester: Zero Books, 2010), 2.

It is my contention that the home represents a crucial (and often overlooked) example of material hegemony in action. Domestic dwellings can be understood as contributing to the solidification of governance through their subtle closing off of options and their contribution to producing generalized consent to an existing order. But there are many possible forms of domestic arrangement—both spatial and relational—aside from the atomized and depoliticized family residence that we most closely associate with the idea of home today. Indeed, it is important that we understand the built environment and its infrastructures not only as means of registering and consolidating dominant political positions but also as potential sites for intervention and as territories for contestation. Interrogating the spaces of reproductive labour (cleaning, cooking, caring, and so on) may be one way of contributing to the construction of a new kind of explicitly feminist and anti-work common sense. But if we are to challenge domestic realism in the twenty-first century, we must first take stock of where we are. What are the contemporary conditions shaping our understanding of the home and determining whether or not we are able to recognize it as a workplace? What currently present the most intractable barriers to emancipatory change? These are the questions underpinning this essay.

Sizing Up the Home

We might start this process of diagnosis by noting the demographic and spatial shifts that have characterized recent decades. Across the core Anglosphere, households have shrunk as houses have grown.[3] While more space per person may sound desirable in the abstract—and clearly, people are continuing to purchase houses built on a larger scale—there are also downsides to the prevalence of massive properties (including higher bills and greater energy

3 In Australia, New Zealand, and the United States, new residential dwellings have at least doubled in size since 1950. See André Stephan and Robert Crawford, "Size does matter: Australia's addiction to big houses is blowing the energy budget," *The Conversation*, 2016, https://theconversation.com/size-does-matter-australias-addiction-to-big-houses-is-blowing-the-energy-budget-70271; RNZ Nights, "New Zealand's ever expanding houses," *Nights*, Radio New Zealand, 14 September 2017, https://www.rnz.co.nz/national/programmes/nights/audio/201858580/new-zealand-s-ever-expanding-houses; and Robert Gordon, *The Rise and Fall of American Growth: The U.S. Standard of Living since the Civil War* (Princeton: Princeton University Press, 2016), 355. Something similar holds for Canada where, since the early 1950s, properties have been "progressively ballooning into one of the largest domiciles in history," and have only recently shown signs of beginning to contract again. Tristan Hopper, "The incredible shrinking home: Why Canada's houses are getting smaller," *The National Post*, 14 July 2012, https://nationalpost.com/news/canada/the-incredible-shrinking-home-why-canadas-houses-are-getting-smaller. The UK is something of an outlier in this discussion, given that its homes are in general much smaller than those of its core Anglosphere cousins. However, a similar broad trend can be detected in England: dwellings constructed between 1945 and 1964 have a mean usable floor area of eighty-six square metres, which was found to increase to ninety square metres for dwellings constructed after 2002. Ministry of Housing, Communities, and Local Governments, *English Housing Survey: Floor Space in English Homes – Main Report* (London: Ministry of Housing, Communities, and Local Governments, 2018), https://assets.publishing.service.gov.uk/government/uploads/system/uploads/attachment_data/file/725085/Floor_Space_in_English_Homes_main_report.pdf, 12.

usage). For the purposes of this essay, there is one particularly key drawback: more space means more maintenance and upkeep work, which translates to an increase in the temporal burdens of reproductive labour—or rather, to the offsetting of any potential benefits for feminized reproductive labourers that might otherwise accrue from smaller household sizes. Bigger does not necessarily mean better when it comes to domestic spaces—at least, not from the perspective of those who have to clean them or who might have ambitions to refuse the more odious burdens of care work and housework.

Just as houses are expanding, Western "society is heading toward the point where the classic family no longer represents the majority."[4] We are moving ever further away from an era in which the nuclear family—as a cohabiting conjugal pair with a small number of school-aged, non-wage earning dependents living with them at home—could be seen as the statistical norm. This kind of family, which, although unevenly distributed, dominated across much of the Anglosphere in the mid-twentieth century due to an unprecedented standardization of the structure of the reproductive unit across socioeconomic classes,[5] has shaped our vision of what a home should be, just as the available housing stock has shaped our sense of what might be possible for our intimate lives. Over the past fifty years or so, however, the nuclear family has persisted as a cultural ideal while also becoming less common as a lived reality. In short, we have witnessed the breakdown of consensus and standardization in terms of the actual organization of social reproduction in the wealthy Anglophone nations.

People are increasingly finding themselves in more varied—and sometimes less extensive—living formations.[6] A trend starting in the 1970s and reaching its peak at the *fin de millénaire*, "smaller households [have become] the norm, including single parents, childless couples, single people, retirees, and couples with fewer children."[7] As households shrink while "houses continue to grow, overcrowding ... is at an all-time low," leading to a "mismatch between people and the housing stock: too many large houses, and too few large traditional families to fill them."[8] To reiterate the point, the kind of households for whom most houses have been designed no longer exist as a numerical norm, even if they continue to exert a powerful hold on our cultural imagination. Today, it seems that neither the housing stock nor the dominant domestic imaginary are maximally compatible with people's existing material needs.

There is a marked incompatibility when it comes to expanding houses and contracting households—a schism between the structures in which we are expected to live our daily lives and the organization of those lives themselves. This becomes all the more obvious

4 Niklas Maak, *The Living Complex: From Zombie City to the New Communal* (Munich: Hirmer, 2015), 14.

5 See Wally Seccombe, *Weathering the Storm: Working-Class Families from the Industrial Revolution to the Fertility Decline* (London: Verso, 1993) and Helen Hester and Nick Srnicek, *After Work: The Fight for Free Time* (London: Verso, 2022).

6 In his empirically driven comparative analysis of the global history of the family, Göran Therborn notes that, within today's wealthy nations, "the secular decline of fertility, in conjunction with the postponement of death at all ages, has created new, or much more common 'non-traditional,' domestic situations, and new life-course stages: the deliberately childless couple, the only-child-childhood, the empty-nest middle-aged couple ..., the single elderly person household." See Göran Therborn, *Between Sex and Power: Family in the World, 1900–2000* (London: Routledge, 2004), 292. Various studies bear this out. In the United States, to take one example, between 1970 and 2012 "the percentage of households composed of married couples with children dropped from 40% to 20%. Non-traditional living arrangements are steadily increasing both in absolute numbers and as a percentage of households." Rigel C. Oliveri, "Single-Family Zoning, Intimate Association, and the Right to Choose Household Companions," *Florida Law Review* 67, no 4 (2016): 1448.

when one considers the challenges involved in living differently within the existing housing stock. It is clear that repurposing a dwelling designed with a nuclear family in mind requires a certain amount of effort and going-against-the-grain. Student house shares, for example, often struggle with how to equitably allocate space and organize resources within such settings: Should the household convert a reception room into additional sleeping quarters to increase occupancy and save on rent? How should residents equitably decide who takes the master bedroom and who gets the box room? How should they schedule access to the bathroom, allocate storage space, and coordinate the movements of multiple people within a poky galley kitchen? In addition to these kinds of quotidian logistical issues, there are wider material hegemonic barriers to life beyond the family within a single-family house. Things like policy and legislation, for example, work to solidify specific spatial and relational living arrangements, making it impossible—or at least, extremely inconvenient—to inhabit the world in any other way.

Take single-family zoning ordinances in the US: "Such ordinances may place whole neighborhoods, or even entire towns, off limits to people who wish to live together but who do not fit into a traditional definition of 'family,' which requires that members be related to one another through blood, marriage, or adoption."[9] In these areas, even a set-up as banal as a student house share is impermissible. As Rigel C. Oliveri notes, "restrictive single-family ordinances and the judicial decisions that uphold them ... are filled with value judgments masquerading as facts about what families look like and why people should live together."[10] Given that people with less economic mobility and racial and ethnic minorities have generally "been more likely to live in multi-generational family arrangements,"[11] the restrictions enacted by these ordinances are likely to particularly affect households whose members are neither white nor middle class. Furthermore, they serve to entrench the disjuncture between housing and households. A housing type that would likely prove outsized in terms of the needs of many contemporary families not only continues to be enshrined as an aspirational norm but is also more directly upheld via legislation that actively prevents the accommodation of other kinds of reproductive units. The intimate arrangements that we seek for ourselves are shaped by the dynamic interplay of desire and possibility; the result, in this case, is that increased childbearing or under-occupancy become the most feasible outcomes.

After the Crash: Generalized Reproductive Crisis

Today, a house's "primary function—accumulating value on the market ... —bears little or even no relation to its ability to perform as a dwelling, any more than a collectible car's value is related to its

7 Dolores Hayden, *Building Suburbia: Green Fields and Urban Growth, 1820–2000* (New York City: Vintage, 2004), 190. While such changes may seem to be imbued with emancipatory potential and may indeed help to prise open a cultural space for new and less restrictive domestic imaginaries, we must also be sensitive to the reasons behind their emergence. Often, these smaller households are the result of divorce or of widows and widowers living alone after their children have grown up; while not necessarily unhappy states of affairs in and of themselves—being a single adult can have many advantages and pleasures—we must not pretend that such situations are widely chosen, welcomed, or envisioned as part of what constitutes the good life. As we shall see throughout this essay, even if alternative household arrangements are increasingly proliferating, domestic realism as an aspirational ideational vision is holding strong.

8 Oliveri, "Single-Family Zoning," 1449.

9 Oliveri, "Single-Family Zoning," 1403.

10 Oliveri, "Single-Family Zoning," 1447.

11 Richard Fry and Jeffrey S. Passel, "In Post-Recession Era, Young Adults Drive Continuing Rise in Multi-Generational Living," Pew Research Center, 17 July 2014, http://www.pewsocialtrends.org/2014/07/17/in-post-recession-era-young-adults-drive-continuing-rise-in-multi-generational-living/.

12 Joseph Grima, "Home is the Answer, but What is the Question?" in *SQM: The Quantified Home*, ed. Space Caviar (Zürich: Lars Müller Publishers, 2014), 12–17 and 16–17.

usefulness as a means to go shopping."[12] The result of this has been "an oversupply of luxury housing and a lack of affordable housing in many cities across the world,"[13] in a context in which the costs of both buying and renting have continued to skyrocket.[14] The full implications of the financialization of, and the affordability crisis in, housing—from poor living conditions to dangerously (even murderously) low-quality buildings and from land banking to houses used solely as investment vehicles being left to rot—have been widely discussed by more expert scholars, non-profits, and policy makers.[15] My interest here is in pointing to the chilling effect that this has upon the diversification of available models of domesticity and, therefore, upon the possibility of reimagining the home from an anti-work feminist perspective. As Richard J. Williams points out, in a "highly developed market economy, buildings are commodities as much as lived spaces; their cost and enduring value as investments inhibit experimentation."[16] As long as housing is seen and treated predominantly as a commodity and an investment vehicle, there will be major barriers to the creation of more emancipatory and politically radical housing forms and to efforts to uproot domestic realism.

It's worth remarking that, whilst the single-family residence retains its grip on the cultural imagination in the form of an aspirational norm, the current lack of affordable housing has prompted its own modes of living beyond conventional ideas of the household, resulting in expansion as well as contraction. Across the core Anglosphere, evidence can be found for an intensification and extension of interest in multi-generational living,[17] including within communities "where this has not been a traditional practice."[18] Of course, collective approaches to ensuring quotidian survival and intergenerational thriving pre-existed any current housing crisis. Typically, however, they have manifested themselves in households with below average incomes, particularly those of racial and ethnic minorities. Solangel Maldonado notes, in relation to the United States, that a substantial number of "families of colour, immigrants, and economically vulnerable families ... reside with extended family members for cultural and economic reasons."[19] Much of the current trend, however, can be seen to be the result of changes experienced by once-affluent white families for whom the increasingly generalized conditions of precarity and crisis are now beginning to bite.

As Bella DePaulo notes, households of this kind have advantages not just in terms of surviving a dearth of waged work (by, for example, the pooling of resources, sharing of expenses, and provision of a collective safety net for individuals in crisis) but also of coping with a surplus of unwaged work: "Most people living in multigenerational households said that their arrangements made it easier to provide

13 Richard Florida and Benjamin Schneider, "The Global Housing Crisis," *CityLab*, 11 April 2018, https://www.citylab.com/equity/2018/04/the-global-housing-crisis/557639.

care to the people who needed it, whether they were aging relatives or little kids."[20] Commenting on the renewed trend for multi-generational living in Australia, an article in the *Sydney Morning Herald* points to similar concerns. When we consider "housing

14 This is evident across the core Anglosphere. The "average Australian living in a capital city spends between 20% and 30% of their weekly income on rent," in many Canadian municipalities and urban regions, the cost of renting has risen by more than twenty percent since 2000, and forty-four percent of "New Zealand households in rental accommodation pay more than 30% of their income in housing costs," Richard Whitten, "How much of our wages do we spend on rent in Australia?" Finder, 1 October 2020, https://www.finder.com.au/how-much-of-our-wages-do-we-spend-on-rent-in-australia; Federation of Canadian Municipalities, *No Vacancy: Trends in Rental Housing in Canada*, (Ottawa: Federation of Canadian Municipalities, 2012), https://data.fcm.ca/documents/reports/FCM/No_Vacancy_Trends_in_Rental_Housing_in_Canada_EN.pdf; and Elinor Chisholm, Philippa Howden-Chapman, and Geoff Fougere, "Renting in New Zealand: perspectives from tenant advocates," *Kōtuitui: New Zealand Journal of Social Sciences Online* 12, no. 1 (8 January 2017): 95–110. It's a similar picture in the UK, with the capital being especially unaffordable—data released in 2017 show that tenants in London spent an average of forty-nine percent of their salaries on rent. Kevin Peachey and Daniele Palumbo, "How much of your salary is spent on rent?" *BBC*, 1 December 2017, https://www.bbc.co.uk/news/business-42179119). Residential rents in the US "increased by 22 percent on average between 2006 and 2014, while average incomes decreased by 6 percent," resulting in nearly half of all renters "spending more than 30 percent of their income on housing." Florida and Schneider, "The Global Housing Crisis."

15 See Florida and Schneider, "The Global Housing Crisis"; James Meek, "Where will we live?" *London Review of Books* 36, no. 1 (9 January 2014): https://www.lrb.co.uk/v36/n01/james-meek/where-will-we-live; and Robert Booth, "Tories are taxing poor while ignoring 'Billionaires Row' scandal, says Labour," *The Guardian,* 2 February 2014, https://www.theguardian.com/society/2014/feb/02/tories-taxing-poor-ignoring-billionaires-row-scandal-labour.

16 Richard J. Williams, *Sex and Buildings: Modern Architecture and the Sexual Revolution* (London: Reaktion Books, 2013), 26.

17 For example, "multigenerational living arrangements thought to be more commonplace in many parts of the world are quietly emerging in Australia," with research indicating that "one in five Australians live in a multi-generational household," Edgar Liu, "Moving back in: The rise of intergenerational households," B News, UNSW Sydney, 10 January 2020, https://www.be.unsw.edu.au/news/moving-back-rise-multigenerational-households; in Canada, data indicates that multigenerational homes were the fastest growing category of household between 2001 and 2016, Caroline Alphonso and Xiao Xu, "Multigenerational households face unique challenges in battling spread of coronavirus," *The Globe and Mail*, 19 March 2020, https://www.theglobeandmail.com/canada/article-multigenerational-households-face-unique-challenges-in-battling-spread; and research suggests that extended family households are increasing in New Zealand, and that the current housing stock is insufficient to meet the needs of these households, including Māori and Pasifika families in long-standing multigenerational arrangements, Penny Lysnar and Ann Dupuis, *Meeting the housing needs of multi-generational households* (Porirua: BRANZ, 2015), https://cdn.auckland.ac.nz/assets/creative/about/our-faculty/School%20programmes%20and%20centres/Transforming%20Cities/ER4-Housing-Multi-generational-Households.pdf. UK statistics indicate that the category "Other households," which includes multi-generational families, had "the largest percentage increase in all household types over the decade 2001–2011," Lynsnar and Dupuis, "Meeting the household needs," 19; and finally, the Pew Research Center found that the number of multi-generational families in America "spiked during the Great Recession of 2007–2009 and has kept on growing in the post-recession period"—a fact partly attributable to "the declining employment and wages of less-educated young adults… undercutting their capacity to live independently of their parents," Fry and Passel, "In Post-Recession Era, Young Adults Drive Continuing Rise in Multi-Generational Living."

18 Lynsnar and Dupuis, "Meeting the household needs," 9.

19 Solangel Maldonado, "Sharing a House but Not a Household: Extended Families and Exclusionary Zoning Forty Years After Moore," *Fordham Law Review* 85, no. 6 (2017): 2641.

20 Bella DePaulo, *How We Live Now: Redefining Home and Family in the Twenty-First Century* (New York City: Atria Books, 2015), 32.

affordability, dual careers, childcare, the frightening quality of a lot of aged care," the author suggests, the multi-generational family starts to "seem like a fine idea, even if it does come with a few inconveniences."[21] (It is particularly a generationally extended version of the conventional, "biological" family that is at play here; the more radical possibilities of multi-generational living are—as is so often the case in mainstream media coverage—left undiscussed.)

One of the households interviewed includes two older people—grandparents who handed over their three bedroom home to their daughter after she was forced to leave a rental property at short notice, with her young family in tow. They are now living in a purpose-built tiny house in what was once their back garden—an arrangement which, despite the sacrifice and space squeeze it implies, could only be made possible by their comparatively privileged position as owner-occupiers of a spacious dwelling set on generous grounds. These grandparents "like being so near to the grandchildren, being able to help with breakfasts, school runs, etc.,"[22] the reader is assured, and the benefits for everybody of having an on-site support network appear to be considerable.

Whilst expanding the household may indeed present ways to mitigate the temporal demands of domestic social reproduction, we must also recognize that the circumstances under discussion here hardly offer a broad-based model of emancipatory opportunity. For one thing, despite multi-generational living having its advantages, "more than three-quarters of those living in such households said that the arrangement sometimes added to their stress."[23] In our Australian example, we learn that the arrangements in question have only been in place for a few weeks, meaning that there is still plenty of time for the novelty to fade. The issue of how the "middle generation" of the household is finding the transition is also left unresolved. It may be that, as time passes and the elders become more vulnerable, the grown-up daughter will find herself responsible for (and torn between) the needs of two different generations, resulting in her reproductive workload intensifying—unless this workload can be redistributed amongst the members of the household.

Beyond this specific case study, it appears that a generalized move toward multi-generational households across the Anglosphere in recent years is built not upon reasoned personal or group preferences but upon economic compulsion and a concomitant absence of choice. A number of studies point to the influence of the 2008 financial crisis in this regard.[24] This is quite obviously less than ideal for any of those involved and needs to be borne in mind lest we risk automatically romanticizing multi-generational arrangements as a defiant and desirable response to current forms of material

21 Fenella Souter, "Family embrace: the rise of multi-generational living in Australia," *Sydney Morning Herald*, 6 March 2020, https://www.smh.com.au/lifestyle/life-and-relationships/family-embrace-the-rise-of-multi-generational-living-in-australia-20191230-p53nmr.html.

22 Ibid.

23 DePaulo, *How We Live Now*, 32.

24 See footnote 29 for several examples.

25 And indeed, in a historical moment in which the daily actions of those closest to us have the potential to generate significant health risks, it seems particularly pressing that we be given the opportunity to exercise meaningful choice over the people we live with.

hegemony. A defensive reorganization of domesticity prompted by a winnowing of options and opportunities is unlikely to scale up into a new socio-spatial common sense and may, in fact, serve to shore up domestic realism by making an inaccessible cultural ideal seem even more desirable.[25]

Domestic realism already encourages us to view deviations from the single-family home and the nuclear-family household as a failure to obtain a self-evidently preferable way of life. To hold up alternatives born (at least in part) of particularly acute economic necessity as the basis for an ideal risks inadvertently lends credence to this idea. If there is a germ of emancipatory opportunity to be found within this general trend, we must be careful to embrace its possibility without lapsing into uncritical idealization. Nevertheless, detached from naturalizing discourses of the nuclear family, it becomes painfully apparent just how unsatisfactory the home is as a place of work and how much domestic labourers (be they waged or unwaged) might have to gain from agitating against it and redistributing their work within it. Seeing the home in this way encourages us to recognize where and how spatial arrangements and working practices might inform the visibility and valuation of reproductive labour and how rarely concerted collective efforts are made to reduce domestic workloads.

Commercial Co-living: Selling an Alternative

A further example of "alternative" living arrangements emerging in response to the housing crisis can be found in the form of commercial collective living facilities. Around the world, private property companies are backing "a new form of shared housing where residents have common interests and lifestyles."[26] Unlike traditional flat shares, these co-living spaces "are professionally managed rather than informally arranged"[27] and typically feature shared amenities like gyms, cafés, and cinema spaces. Aimed primarily at millennial professionals, this type of co-living arrangement is gaining traction across the Anglosphere, a trend that has been accelerated by start-ups like PodShare in California and developments such as The Coh in Auckland.[28] Often bolstered by housing shortages in local markets, co-living has become a "focus of development interest internationally, because it is one of the most profitable forms of housing development possible."[29]

London is one city at the forefront of the rise of this kind of accommodation, which commentators have compared to students' residence halls, boutique hotels, and high-end youth hostels.[30] COLIV—the first fund for large-scale, purpose-built co-living facilities in the city—recently forward funded a 310-room complex in South London. COLIV is now looking to "acquire or fund between six and ten developments in [London] over a ten year

26 Micheal Gerrity, "Residential Co-Living Trend Accelerates in Asia." *World Property Journal*, 2 February 2018, http://www.worldpropertyjournal.com/real-estate-news/hong-kongjll-report-bridging-the-housing-gap-millennials-coliving-in-asia-report-millennials-housing-trends-in-asia-china-housing-report-2018-china-real-estate-news-10737.php.

27 Ibid.

28 Indeed, research for Savills in Australia indicates that co-living is a "global metropolitan housing trend." Conal Newland and Paul Savitz, "The global trend in co-living spaces," Savills, 24 February 2020, https://www.savills.com.au/blog/article/180712/student-accomodation/the-global-trend-in-co-living-spaces. Within the core Anglosphere, it is particularly taking hold in the more expensive cities, such as San Francisco, New York, and London, but is increasingly gaining a foothold in places like Auckland, Melbourne, and Ottawa as well.

29 Mark Southcombe, "When 'co-living housing' is just a fancy name for exploiting a crisis," *The Spinoff*, 21 June 2019, https://thespinoff.co.nz/auckland/21-06-2019/when-co-living-housing-is-just-a-fancy-name-for-exploiting-a-crisis.

30 Winnie Agbonlahor, "Co-living in London: Friendship, fines and frustration," *BBC*, 23 April 2018, https://www.bbc.co.uk/news/uk-england-london-43090849.

31 Jessica Clark, "DTZ Investors backs London rental market with £70m co-living project," *City A.M.*, 5 October 2020, https://www.cityam.com/dtz-investors-backs-london-rental-market-with-70m-co-living-project.

period."[31] Although this trend seems to be accelerating at present, complexes of this kind have been taking hold in the city for several years. An article for *i-D* looked at one of the first developments of this kind, Co-Living Old Oak, back in 2017, and pointed to a litany of facilities: "over 500 rooms, a spa, cinema, bar and restaurant, a gym, games room and roof terrace."[32] The space is supposed to offer a "new mode of living: accommodation, laundry, tax and Wi-Fi bundled into one easy payment of about £1000 a month."[33] Could this represent a step toward an anti-work domestic dream? Will living arrangements be revisited in the name of reducing the drudgery of housework, streamlining household organization, and enhancing both individual and collective autonomy?

Certainly, there are echoes of emancipatory experiments from bygone eras here. Amenities that exceed the functional to incorporate the potentially luxurious are reminiscent of some of the most desirable elements of European interwar social housing—municipal visions in which the proximity of services to individual dwellings was intended to lessen the burdens of the home in order to free up the reproductive labourer for civic engagement and political participation. The most famous example is Vienna's Social Democratic city council's introduction of large housing complexes designed and built as part of a swath of municipal reforms between 1919 and 1934. In this case, "dwellings were incorporated with kindergartens, libraries, medical and dental clinics, laundries, workshops, theatres, co-operative stores, public gardens, sports facilities, and a wide range of other public facilities."[34] If one squints hard enough, one can detect similarities between this historical example and the vision of the good life that commercial co-living is so keen to market. It will come as no surprise, however, to learn that these echoes are merely the ghosts of unrealized potentials, which become particularly apparent when one turns to the question of work.

In many ways, commercial co-living projects in metropolitan centres represent a response to the challenges of paid work in an era of generalized precarity. I mean this not simply in the sense that they represent a package targeted at time-poor young workers who lack the means (and in some cases the will) to get onto the property ladder but also in the sense that they are oriented toward remote and freelance working (and workers). This form of co-living is, after all, the domestic equivalent of co-working; it is no coincidence that WeWork went on to launch WeLive: co-living units situated in several American cities. We see this with the new COLIV facility in South London, too, which will have "a dedicated co-working space to help bring that richness of experience and creative contact"—a space designed to meet people's assumed need for "vibrancy and contact in their daily working lives."[35]

32 Tom Harrad, "This new co-living space is the dystopian symptom of a London failing young people," *i-D*, 20 June 2017, https://i-d.vice.com/en_uk/article/43xgx9/this-new-co-living-space-is-the-dystopian-symptom-of-a-london-failing-young-people.
33 Ibid.
34 Eve Blau, *The Architecture of Red Vienna 1919–1934* (Cambridge, MA: The MIT Press, 1999), 2.
35 Chris Cooper, "The Co-Living Sector is Here to Stay," *Property Week*, 21 October 2020, https://www.propertyweek.com/insight/the-co-living-sector-is-here-to-stay/5110700.article.

However, this attempt to (literally) accommodate changing conditions around some forms of wage work in urban centres resolutely fails to address related problems with reproductive labour. Reports make clear that unwaged work remains a problem in these co-living projects. A journalist who tried out two London co-living projects for the BBC noted that "there are drawbacks to this style of living: finding basic utensils in the kitchen on my floor was not easy, with many dirty or broken. Dotted around the building are signs urging people to clean up after themselves."[36] The developers, we are told, no longer provide utensils and equipment for shared spaces, presumably because, in practice, residents were unwilling to do the work of maintaining them.

To add insult to injury, London-based co-living projects appear to deliberately wrap their profit-driven activities in a mantle of radicality, borrowing from "the language of progressive, alternative modes of living, in order to promote an exclusive housing development."[37] Tom Harrad points out, words like "common" and "collective," which are often thrown around in relation to these facilities "imply ownership, responsibility, cooperation, freedom. They come weighed down with historical connotations—from forced land enclosures to the counterculture movement."[38] To his mind, creative professionals find themselves "attracted to these inauthentic capitalist shadows of progressive spaces because genuine progressive spaces in London are now almost nonexistent. The criminalisation of residential squatting in 2012 effectively ended the possibility of young people starting cohabitation projects in the city without serious financial investment."[39] Emerging from a profound crisis in housing affordability—one tied up with the treatment of homes as repositories for capital—schemes like these seek to absorb the energy of autonomous communities and politically conscious ways of living together, in order to package them up as a ready-made, rentable commodity, from which developers can extract a profit.

How such commercial experiments, with their erosion of personal space and emphasis on shared facilities, might hold up in a post-pandemic world remains an open question. The bigger picture is that domestic realism has in fact been fortified in the era of financial capitalism and, indeed, appears to be holding strong in the vertiginous interregnum in which we now find ourselves. There is still widespread acceptance that the single-family home is a mark of entry into adulthood; any alternatives to it are seen as a matter of making a virtue out of necessity—the expanded dwellings of multi-generational families are seen as attempts to access a safety net and ride out a crisis, the contracted small flats of commercial co-living projects are understood as a stop gap while one establishes their career or as a first half-step on a property ladder that

36 Agbonlahor, "Co-living in London."
37 Harrad, "This new co-living space."
38 Ibid.
39 Ibid.

would otherwise remain inaccessible. None of this is intended to deny the existence of more meaningful and politically radical contemporary experiments in domestic organization. As has long been the case, pioneering groups and individuals continue to experiment with both the social and the spatial relations of the home.[40] However, many of these experiments are piecemeal, limited in scope, or lacking in material support. Indeed, some appear to be as isolated and atomized as the single-family homes that they criticize. These limitations are not necessarily failures, and many spatial interventions succeed when considered on their own terms. However, if the aim is to disembed domestic realism and initiate a program of material counter-hegemony in the name of decisively breaking open the options that people have available to them in regards to their intimate lives, then a wider-reaching cultural shift is required.

Conclusion: Dismantling Domestic Realism

How might one seek to engineer this? There are certain interventions we could tentatively propose, with the understanding that any attempt to build material counter-hegemony will depend on the synthesis and co-operation of a broad range of specialist knowledges oriented toward a similar goal. If we are invested in dislodging domestic realism and in creating housing that is responsive to different kinds of human and environmental needs, an important first step might be to undermine the various cultural, political, and legislative supports that artificially bolster and preserve the privileged status of the single-family home and nuclear family and work to supress the possible flourishing of any alternatives. There are a multitude of regulations, financial incentives, tax breaks, and so on that encourage the continuation of the conventional domestic residence at the expense of spatial alternatives across the countries of the core Anglosphere.

40 Indeed, some of the most inspiring experiments have emerged as a direct response to the crisis in affordable housing. The Focus E15 Campaign, for example, saw young and expectant mothers occupy abandoned flats on the Carpenters Estate in East London in protest of their eviction and proposed relocation to less expensive parts of the country. The squatted flats were temporarily transformed into a social centre, with play spaces for children and a scheme including an "evolving program of daily events, including workshops, meetings, and music and comedy gigs." See Focus E15, "About Us," Focus E15 Campaign, https://focuse15.org/about. Elsewhere, collectives of older women have turned to co-housing as a means of extending their independence and circumventing the loneliness that can sometimes plague those who decide to "age in place." The London Older Lesbian Co-housing project started from the realization that residential care homes are not necessarily comfortable places for those whose lives have not revolved around a heterosexual nuclear family, and that older people who identify as LGBTQIA+ could therefore feel as if they were being pushed back into the closet as they aged. The co-housing project is currently looking for support from a developer and a local authority in order to build flats with common areas, in the hope that this will enable residents to avoid reliance on external health and social care agencies for as long as possible. Older Women's Co-Housing, meanwhile, is further along in the process, having established a community in "a new, purpose-built block of flats in North London." The development features mixed tenure properties, including social rental units, along with communal facilities and grounds. See Heather Saul, "How the older women who built their own co-housing community found the first year together," *i news*, 19 October 2017, https://inews.co.uk/essentials/older-women-built-pioneering-new-community-98499.

In New Zealand, for example, efforts could be made to target a tax system that works to artificially inflate demand for increasingly enormous single-family homes. At present, "income from residential property, New Zealand's largest asset class, is taxed at lower rates than income from other assets,"[41] a policy that incentivizes investment in property and encourages "people to build houses that are maybe 25% larger" than they would be otherwise.[42] If these homes are not being used to house multi-generational families or other reproductive groupings that are larger than the nuclear family, then moves might be made to rebalance the taxation system to remove this kind scaffolding for domestic realism. The issue of American single-family zoning ordinances discussed earlier would fall into this same camp. In Oliveri's opinion, the Supreme Court should revisit these ordinances, and "make a clear statement that the right of intimate association includes the right to choose household companions, and therefore all efforts to regulate internal household composition are suspect."[43] Seeking to identify and challenge policies and ordinances of this type, which unevenly support certain kinds of dwellings and living arrangements over others, may be one relatively modest starting point via which to start unpicking domestic realism and around which to begin organizing around spatial justice.

Such a move is crucial if we do not want housing advocacy to unwittingly enforce material hegemony as it stands. Can we point our organizing efforts toward a horizon more emancipatory than that offered by the labour-intensive single-family dwelling and the idea of the house as a financial instrument? Can we approach living space in a way that facilitates the accommodation of different needs and makes the mitigation of the worst burdens of gendered reproductive labour a real priority? Given the diversification of household size and organization since the middle of the twentieth century—the rise of reproductive units smaller and larger than that associated with an incorrectly assumed nuclear norm, from single elders and solo millennials to multi-generational families—it seems as though we are now at an opportune moment to seize the initiative and lay the foundations for alternatives. What could be better than home?

With this in mind, we could consider the integration of domestic residences and communal services—not in the sense of providing access to the soulless and shabby common spaces of corporate developments but in terms of making resources accessible and bringing facilities, amenities, and support within arms' reach. Hayden pursues this line of thinking in her classic article, "What Would a Non-Sexist City Be Like?" Imagining a metropolitan cooperative made up of forty households, she envisions collective

41 Andrew Coleman, "Taxing capital income in New Zealand: an international perspective," University of Otago Economics Discussion Papers No. 1902 (January 2019), https://www.otago.ac.nz/economics/otago703148.pdf.

42 Andrew Coleman, "Why does New Zealand keep building such massive houses?" *The Spinoff*, 15 May 2017, https://thespinoff.co.nz/society/15-05-2017/why-does-new-zealand-keep-building-such-massive-houses.

43 Oliveri, "Single-Family Zoning," 1450.

spaces and activities, to be staffed (as far as possible) by residents themselves in return for generous compensation:

> [1] a day-care center with landscaped outdoor space, providing day care for forty children and after-school activities for sixty-four children; [2] a laundromat providing laundry service; [3] a kitchen providing lunches for the day-care center, take-out evening meals, and "meals-on-wheels" for elderly people in the neighborhood; [4] a grocery depot, connected to a local food cooperative; [5] a garage with two vans providing dial-a- ride service and meals-on-wheels; [6] a garden (or allotments) where some food can be grown; [7] a home help office providing helpers for the elderly, the sick, and employed parents whose children are sick. The use of all of these collective services should be voluntary; they would exist in addition to private dwelling units and private gardens.[44]

Hayden's suggested schema feels as innovative now as it must have when it was first advanced in 1980. It offers a vision in which the temporal burdens of social reproduction are substantially mitigated by community-steered services and spaces. Simply reducing the travel time and planning required to access vital community resources would have obvious benefits for those responsible for feminized reproductive labour (and, given the circumstances at the time I'm writing, point to the intriguing possibility of a scaled-up lockdown—one in which the proximity of others is viewed less as a risk factor and more as a resource). Whilst Hayden largely seems to position her non-sexist city complex as a way to deal with the competing pressures of waged labour and unwaged social reproduction, her proposals could easily be reframed as a means of maximizing free time and enhancing collective autonomy: What would an anti-work feminist city be like?

There are several steps one could take to update Hayden's vision for the twenty-first century. A phone and computer repair shop, for example, with a mobile team of technology trouble-shooters might prove to be a useful resource. Communally accessible maker spaces could include everything from screen-printing equipment, sewing machines, and kilns, to top-of-the-line 3D printers; regular classes could be offered for those who wish to learn how to use these technologies; and onsite teachers and technicians could be made available to assist with projects. Something similar could be put in place for media suites (enabling residents to seize the means of content production), as well as for music practice rooms, gyms, and studios. Residents and members could have access to a "library of things," via which cutting-edge technologies could be accessed and borrowed as and when needed. Local doctors' offices could be combined with self-help health facilities and biomedical

44 Dolores Hayden, "What Would a Non-Sexist City Be Like? Speculations on Housing, Urban Design, and Human Work," *Signs* 5, no. 3 (Spring 1980): 182.

education centres. For younger residents and those who take care of them, there could be book and toy libraries, an ecologically-friendly reusable nappy laundry service, a baby clothing rental service, regular breastfeeding support groups (with peer counsellors available for home visits), pre- and post-natal mental health groups, a homework help centre, and so on.

This is clearly a utopian exercise in envisioning the good life—one undertaken with my own personal perspective and circumstances in mind (as well as the influential counter-imaginaries of Red Vienna). The point, however, is not to offer a single blueprint of an alternative, but to engage in a process of *thinking otherwise*. Any attempt to challenge the oppressive conditions of unpaid work within the household depends upon a decisive upending of the perceived inevitability of the isolated single-family dwelling. The house is the physical embodiment of an inequitable gendered division of labour, and the refusal of work begins at home.

Title: Real Humans
Season/Episode: S01E01
Year: 2012
Network: SVT1
Country: Sweden

In this dystopian depiction of contemporary Sweden, a cross between the myth of Prometheus and Issac Asimov's science fiction meets capitalism. Hubots are androids that have been designed to compensate for the shortcomings of human beings—obedience, loyalty, labour, and companionship. Both perfect and impersonal, like dolls for adults, the hubots represent the ghosts of Western civilization's primary obsessions: consumption and homogeneity, and as such are the subjects of discrimination based on neo-Luddism, xenophobia, and gender.

Anna Puigjaner

A Space for a Non-Human Domestic Labourer

The progressive aging of Western societies and the increasing dependency that we experience as we age have fostered the gradual introduction of new care technologies to everyday life. The unbalanced demographic scenario that is being forecasted for the coming decades clearly indicates that we will imminently be facing a lack of a workforce able to provide the degree of care that these societies will require. And, in light of this ongoing social change, advanced technologies with the ability to perform non-human care work have repeatedly been envisioned and advertised as a possible solution by their creators and mainstream media. The market is already filled with a vast range of machines that manage medication doses and provide companionship, from near-invisible apparatuses to doll-like therapy robots and mechanical pets. Despite the benefits that these machines provide, their recent ubiquity raises concerns about the possible consequences they may have—not only in terms of how their commodification fosters social inequity, individualism, and isolation, but also in terms of how they will reshape programmatic needs and, therefore, how they will directly or indirectly reshape our future homes, neighbourhoods, and even the city at large.

Despite the novelty of this phenomenon, the interest in integrating science and technology in care work is not new. As an answer to the progressive incorporation of women into productive labour at the end of the nineteenth century, terms such as "domestic labour-saving devices" and "home efficiency" began to be widely used, especially following the popularization of Frederick Taylor's theory of scientific management. Domestic machinery and technological devices began to fill houses with the intention of cutting down on the time that dwellers had to dedicate to reproductive labour. At the time, any and all work related to caring for the house and the householders was thought to have been magically reduced by means of these new technologies. Over a century later, it has become apparent that the promises made by the manufacturers of these devices were left unfulfilled and that the amount of time dedicated to care was not drastically reduced thanks to machinery. In looking back at these labouring machines, one can also observe how they are not just social artefacts but are, in fact, evidence of a particular political and economic ideology at work. Especially in the American context, after the Second World War, when the technification of the house was less about time saving and more on the privatization of the home and orienting society toward consumerism as a means of promoting mass individuation. The divisions between genders and classes were strengthened, and whatever collectivity still remained at this time was abandoned in favour of the free market: selling more goods and increasing industrial production.

Rather than discussing the necessity of or the pros and cons of this new iteration of caring technologies, we should be questioning the ideology that has allowed them to proliferate and the ways in which architecture might respond to this ideology. This consideration is especially pressing given the risk of the progressive social individualism promoted by consumer life over the course of the twentieth century being further exacerbated. Look, for instance, to the way caring robots are being disseminated in mainstream media. Nothing requires elderly care to be individually performed and supported with individual means yet all of the commercials advertising these new devices present them as being operated in the privacy of the home, signaling their designs uphold an existing ideology. As Walter Benjamin posits, when a new technology emerges it is initially applied in a way that reproduces former cultural aesthetics and social constructs. Something similar is happening here: instead of redefining the existing architectures of care and their systems, these new devices tend to mimetically replicate the existing logic that defines them.

This process of domestic commodification is a call to rethink architecture as a tool for visibility and resistance. Instead of picturing these new technologies existing and being used inside homes, we could start by picturing them as part of municipal infrastructures, where non-human caretakers could provide a form of guardianship to humans. The simple action of reconceiving domestic reproductive labour as a part of the public realm would help rebalance certain existing social inequities by providing visibility, accessibility, equity, and labour regulations for care work, while also allowing collectivity to take shape outside of consumerism.

This new typology of caring could be part of the city as well as an extension of the domestic, on which it could catalyze progressive change. Thinking of domestic spaces in this way could also be an opportunity to counter the diffuse and expansive logic of late capitalism—under which the domestic has progressively become incorporated in the urban sphere—in order to allow for a redefinition of care. If the house has traditionally been the place in which unpaid and unregulated reproductive labour takes place, it might be that by rethinking its limits and its private character we might be able to find another narrative to define the domestic realm—a narrative that not only embraces non-human and technological realities but one that also addresses its economies in relation to caring practices in a manner that is more collective and socially just.

CERTAIN MEASURES
HOME IS WHERE THE DROIDS ARE,
2019

Today, robots are not only functional apparatuses that manage and perform everyday tasks such as vacuuming or grocery shopping, but are increasingly integrated into the quotidian aspects of domestic life, often taking on the tasks of socializing with, providing therapy to, entertaining, and even taking care of children, parents, and grandparents alike. Home is Where the Droids Are responds to this new robotic presence in the contemporary domestic environment by presenting droids as intelligent creatures with free will, rather than as machines that simply perform everyday tasks. These droids are on the verge of being domesticated, and the emotional bonds between them and other members of the household supersede any functional needs they fulfill. Their movements are erratic and offbeat, as though they have yet to fully adjust to their human companions and their everyday routines. As they orbit around the home, this new robotic species calls for the attention and affection of the household's human inhabitants.

Stills from "Home is Where the Droids Are," directed by Charlotte Jansen

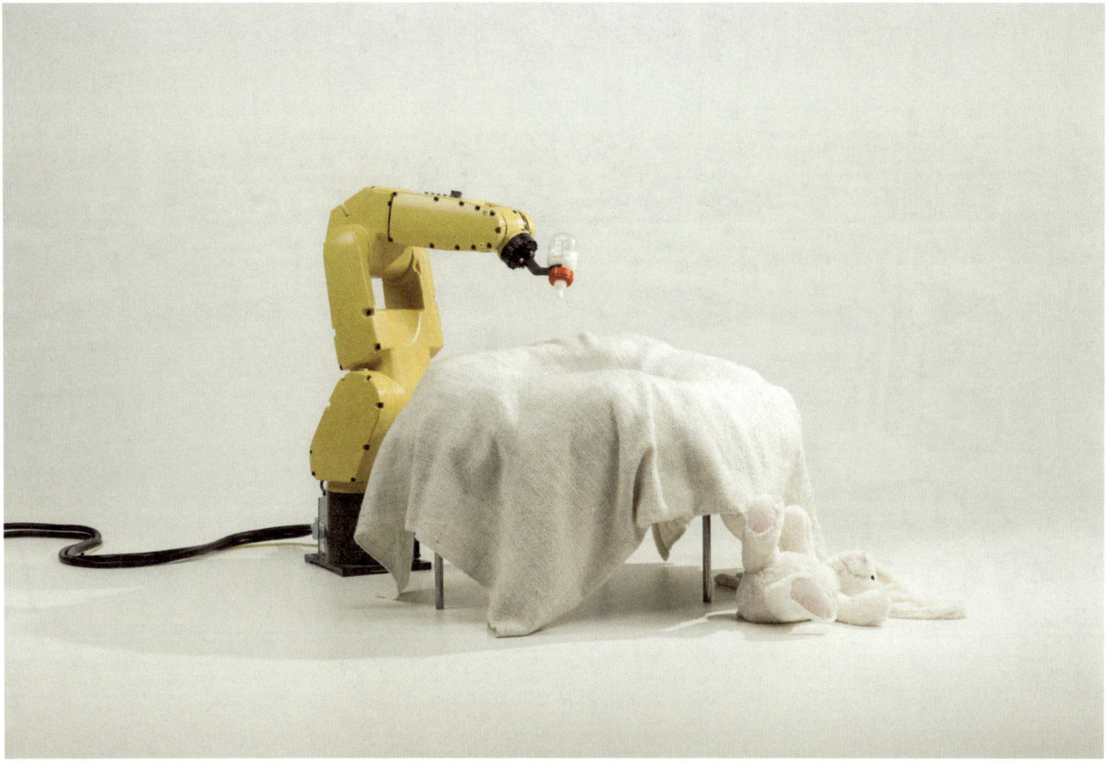

STEPHAN BOGNER, PHILIPP SCHMITT, AND JONAS VOIGT
RAISING ROBOTIC NATIVES, 2016

While virtual assistants have quickly become a normalized part of daily life, the adoption of robotic assistants (apart from the Roomba) remains relatively novel—at least for the time being. Raising Robotic Natives is a speculative design for a near future in which children are *robotic natives*, having been born into a world that has adapted to robots—much like how young adults today are digital natives, raised in the age of the internet. The project proposes an open-source design for a robotic arm that can be adapted to serve multiple purposes. One such adaptation is a baby feeder toolhead that acts as a nursing assistant, while another is a dragon costume that transforms the robotic arm into a childhood companion. Amidst these functions is a robotic kill switch designed to immediately shut down all robotics in the event of an emergency, suggesting that these benign-looking assistants cannot necessarily be trusted.

Kiva Systems (now Amazon Robotics) cobots work to pick and sort items at a Staples warehouse in Denver, Colorado, 2008. Photograph: Joel Eden.

It has long been feared that widespread automation will result in equally widespread unemployment. As collaborative robots—known as "cobots"—continue to become a greater part of the contemporary workforce, the qualms about their effects on employment have shifted focus. A report published in 2019 by the UC Berkeley Labor Center posited that the increasing automation of warehouse work will not reduce the number of available jobs but will instead affect the quality of these jobs—and not necessarily for the better. One potential effect listed by the report was that new technologies will de-skill certain tasks, citing Amazon Robotics' (previously KIVA Systems) robotic picking system as an example. The Amazon Robotics cobot simplifies the human role in picking products by navigating warehouses to locate necessary items, which reduces the need for human skill and training, making it easy for companies to employ a temporary workforce rather than hire and invest in long-term employees.

In 2011, IBM's Watson became a household name when it competed against human players (both of whom had previously earned the title of champion) on the game show *Jeopardy!*. Watson ultimately beat its competitors and won the $1 million prize. Lesser known is the fact that the technology that brought Watson to victory has since come to play a significant role in the contemporary workforce. Chatbots powered by Watson Assistant's conversational artificial intelligence technology are now so ubiquitous that they are part of an emerging professional class of virtual employees working with and for human counterparts referred to as "no-collar workers." While there are many differing predictions as to how this group of workers will affect the future of work—will it create widespread unemployment, or will it make way for universal basic income?—it is likely to require more server space than office space.

AI for professionals, designed for your business

ibm.com/watson

A worker wears StrongArm Technologies' FUSE FLEX, a device that monitors the movements of its wearer in order to prevent injury and increase productivity, 2016. Photograph: Steve Tague

While cobots have in some cases lessened the need for skilled human labour, the unceasing demand for order fulfillment by online retailers continues to create strenuous conditions for (human) warehouse workers as they attempt to meet relentless productivity quotas set by their employers. Within these supply chains, logistical prosthetics—wearable devices that optimize human performance—are being widely adopted. As a tracker that monitors its wearer's movements, FUSE FLEX is designed to alert workers to potential workplace injuries. Despite the advantages this tracker provides, its use also comes with concerns for the wearer's privacy, given that ergonomic data can equally be used for algorithmic management—a form of remote management that relies on employee tracking and surveillance as a means of assessing productivity. Abstracted data is used to decide who is and who is not meeting performance standards and has the potential to inform the fate of employees.

Amidst the relentless distractions of contemporary life emerges the need for "deep work," a term popularized in 2016 by productivity guru Cal Newport that refers to the ability to focus without distraction upon a cognitively demanding task. The wide range of products and services currently on the market that claim to enhance focus and productivity seems to support the idea that achieving this state is more difficult than one might initially expect. One popular approach to reaching an optimal level of focus is the use of neural phase-locking playlists such as brain.fm—so-called "functional music" designed to minimize distractions and direct the listener toward a desired mental state. A deep work playlist on the website features ethereal-sounding tracks with titles such as "Zero Gravity" and "Below the Ocean"—environments that evoke the sense of free floating within an interruption-free environment. While the efficacy of these playlists might be disputed, they provide the possibility of enhanced cognition without the side effects that typically accompany the use of psychoactive substances that serve the same purpose.

Music to focus, relax, meditate, or sleep—control your mental state on demand

brain.fm

Going down together.

Imagine a space for deep work. Not just an ordinary workspace, with a desk and chair and, most likely, some type of recording instrument. No, we desire something more profound.

A fresh moniker for an age-old concept, “deep work” comes with its own predicaments. The notion evokes monastic imagery, a Benedictine life. *Ora et labora*. It demands discipline to embark on long stints of undistracted mind work. During deep work, the brain is functioning at its fullest capacity and is wholeheartedly dedicated to the task at hand. In this space, the mind is acute. It’s not daydreaming or loitering around in its shallower registers, accessing superficial thoughts, gossipy insights, and banal fantasies. No, here, in this space, the brain is “total” and “perfect.”

In an ideal natural state, work grants a sense of purpose. It validates our existence. “I work, therefore I am.” The desire to access a space for deep work presupposes that, as humans, we—or at least a privileged cohort of us—are on this planet to engage in “mind work.” Deferring questions about the consequences of this pursuit, can we imagine a space that aligns our brains perfectly with the tools and interfaces that record our most profound thoughts and transform our most in-depth insights into valuable assets for ourselves and perhaps for others?

Like the strategy employed by Benedictine monks, today, it seems as though depth can only be achieved through voluntary exile, cutting out any sensorial signal that might interfere. As comfort is a phenomenological cocktail of temperature, humidity, airflow, light, and acoustics, optimized wavefields differ from body to body.

We could imagine some sort of "smart" cocoon: a cross between an anechoic chamber, a faraday cage, a float tank, and an infinity pool, drenched in circadian lighting and olfactory infusions, with salubrious psithurism and chirruping birds in the background—all calibrated to each unique individual. But isolation and comfort alone do not yet put us in the "right" frame of mind. Besides eliminating all negative distractions and situating oneself in a perfect soothing sensory envelope, we need positive stimulants. How can a space expand one's mind?

Must we reconsider a renaissance classic, the studiolo? A necessity for every *uomo universalis*, the *studiolo* may be described as a treasury of emblems: it does not contain things but rather images of things. As the result of material and spiritual crafts, these small, image-filled chambers follow the ancient tradition of open-ended models conceived of to activate the imagination and exercise the memory. Niccolò Machiavelli described the kind of personal retreat such a room represented: "When evening comes, I return home and go into my study. On the threshold, I strip off my muddy, sweaty workday clothes, and put on the robes of court and palace, and in this graver dress I enter the antique courts of the ancients and am welcomed by them. ... Then I make bold to speak to them and ask the motives for their actions, and they, in their humanity, reply to me. And for the space of four hours, I forget the world, remember no vexations, fear poverty no more, tremble no more at death: I pass into their world."[1]

1 Niccolò Machiavelli, letter to Francesco Vettori, 10 December 1513, in Niccolò Machiavelli, *The Prince*, trans. James B. Atkinson (Indianapolis: Bobbs-Merrill Company, 1976), 19.

Our contemporary pandemonium has exacerbated the contention surrounding the latest paradigms of office space for being overcrowded, unkind to introverts, surveilled, and mired with distractions. As the pandemic raged, our open landscapes of co-working stations, kombucha taps, huddle rooms, and drop-down desks were abruptly abandoned: no more peer pressure, no more hackathons, no more group churn. New calls for separation and isolation appeared. Yet, we question whether a battery of *studioli* throughout our offices would be a panacea. The modern workspace is implicitly a program that describes a space for collective work toward capital gain, not individual reflection. The issue with deep work, it seems, is that it is work done alone—in the depths of one's mind. *Studioli* produce Renaissance insights.

Today's societal challenges necessitate us to reach beyond our solipsistic, Humanist worldview. Can we liberate our brains from our easily distracted individual bodies? Buddhists, cognitive scientists, and philosophers have all made persuasive arguments that nothing is like a "fixed self." There is no thinker behind our thoughts. Can we descend into deep work together? Genuine sex requires at least a pair and improvisational jazz typically involves a trio or a quartet; how about a fully aligned sports team? Through a plethora of management metaphors, business leaders are already fantasizing about an entire corporation that is fully aligned in deep work. Can we imagine a space for integrated thought that stimulates our shared intelligence and brings the best out of our collective self? What stimuli would such space provide?

Disillusioned with finding meaning in contemporary work, office workers are in a constant search for new ways to lose their minds. Vipassana and Ayahuasca have replaced cocaine and alcohol as ways "out." In collective ceremonies, we attempt to free the brain from the body. Archaic practices such as barn raisings and harvest feasts demonstrate how individuals can subsume into a collective whole. These practices gather manual labour toward shared goals. Does the answer lie in combining these intrinsic desires for shared experiences with new rites and rituals around work? It might be that we do not require new spaces but new spatial practices, new rites, new rituals, and, most of all, a new collective goal.

ROOM object

BUSYPOD

BUSYPOD Large

BUSYPOD Medium Work

BUSYPOD Medium Meet

BUSYPOD XL

Getawayer

Orangebox

Although the open-plan office was intended as a boon to productivity, it is now predominantly reviled as an environment of constant distraction and surveillance. The occasional need for solace and privacy within not only open-plan workplaces but a range of other public environments, such as airports and university campuses, has prompted a proliferation of pods for all kinds of purposes. One such example that went viral in 2018, titled *A Safe Space for Stressed-Out Students Otherwise Known as The Cry Closet*, was designed and constructed by art student Nemo Miller for a class at the University of Utah College of Fine Arts. Although many may not be comforted by or interesting in occupying this space, the closet nonetheless draws attention to a basic human need that is typically not designed for in collective environments: the need to be alone. To address this absence of private space, several start-ups have equally adapted the pod to create spaces for activities such as napping or nursing within their cultures of widespread optimization.

Nemo Miller, The Cry Closet, 2018

How many times have you looked at your phone today? Have you considered rebranding yourself?

Michael Schmelling, *The Real Teens of Silicon Valley*, 2015

Michael Schmelling, *The Real Teens of Silicon Valley*, 2015

Michael Schmelling, *The Real Teens of Silicon Valley*, 2015

N H D M
HQY (PART OF FIVE PROPOSALS FOR YOUTH, DWELLING, CITY), 2017–ONGOING

Societies tend to plan for the young and the old alike, with infrastructures such as kindergartens, schools, retirement villages, and nursing homes functioning to serve unique segments of the public. Youth, however, are rarely the subject of design proposals in spite of the many social and financial challenges this demographic tends to face. HQY imagines hybrid spaces for this ambiguous interim stage of life, acknowledging its frequently precarious reality. Located in a former warehouse complex—the site of Amazon's failed HQ2 headquarters in Queens, New York—the project envisions the transformation of what would have been a private facility with inevitably precarious working conditions into a place for public good. HQY's campus complex includes both housing units and workspaces, creating a new type of public higher education institution that privileges broad accessibility.

Drawing of HQ2, a complex for youth that integrates public higher education, housing, and work units

Traumnovelle

A Space for a 30-Year-Old Retiree

As I write this, I live alone, in the woods, a few miles from a small town that I can access by foot, in a home that I built with only the power of my bare hands, and I no longer need to earn my living.

To the surprise of many, I retired at the age of thirty-two from a high-income job. Though I had been a high earner, I openly rejected the lifestyle that many of my peers had considered to be normal, and that many others considered desirable. Those who knew me best had observed my shift away from city living, favouring a more affordable suburb instead. Most knew that I preferred hiking a mountain or visiting nature over any work-related social event, where the undertones of comparison and competition were overwhelming. Most knew my aversion to the fashion, cars, and houses that others desired and boasted. The gatherings I hosted were humble, my closet was devoid of frivolity, and my pantry was sensibly purchased in bulk.

My frugal lifestyle allowed me to retire as a millionaire. I set up my bank accounts and adapted my investment plan such that they could perform optimally within the current economic climate. After I sold my house and my few superfluous possessions, I purchased the acreage on which I would construct the abode in which I would spend my retirement.

During the first summer of my retirement, I roamed my forested site, observing and learning the land. On a south-facing rocky slope surrounded by tall oaks, I discovered a small cave, which immediately appealed to my sense of the primitivity and fulfilled the rough warmth that I had been in search of. I spent the summer working the earth with simple tools and carving out new openings into the cave to bring light into its depths, with no plan in mind other than the desire to sculpt it. I was ecstatic in my determination to set up a home perfectly fitted to my needs, in which I would lead a life of joy, learning, and creation—a life that I had yearned for throughout my years of being employed. It was to be a life in which I could be in touch with nature and with myself and in complete control of my impact on the world.

Throughout the autumn, I hunted and harvested the forest's berries and mushrooms to fill my pantry. I canned and smoked as much of the Earth's generosity as I could and stocked up on staple dry goods from the supermarket. The discount stores found within the city sprawl had previously always left me with a feeling of ambivalence, but, they have always allowed me to save my pennies, and since I F.I.R.E.-ed, I have found an added sense of peace in their bulk opulence.

During my infrequent visits to town, I would also check on the general state of the economy. Each time I did, I found the market to be in an increasingly worrying condition, which eventually led me to install a satellite internet connection that would allow me to constantly keep in touch with the state of my finances. I set up a projector that displayed all the changes to my equity live. I would monitor the numbers on the rough curvature of the darkest corner in my dwelling during my days and through some of my nights.

The market collapsed that winter. Though I lost everything I was worth and was left penniless, I managed to maintain ownership of my land. In retrospect, I think the idleness I found in my retirement kept me too close to my worries. I was not living the life full of meaning, self-love, and exploration that I had envisioned for myself, rather I remained a slave to the money I had earned, just as I had been a slave to it while earning it. During the long and dark evenings that winter, I did not read a single book or knit a single scarf. Instead of the calm winter days of mindful fabrication that I had planned for myself, I agonized. Terrified, I considered what would happen if I were to have an accident, if I wished to eventually have a family, or if I wanted to travel, all of which my cautious planning and restraint would have previously allowed for.

As the days lengthened, I set out to prepare for the spring. As I witnessed the green shoots of seedlings push through the earth, rays of sunlight reaching the central stone I used as table, and echoing of the morning chatter of birds through my cavern, I began to find a profound sense of belonging. My worries ebbed as the land surprised me with its generosity. By summer, I had withdrawn the last of my cash, closed all my accounts, and set out to live solely off the land. I came to observe that my concerns had shifted rather than disappeared: from health of the stock market to the weather, from points and dollars to crops and seeds, from interest rates to water supply. I no longer had numbers to reliably predict and abstract my survival.

wikiHow, an open-source how-to guide database founded in 2005 by Jack Herrick, is premised on the ethos of teaching anyone "how to do anything" through a series of illustrated steps, tips, suggestions, and warnings that address a wide-ranging set of topics. From how to cope with a dysfunctional family to how to speak like a New Yorker, wikiHow has an instructional to guide users to their goals step-by-step. While historically, everyday information and advice was predominantly shared informally within one's community and social circles, wikiHow responds to the growing contemporary compulsion to consult the internet for all problems—regardless of their scope or complexity—by offering a comprehensive manual and clear set of instructions describing how to approach and operate in virtually any conceivable situation.

Learn how to do anything on the world's most popular how-to website

wikihow.com

A row of self-help books, a genre that advises its readers on how to navigate their problems in life. Photograph: Matthieu Brouillard, CCA

In a global economy that is constantly becoming more competitive and in which the few social programs that provide safety nets are becoming dangerously underfunded, there has been a growing interest in self-help and self-improvement books to make oneself more marketable. Having gained mainstream prevalence in the 1970s, the titles published in this genre capture the shifting beliefs, values, and goals of the period in which they were each written. The genre's current iteration focuses on measurable forms of self-optimization in all areas of life—productivity, romance, organization, well-being—through the lens of efficiency and, in turn, an outward projection of how to live an improved and seemingly more perfect life (oftentimes in areas of life that the reader did not even know needed improvement). Endemic within the genre is an ethos of self-determinism, fully placing the onus of one's current life circumstances solely onto the individual, while dismissing any of the larger structural and systemic forces that shape and affect individual realities.

Title: Black Mirror
Season/Episode: S02E03
Year: 2013
Network: Channel 4
Country: UK

Black Mirror revitalized the anthology series format and made technological dystopia its own televised genre. From the UK to the USA and from Channel 4 to Netflix, Charlie Brooker, the creator of the show, has rightfully entered the ranks of the greatest visionaries of all time. Through the series, Brooker has intercepted, recorded, and foreseen all of our obsessions: from device dependency to loss of control over reality, the distortion of perception, immersion in the digital realm, and, in 2013, the advent of populism, with the episode "The Waldo Moment."

Nina Power

One or Many Selves?

Of all of the ways of describing who or what we are, our age encourages terms that separate us from others the most: we are, above all, an individual, an identity (or several), a *self*. Where previous ages would have emphasized certain kinds of belonging—kin, family, tribe, community, region, or nation—today, it is the solitary person, the human atom, that comes first, that most represents who we "are." Some of the reasons for this are obvious: we are living in the endgame, or perhaps collapse, of liberalism, the political project that permitted individual freedom and choice in all things and took as its rational unit, the autonomous adult. This idea of the rational adult became the basis upon which economic liberalism could progress: aren't we all seeking to maximize our own interests? Why shouldn't we all just do what we want to do? The liberal idea of freedom—of expression, of choice—has indeed liberated us "modern subjects" from certain kinds of frameworks, but it has undoubtedly also caught us in new and unforeseen kinds of traps.

Unlike traditional forms of living—the family or church-base communities, for example—today, we are generally not beholden to any ties that we do not choose for ourselves. Existentialism runs wild—and the market is the best way of "giving people what they want," what they think they want, or what they say they want. We can remain relatively unencumbered beings, without obligations, or with only those ties that we choose. Technology increasingly encourages and maintains isolation, whether we are in lockdown already or otherwise. We might even come to *like* being on our own, even when loneliness is endemic and widespread, and even politically dangerous. As Hannah Arendt puts it:

> What prepares men for totalitarian domination in the non-totalitarian world, is the fact that loneliness, once a borderline experience usually suffered in certain marginal social conditions like old age, has become an everyday experience of the ever-growing masses of our century.[1]

So, we are each little selves, individuals, atoms, and increasingly alone. The "totalitarian domination" that Arendt warns us about would today most likely come about through acephalous online platforms rather than a populist demagogue, though the two modes are not incompatible. Can we think properly if we think too much alone? Can we protect our thoughts from becoming unstable in the absence of a secure place to think, emotionally and physically?

Each one of us sits alone in a room, perhaps by the window, gazing outwards. What does the architecture of our existence tell us about our moral beings, and what kind of self can be cultivated in these situations? To begin with the isolated subject of course does not imply that people can't or don't enter into relations, have families, or live in communities. It is rather that, from the standpoint of a larger political condition, we should recognize that this is the dominant mode of how we are counted and how we are seen. The state and corporations see us as units of a population first and foremost, as nodes in a network, rather than as, say, meaning-producing, cooperative beings. Our "tastes" and "preferences" are registered and sold back to us, queued up by an algorithm. We have come to be amazed that machines "know" us so well, but we shouldn't be, as by submitting ourselves to the regime of data, we become more and more homogenous, even where we feel our individual interests, preferences, and tastes to be niche or unusual. The self becomes a reinforcing loop, an ouroboros.

It is a cliché to say that we live in a consumer age—who you are is what you can buy—but there is no way around this truth. Your identity is a symptom or a function of your purchasing power, and your tastes and forms of expression are largely what make you "you."

1 Hannah Arendt, *The Origins of Totalitarianism* (New York City: Harcourt, 1973), 468.

At the same time, culture and the online platforms that promulgate it are increasingly homogenous, policed, censored, and controlled. We might all be encouraged to "be ourselves," but it is harder and harder to be a personality, a character, or anything more eccentric than just another IP address, or your national insurance number, or the (likely negative) figure of your bank balance and the sum of your accumulated debts. Furthermore, what you can and can't say is, in actuality, very narrow and what you do say is frequently monitored and "reported" by others. In the chaos of selves, there is a chilling atmosphere: say the "wrong thing" and you could be "cancelled," you could lose your job and your friends. You become a scapegoat-self, a hated-self, a self that only serves to strengthen the group that shores up its own identity by destroying yours.

But what is the deeper notion of the self behind all of this? When did it emerge historically? Is there an idea of the self, a spiritual, moral, collective self, perhaps, that is capable of transcending the restricted image of today's self? We all live, whether we like it or not, as what we could call the "capital-self," the self that is both a consumer and a brand and that undertakes the multi-dimensional job of promoting itself, selling itself, monitoring itself, putting itself forward for employment, and competing with other "selves" for work, recognition, and attention, via images and words and involving everything from selfies to CVs, profiles, networking, and so on.

There are certainly ways of pulling back from the capital-self—by getting offline, by cultivating modes of life that don't require selling oneself. But for many, there is only one meta-marketplace where selves circulate: online, one is a curious combination of advert for oneself, "individual," potential employee, possible friend, and maybe someone to date. The internet has become the fulcrum for many future relationships and branding opportunities. There is still the world outside, of course, the offline world, but more and more it is entangled with the online one. Economic crises to come will no doubt see more desperate scrabbling around in the attention economy, as selves, facing the world as if shields, facing the glare of the sun from screens, compete even more ruthlessly for time and money.

What of the philosophers? What deeper notion of self do they understand? To use "self" as a reflexive pronoun, as in "myself" or "oneself," creates a certain kind of subject, the subject of a sentence. But today's capital-self is largely an outward creature: spatial, communicative, a bubble in touch with other bubbles. The problem of personal identity, particularly of identity over time, is an old philosophical question: If you can't remember what you did while you were sleepwalking or drunk, are you the same person? In what sense? How are you the same person as you were last year?

What relationship does the fifty-year-old you have with the five-year-old you? Summarizing Derek Parfit, Canadian philosopher Charles Taylor puts it as follows: "It is perfectly defensible for me to consider (what I would conventionally call) my earlier, say, pre-adolescent self as another person and, similarly, to consider what 'I' (as we normally put it) shall be several decades in the future as still another person."[2]

The self is thus something of a legal fiction—our individuating names and who we "are" cover up a multitude of forgetting, lost memories, and previous identities. Far from a coherent identity, David Hume thought that we are, instead, only a bundle of perceptions. What ties these impressions together? We tend to think that we are the same person over time—we have the same names that we have always had and we have all these documents that tell us who we are—but, in fact, our grasp on identity is surprisingly tenuous. Maintaining the self requires a surprising amount of effort. Between sleeping, dreaming, exhaustion, and other states of intoxication, we are frequently not "ourselves," if by that we intend something like conscious, coherent, and able to give an account of who we are and what we think and why.

We are all introspective from time to time. We all think about what we are doing, think about our thoughts, indeed, but how and when our selves meet the outside world is a complex question. How much of our selves are composed of our encounters with the world and with others, and how much of it belongs only to us? Do we "own" ourselves—are we a kind of property, as some liberal and libertarian thinkers would suggest? Or does this image of the self restrict us to the particular historical moment, one which we undoubtedly still occupy, as discussions of "my body, my choice" now circulate to cover everything from abortion rights, to sex work, to not wearing a mask during the COVID-19 pandemic?

The question of the relationship between the self and space is opened up when we think about the inside and the outside—whether we are discussing being inside during a lockdown, for example, or online on the internet, or outside in the world. Who is the self that unites these different orientations? *Orientation* originally comes from the Latin "orientem" which refers to the part of the sky where the sun rises, putting us in the mind of a compass: looking around, working out where we are first before we move on. It has a geographical meaning, of course, but also a moral one (think: "moral compass"). If we do not know where we are, morally, we do not know who we are.

In his 1989 book *Sources of the Self: The Making of Modern Identity*, Charles Taylor clearly makes this point:

2 Charles Taylor, *Sources of the Self: The Making of Modern Identity* (Cambridge, MA: Cambridge University Press, 1989), 49.

> But then what emerges from all this is that we think of this fundamental moral orientation as essential to being a human interlocutor, capable of answering for oneself. But to speak of orientation is to presuppose a space-analogue within which one finds one's way. To understand our predicament in terms of finding or losing orientation in moral space is to take the space which our frameworks seek to define as ontologically basic. The issue is, through what framework-definition can I find my bearings in it? In other words, we take as basic that the human agent exists in a space of questions. And these are the questions to which our framework-definitions are answers, providing the horizon within which we know where we stand, and what meanings things have for us.[3]

Taylor links orientation—as place—to what it means to be human. Yet we are often lost, emotionally, if not also physically. We do not necessarily know what to think or where to begin to think. We walk around in circles. Our notion of self is double-edged here—we are a body in space, but we are also a mind attempting to locate itself in the realm of its own thoughts. Space is not only geography, but also "a space of questions." What, for Taylor, is the relationship between an orientation and a framework? Before we can orient ourselves, we must understand ourselves as being in a world or, morally, as being within a particular frame. Living in the end-times of liberalism often reveals to us the absence of frameworks, meaning that we are apt to live in disorientating ways. What can our values be when we do not know what framework we live within, or where there are multiple frameworks to choose from, or where we have to make up our own framework from scratch?

What are the questions that Taylor imagines that we might ask, if we are able to find ourselves thoughtfully in space? How does our geographical orientation link up with our moral state of being? It is no coincidence that Taylor uses the word "horizon" here: the horizon is where our vision and the land meet. It is what we look toward, it is the limit from which we understand what meanings are generated by our own questions and the answers to them. If I ask myself, "What is a good life?" I am presented with multiple answers from outside: it may be that a good life is a life of enjoyment, it may be that a good life is a life in which I help others, or it may be that a good life is one in which my own self is ultimately subsumed in the service of a higher cause. But before we answer this question, or any moral question, it is necessary to understand the place that such a question has in the "space of questions": Why this question and not others? What is this space? If it is intangible and mental, how can we access it, and how often? What if we get cut off from the space of questions altogether, because any questions that we might proffer have already been answered for us by others, or by the culture around us?

3 Taylor, *Sources of the Self*, 29.

To erode the space of questions or to eliminate the framework would take some effort, yet we are in danger of frequently being in states of being far removed from what Taylor imagines must be in place for our senses of self as spatial and as moral beings to flourish. The possibility of the framework that he imagines is indeed deeply connected to the question of value and the good:

> On the contrary, we come here to one of the most basic aspirations of human beings, the need to be connected to, or in contact with, what they see as good, or of crucial importance, or of fundamental value. And how could it be otherwise, once we see that this orientation in relation to the good is essential to being a functional human agent? The fact that we have to place ourselves in a space which is defined by these qualitative distinctions cannot but mean that where we stand in relation to them must matter to us. Not being able to function without orientation in the space of the ultimately important means not being able to stop caring where we sit in it.[4]

Here we see more important spatial metaphors enter the fray: where we "sit" in space and where we are "in relation." These are qualitative questions, though Taylor's use of "functional" here seems to be a little at odds with his otherwise resolutely non-utilitarian image of values and aspirations. Nevertheless, here we are. We place ourselves in a space and we are in relation to qualitative distinctions that fundamentally matter to us. Where we sit is important, we care about it and we are concerned. In order to feel ourselves in a room, a moral room, we must pause.

But who can pause today? The global pandemic that occurred in the midst of the end days of liberalism, was the culmination of a global, connected world, in which air flight and mass movement were central features. Suddenly, many countries were tipped abruptly into lockdown, and "indoors" was the reality that many faced, even as others had to continue to work outdoors and in danger. We will likely never go back to that world, and elites may be discussing "the great reset," seeing an opportunity to reorganize energy, cities, and labour, but on a more personal level, what Taylor means by caring about where we sit reveals a missing aspect of the story we tell ourselves about our individual selves and the larger structures in which we try to find somewhere, anywhere at all, to sit still for a moment in the first place.

Can we salvage this kinder, calmer, more patient sitting self from the self that is generated and exploited by consumer capitalism and employed (sometimes) by the labour market? This philosophical, moral, reflective self is also, and Taylor's work indicates this very

4 Taylor, *Sources of the Self*, 49.

clearly, an architectural self, a self in space, a body and a mind oriented and located in a particular place, and aware of its situatedness. This self, crucially, is the self that asks questions. It is the polar opposite of the self that feels compelled to assert its identity at all costs and at all times, that tells others compulsively who or what it is. It is not the self that defines itself in relation to its belonging to a group or as a particular kind of individual. It is not at all over- or pre-determined in any of these ways. Behind the outward-facing self is this much more cautious, undefined being. The moral being is an incomplete being: incomplete because it is open and open because it is questioning.

How to protect this vulnerable moral self? When people talk about "self-care," today, it is often a casual way of referring to maintaining one's body, often in conventional ways, so that the self is presentable, visually acceptable, and ready to participate in the world of work, self-promotion, and self-circulation of all kinds. There is of course nothing wrong with wanting to look after oneself, to stay as fit and healthy as possible, with wanting to maintain oneself to avoid incurring illness wherever possible. But there is, perhaps, a private kind of health as well as a more public one: does your health belong to you, to the state, or to corporations? Does your image belong to you and the people around you, or does it belong to the world—however amorphous that world might be?

The pandemic troubles the image of self-care and the separation of public and private, because it reveals the extent to which we are all intertwined in extraordinary ways. We are completely interdependent, even as we are encouraged to imagine ourselves as self-branding, self-promoting, and self-protecting beings. We rely on each other constantly and not only in ways that we do not choose—in the ways in which global commercial networks create national interdependencies, for example—but also in ways that bind us to others emotionally, practically, and virally. Caring about one's own health is inextricably linked to caring about the health of others. The very different responses people have when evaluating risk point to deep political divides in the ways in which people conceptualize of themselves—do people understand themselves first and foremost as free, liberal agents, or, instead, primarily as social, cooperative beings and as fragments of a larger social whole?

Liberalism has caused these kinds of confusions, because of the multiple ambiguities it has engendered in our understanding of what a self is in the first place. The erosion of collective values has led to a rather depressing situation in which governments feel compelled to put up posters instructing citizens to "Be Kind"—a dominant feature of London in the summer of 2020.

There is, however, the other side of the private, self-promoting individual, also in evidence in 2020. This self is the self of the crowds, of protests, of coming together in the streets to fill squares and occupy the outside. Several countries saw Black Lives Matter protests over the summer, with people defying lockdowns to come together in opposition to police and structural racism. There were also anti-mask and anti-lockdown protests. There were arrests and fines. The relationship between the values of lockdown and the values of the right to protest pushed up against one another in a fierce way. The insideness of many weeks of self-isolation often spilled over into huge collective gatherings of one kind or another—we shouldn't forget that in addition to protests some of these gatherings were also illegal raves, weddings, and parties. Here, the questions of moral values and frameworks and the architecture of the world come in view in a slightly different way.

What is the morality of public space compared to the morality of indoor architecture? What is the difference between sitting alone in a room and being outside with others under the sky: what transformations in moral thinking occur in these different scenes? How does the architecture of one position segue into the structure of another?

The world today seems to be flipping between extremes of insideness and outsideness, between enforced isolation and potentially illegal togetherness. The consumer-self is already a kind of locked-down self, the self of identity is already boxed-in. It is no wonder, particularly in times of crisis and anxiety, that the question of what people value, what they stand for when they have sat down and understood what their concerns are, and how they want to answer the questions that they ask regarding what they believe in, are sometimes answered in extremely direct ways.

Are we self-possessed these days, or are we haunted by images of who or what we might be, a fragmented self, a self of shards? The spaces we inhabit—moral and architectural—are not always freely chosen: we might not be able to afford to live somewhere inhabitable, we may be without stability or an anchor. We may resent the rules, even if we understand there is good reason for them: our comprehending-self rubs up against our self that desires freedom.

What will the self of the 2020s look like? Will we be able to integrate the many selves we feel compelled to present to the world, leaving, we might hope, a small remainder of self for ourselves? How and where will we sit, without being disturbed, for long enough to reflect on what moral and spatial questions mean the most to us, and how will we begin to answer them? The architecture of the future must include this moral dimension: if we do not design a world that permits such questioning, we will find the answers to already be pre-given, and we will be told only to “sit down” by others who are keen that we use our time only to consume and to worry, but not, at any costs, to think.

Michelle Groskopf, *Hype House*, 2020

Michelle Groskopf, *Hype House*, 2020

Michelle Groskopf, *Hype House*, 2020

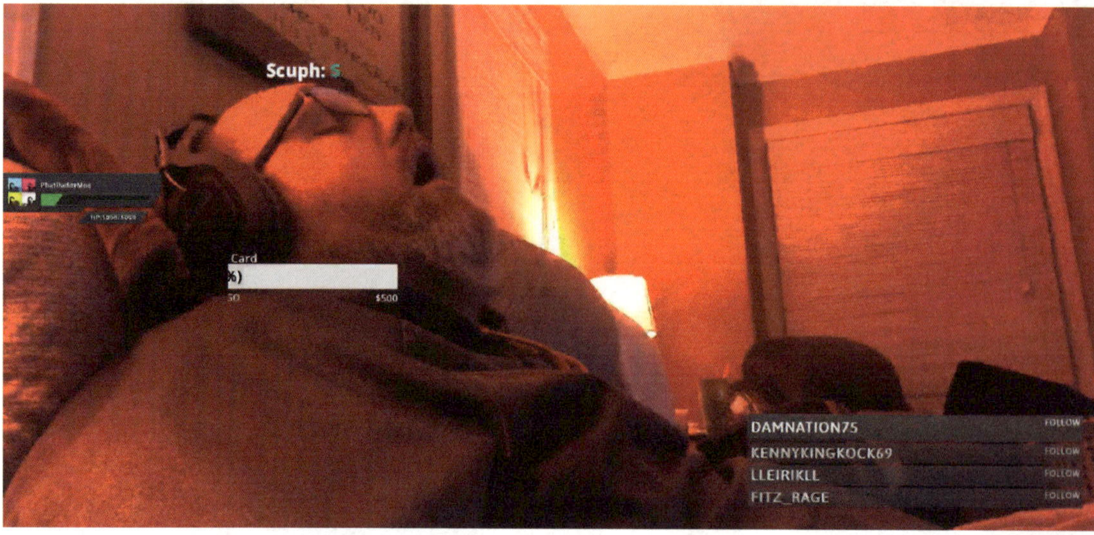

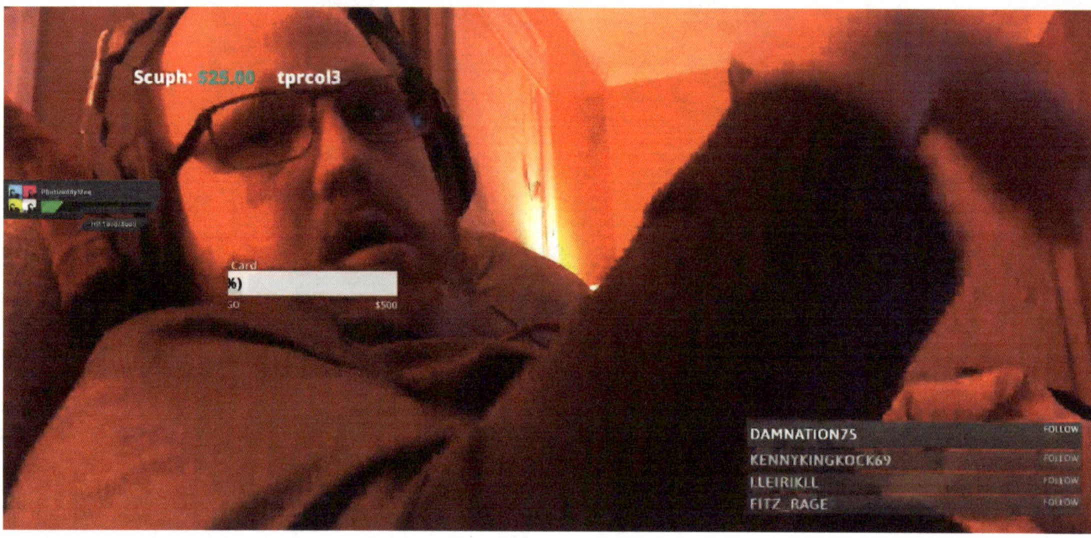

Twitch sleepstream by JesseDStreams, 2019

Under the demands of late capitalism, there is a constant pressure to be and perform online. Twitch, a popular social platform most often associated with videogame livestreaming, has emerged amidst this societal shift. The platform's interface is composed of multiple windows: the videogame being played, a chat bar, and, most importantly, a window showing the gamer. While this common format has become the backbone of the platform, Twitch is also commonly used by non-gamers to livestream just about anything. Deviating from the typical mode of gameplay performances, a popular trend emerging on the platform is that of players livestreaming themselves sleeping, also known as "sleepstreaming." Streamers, many of whom have ardent and loyal followings, have accrued thousands of dollars during the broadcast of a single night's sleep—a sum that is generated through fan donations. The trend allows streamers to turn the most mundane and inevitable moments of their lives, sleep, into content that can be commodified and consumed.

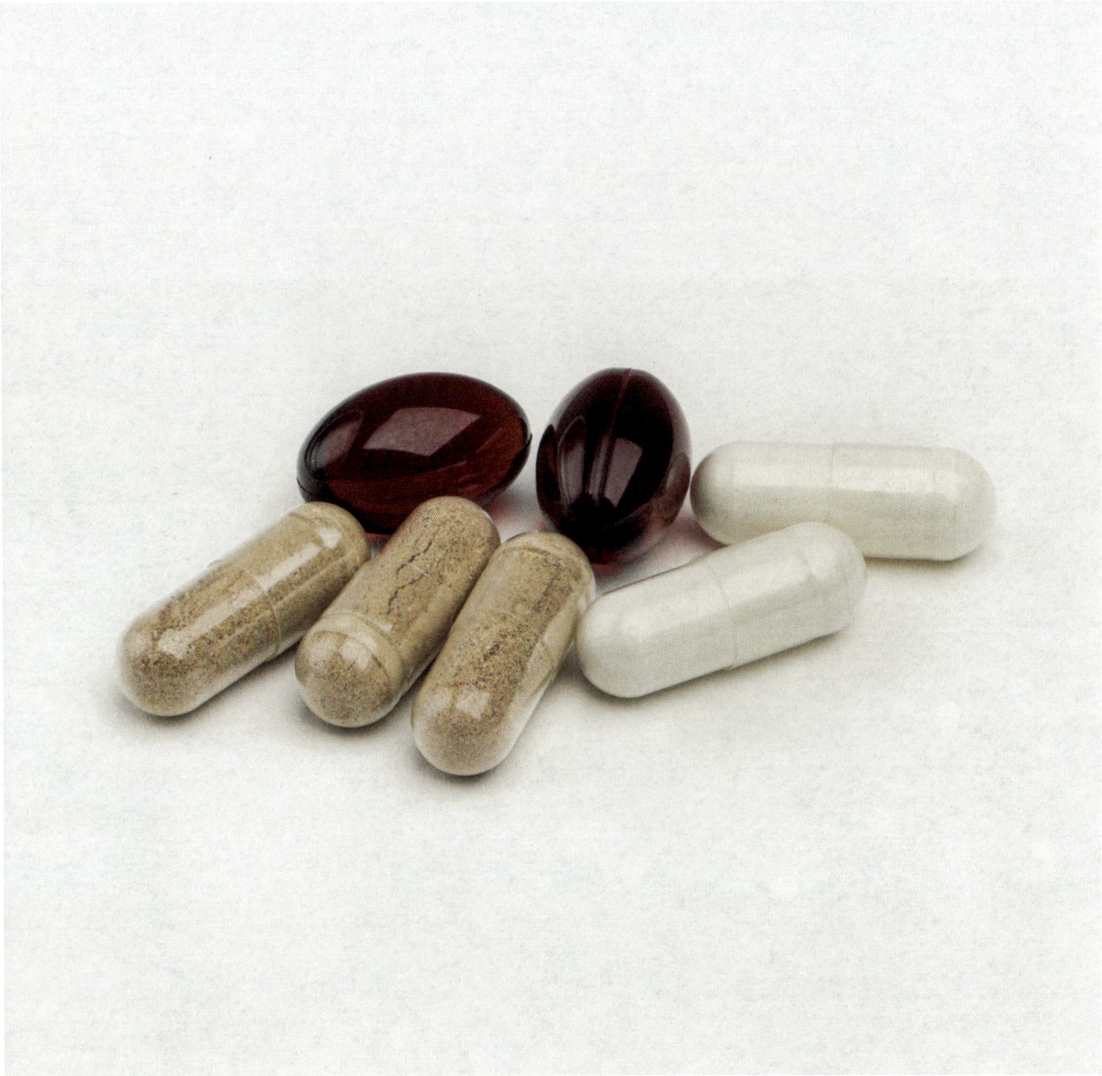

Nootropics, a type of substance meant to improve cognitive function. Photograph: Matthieu Brouillard, CCA

Contemporary office culture is largely defined by an ethos of what has been termed "workism" where, amidst an absence of religious affiliations and strong community ties, a significant cohort of white-collar workers have begun to derive their identity from their work. As a result of an engrained notion that what you do is who you are, overtime and burnout have displaced John Maynard Keynes' oft-quoted prediction that the fifteen-hour workweek would be a standard feature of the twenty-first century. In order to maximize productivity, self-optimization is a must—especially when everyone else is doing it. Nootropics are the subset of supplements and drugs related to cognitive enhancement, and they have become an essential part of the daily routines of many knowledge workers. This fact has been made particularly evident through subscription-based supplement packs branded with buzzwords such as "rise" and "sprint" that claim to support and enhance a range of cognitive functions, from memory and mood to energy and focus.

Title: Weird City
Season/Episode: S01E01
Year: 2019
Network: YouTube
Country: USA

Weird City is divided in two by the Line. Above the Line, where the Haves live, and Below the Line, where the Have-Nots reside. Stu lives Above, but he was born Below. He had never had a partner, until a dating app matched him with Burt, who lives Below. In the tradition of Romeo and Juliet, their love story treads perilously as they cross the Line to be with one another, until they decide to move Below the Line in order to stay together. With this series, YouTube enters television production, offering an anthology of contemporary digital obsessions to watch on its digital platform.

Joanne McNeil
Goodnight, Login

Somewhere in Minneapolis, a woman has taken off her makeup. She has bleached blonde hair and a wiry posture. Her name is Ana. She will sleep on a futon with a black-and-white micro-dotted pattern that looks like television static.

Somewhere in Berlin, a young man lies already asleep on a mattress on the floor in his room. The walls appear to glow deep mauve on camera. His face looks pink and his hair is the colour of an aubergine. I suspect that his duvet cover is white, but, on screen, it also looks purple to me. I take a screenshot of a small square of the fabric and upload it to a colour-recognition app. The colour names it suggests are "Voodoo (90%)," "Mortar (84%)," and "Mulled Wine (83%),"[1] but these swatches don't quite capture the blue undertones of the bright plummy colour that I see. Another app matches my screenshot as RGB (88,59,91).[2] I don't know his name; I'll call him Torr.

1 The first colour recognition app is freely available on the web at https://www.ginifab.com/feeds/pms/color_name_in_image.php.

2 The second colour recognition app I used is the website https://imagecolorpicker.com/en.

One of Ana's black-and-white Japanese Spaniels is curled up on the futon with her. In the grainy webcam footage, the tiny dog looks more like a rabbit or a cat than a dog. Ana has set up a Tripod page for her accidentally micro-famous pets. In candy-colour typeface over a black background, she explains that Pooka's favourite toys "include stuffed animals and a squeaky red triple rubber monkey," and that Deiter, her younger dog, was "born on August 29th, 1998 to Lord Master Chin Wolfgang and Empress Lady Chin Samantha."

The rest of Ana's apartment is a mishmash of vintage furniture and knickknacks throughout which a tangle of telephone wires, fairy lights, and computer cables run. From other angles, you might see her television in the living room or her kitchen; but, for now, the webcam is fixed on Ana, her pet, and her TV-static futon.

She lifts the dog up before the camera: it's Deiter.

Sometimes she sleeps alone on camera. Tonight, she's sleeping with people from all over. These days she can count on at least nine people to join her at a time. They each broadcast themselves while sleeping from their respective beds to an online audience. Some of them timestamp their broadcasts and post their locations. Most of them come from North America—these particular bedtime hours favour sleepers in time zones from Eastern Standard to Pacific.

The images of the sleepers are displayed on The Universal Sleep Station, another webpage that Ana created. They appear as squares in a neat tic-tac-toe grid. If a viewer stays up late enough and has some luck, they might click on The Universal Sleep Station page and find all nine participants asleep in unison.

"It's eerie to sleep with the cam on you. i'll wake up and see it shining and blinking at me and it's like a dream," Ana wrote in her online journal sometime earlier. "it's really ultra strange to watch another woman on cam while they are watching you! the technology of all of this is so astounding, mind-blowing, yet so incredibly archaic at the same time. people starring at computers all over the world waiting for minutes for a picture to refresh. it's endearing and insane. i like it. i'm glad to be part of this whatever-it-is. [*sic*]"

Torr is still asleep. There's a chat box next to his image:

- weck den mal, 4 stunden sind genug!
- HAHA ja ne er hat Praktikum und sein Wecker läutet um 7:15 oder so
- schlaft er einfach on stream
- wetten du pennst bis 8
- Gut Nacht ich geh jetzt auch pennen

- warum guckt man leuten beim pennen zu?
- warum bannt twitch sowas nicht
- wird sicher moderiert, der chat
- yo HE dead

I don't speak German, so I turned to Google Translate to help me out:

- wake him up, 4 hours are enough!
- HAHA yes he has an internship and his alarm clock rings at 7:15 or so
- he just sleeps on stream
- bet you're sleeping until 8
- Good night, I'm going to sleep now too
- why do you watch people fall asleep?
- why doesn't twitch ban something like that
- the chat will be moderated for sure
- yo HE dead

That last line, "yo HE dead," received a number of "lol" and "HAHAHA" responses—responses that I don't need machine learning to understand.

***

The woman on the TV-static futon is camgirl Ana Voog. She hosted her livestream sleep parties in the late 90s. Above is a composite sketch inspired by all the public archives that are left of her online sleeping sanctuary. Still images of Ana and her sleeping companions can be accessed through the Wayback Machine, but for the actual video, you would have had to have surfed to the right website at the right time, more than twenty years ago.

As for Torr, I know even less about him, but I briefly watched him as he slept on camera. I came across his channel on Twitch one evening in November of 2020. I had heard about contemporary internet users who broadcast themselves asleep. When I entered the search term "#sleepstream" on Twitch, sometime before midnight EST, his was the first livestream that I found.

Torr's stream appeared to be a puzzle piece that could have perfectly fit in The Universal Sleep Station. His purple room could have easily been a square in Ana's grid. But Torr and Ana were sleeping at different times and their experiences were captured on entirely different internets.

I only briefly glanced at Torr's livestream. It made me feel uncomfortable—like I was prying, even if he wanted an audience. Knowing Ana's performance, I thought #sleepstream might make for an intriguing and whimsical story, just the same, but what I witnessed seemed more like degradation. I took a screenshot to record the chat conversation. When the young man on camera rolled over in bed, I closed the browser tab before I could see his face any more clearly. The whole thing seemed exploitative for reasons that I wasn't able to place in the moment.

The "About" section on Torr's Twitch page was very sad: "schlafstream/sleepstream weil ich keine hobbys hab uwu."—which Google translated as "because I have no hobbies."

He was livestreaming himself asleep in order to gain followers. Torr is a user on Twitch, a livestreaming platform and subsidiary of Amazon. This hazing ritual—someone asleep on camera, as others watch and joke in the chat box—isn't exactly encouraged by the company, but it isn't rare either. There was once vague language in the "Terms of Service" page prohibiting "unattended content," but this rule was removed for unexplained reasons (users on Reddit suspect it was to make space for popular "unattended" accounts that broadcast things like tropical fish in an aquarium or views of city streets from cameras in a window.)[3] Though some #sleepstreams are enormously popular—Twitch users seem to especially enjoy watching attractive women wake up—there were only a handful of people commenting in the chat section on Torr's page. Most of them, like me, arrived at his page by clicking on the hashtag #sleepstream.

In 2019, Twitch streamer JesseDStreams woke up to two hundred viewers after falling asleep on camera. They were attentive viewers—and generous too. Sometimes users send money to their favourite streamers as a sign of appreciation for their skills executing a difficult manoeuvre in a game or otherwise providing entertaining content. JesseDStreams received donations of this kind while he slept like an absurd joke, but one to which no one knew the punchline. Soon others tried to mimic his success through #sleepstream. There were sleepers on Twitch before 2019, but this was only incidental to labour that demands the maximum hours. Livestreamers lose followers and cash donations when their streams are shut off. Some of the streamers who rely on donations keep their cameras on, even while they sleep, just so users will see the word "live" and not "offline," when they click onto their pages. In *Wired*, Cecilia D'Anastasio writes that the practice of sleepstreaming has another "more obvious reason: They're tired. Occasionally, they'll take an unplanned nap after a full day of gaming and vigilantly entertaining thousands of people."[4]

Torr is a user on a commercially owned, ad-driven platform, which, in 2020, was valued at US$15 billion,[5] but Ana Voog carved out

3 rick9k commented on a thread in r/Twitch, "That unattended content rule was removed. I do remember it, when I went looking for it recently it was gone. I asked around and the ppl who knew about it said it was gone. Explains why there are so many new animal cameras and fishbowl streams where nobody is even watching chat." rick9k, "r/Twitch," Reddit, 13 July 2020, https://www.reddit.com/r/Twitch/comments/hpvc0x/tos_about_unattended_content.

4 Cecilia D'Anastasio, "Twitch Streamers Make Thousands Literally by Just Sleeping," *Wired,* 22 December 2020, https://www.wired.com/story/twitch-streamers-make-thousands-sleeping.

5 Ari Levy, "Amazon's Media Business Is Worth $500 Billion Based on 'Hidden Value,' Says Needham Analyst," *CNBC*, 16 June 2020, https://www.cnbc.com/2020/06/16/amazon-media-assets-worth-500-billion-almost-as-much-as-aws-needham.html.

a place for herself in the free and open, non-proprietary world wide web. Voog built and hosted her own webpages and maintained Internet Relay Chat (IRC) channels, another communication tool based on open-source protocols.

Torr could build a website like Ana's. He could code it in HTML and upload files through FTP. The tools he has at his disposal might be the same, but he doesn't have the internet culture of 1997. Back then, there were just over one million websites on the internet; now, there are over one and a half billion websites.[6] On Twitch, just one of these websites, there are fifteen million daily active users. There are over seven and a half billion people on earth.

There's also a stark difference in their intentions. Voog interfaced with webcams as a deliberate performer. In her reams of online diary entries and in interviews with the press, she is careful to dissuade others of the notion that her livestream is an unfiltered, authentic presentation of her life. Voog kept her webcam recording from 1997 to 2009, and she considers all twelve years of her livestreamed footage on *anacam* to be a single performance piece.[7] *anacam* was included in the exhibition *Fame After Photography*, which was presented at the Museum of Modern Art (MoMA) in 1999. In the exhibition catalogue, curators Marvin Heiferman and Carole Kismaric presciently allude to Voog's work and what it prefigures: "On the Internet, fame is self-appointed for the first time as hundreds of individuals worldwide point their camcorders on themselves to record and broadcast their every move in streaming video images available round the clock and around the world to anyone interested in looking."[8]

A week after I found his sleepstream, I checked Torr's page again and he was playing a videogame. At the bottom of his screen was a bar graph that showed that he was forty-five percent of the way to his goal of "250 followers on Twitter." I can't tell whether he's a talented gamer or just wants some online company, but I noticed that, since I had last looked, he had changed his profile description: he has listed some of his hobbies and his age, he's fifteen years old.

Torr is a child—a child that random people in an online chat once joked might be dead.

Ana was already more than twice Torr's age in 1999 when she first streamed her sleep—two years after she launched *anacam*. Before she turned on her webcam, Voog had been the lead singer of an indie band called The Blue Up? that had a stylishly dark XTC and Siouxsie Sioux-inspired sound. The band had a fanbase who followed Voog to this second act—an act through which she would accumulate more witnesses (and more fans) as her performance

6 Real Time Statistics Project, Internet Live Stats, accessed 1 March 2021, https://www.internetlivestats.com.

7 On her Vimeo page, Voog calls the archive of anacam a "complete piece... you really need to consider the ENTIRE 12 year piece." Ana Voog, "ana voog," Vimeo, https://vimeo.com/anavoog.

8 Marvin Heiferman and Carole Kismaric, "Fame After Photography," in *Fame After Photography*, eds. Marvin Heiferman and Carole Kismaric (New York City, New York: The Museum of Modern Art, 1999), 12.

became a notorious spectacle on the internet. The web had only become publicly available in 1991 and internet users were all still finding their feet when Voog began her livestreaming project. She appeared as a guest on programs like *Entertainment Tonight*, and Sinbad interviewed her on the TV talk show for the magazine *Vibe*. *anacam* offered viewers a window into Ana's life, but their presence also shaped her life. She met her husband through her webcam.

Over the years, Voog has offered many reasons as to why she maintained this project. Most recently, in a 2018 essay for *Vice* in which she looked back on the experience, she wrote, "I wasn't an exhibitionist. I was an anarchist. I wanted to crush all the archetypes people held about me—like thinking I was a dumb blonde, for example—by slowly disintegrating them from within."[9] It was also a way for her to make money. Sometimes she had sex on camera—once she gave birth on camera[10]—and anyone who paid $10 a month[11] to access *anacam* could see the parts of her life that most of the world keeps private. But this all seems incidental: natural moments in the life of someone who was already sharing so much. As Voog wrote in the bio for *anacam*, last updated in 2007, "sexuality and SENSUALITY is a PART of this site because that is part of my life."[12]

The Universal Sleep Station is reminiscent of Sophie Calle's 1979 photography series *The Sleepers*. In her first major project addressing voyeurism and surveillance, Calle invited twenty-nine strangers and acquaintances to sleep in her bed. She photographed each of them as they slept—some paired up, others slept alone. Calle infiltrated their private and vulnerable moments; creating an unusual relationship with her participants, just as Voog knitted herself into a community of sleeping strangers and acquaintances. But The Universal Sleep Station's participants weren't taking over Voog's space. She wasn't displaced by their sleep, she had, after all, set up a unique URL for this assembly of co-sleepers (*anacam*, her streaming site, had a unique domain name). The Universal Sleep Station wasn't transactional—it was communal. Calle's project was free to access, unlike *anacam*. In retrospect, part of the innocence of the project is the rudimentary equipment—albeit "high-tech" for the times—that was used to broadcast it and the bewilderment over what the technology might do and what relationships could be formed through it. The participants had webcams that broadcast over dial-up. Every three seconds, the uploaded images would update on the web with noticeable zoetrope-like gaps. It wasn't like being with someone in person, but it was a way of being there with somebody. It was no utopia, but the internet was an unknown—new endeavours like The Universal Sleep Station were launched out of a sense of promise and opportunity.

Joanne McNeil

9 The URL for the Universal Sleep Station page expired about ten years ago, but the website is archived on the Wayback Machine at http://web.archive.org/web/19991012223749/http://www.voog.com.

10 Jim Walsh, "Ana Voog: 'I'm Sort of the Anti-Kardashian,'" *Star Tribune*, 17 January 2013, https://www.startribune.com/ana-voog-i-m-sort-of-the-anti-kardashian/187324801.

11 Marisa Helms, "The Surveillance Society: Webcams." News & Features, Minnesota Public Radio (MPR), 15 November 1999, http://news.minnesota.publicradio.org/features/199911/15_newsroom_privacy/watched.html.

12 Ana Voog, "anacam, the internet's 1st 24/7 art+life cam!," Ana Voog, last revised 1 February 2007, http://anavoog.com/anacam.com/anatomy/index.html.

"To me, the nascent World Wide Web seemed to be a non-hierarchical, destabilizing system of power," writes Voog. "I thought that the Internet would be a way for me to circumvent everything that stood in my way: a tool for the unheard. We could speak out and completely bypass the hierarchical, patriarchal system in place to keep us silent. Or at least this is how things felt like they might be in 1997."[13]

It seems as though Torr wants the contemporary version of fame that Ana Voog once had: not necessarily visibility in a MoMA exhibition or to be interviewed by Sinbad but name recognition and what we now call a "following." There are major livestreamers—professional gamers—who have made millions from streaming on Twitch, such as Ninja and Dr Lupo. Their incomes typically come from a mix of "donations" from fans and revenue generated from advertising, including brand partnerships and sponsorships. To answer the question as to why viewers send money to superstar streamers who already have a lot, Nathan Grayson, writing for *Kotaku*, spoke with Twitch stream followers, including many young people who work minimum-wage jobs. These followers donate to "streamers who they feel regularly enrich their lives," as a sign of respect.[14] They might feel a thrill when a livestreamer shouts out their name to thank them for their donation, but there's also a sense of obligation. If they have to pay for movie tickets and comic books, why wouldn't they pay their favourite entertainers? Another Twitch user told Grayson that he donates to one of his favourite livestreamers out of a sense of anxiety over his future:

> If the game ever flames out, [the livestreamer] doesn't really have a path to migrate to another game or maintain the same level of success. It's possible he could lose all of his subscribers due to attrition and go back to just getting by ... so I'll support him with my five bucks even though he owns his own home and I might never.[15]

The internet can be a cheat code for those without the alumni networks and family connections that traditionally pave the way to broad recognition, but of the fifteen million users on Twitch, most are followers rather than followed. Torr is not unique. Even those who find success online may still yearn for the long-term stability of a more traditional career.

***

Some elements of Twitch remind me of the first several years of the world wide web. A similar air of leisure and serendipity comes through in the mélange of clubs that host virtual events through it and random users that play archival material on its streams.

13 Ana Voog, "I Was One of the Most Famous People Online in 1998-Then I Disappeared," *VICE*, 22 June 2018, https://www.vice.com/en/article/ywe9wv/anacam-anna-voog-livestream-web-cam-art.

14 Nathan Grayson, "Why Twitch Fans Donate Money To Wealthy Streamers," *Kotaku*, 5 February 2020, https://kotaku.com/why-twitch-fans-donate-money-to-already-wealthy-streame-1841456196.

15 Ibid.

Forgotten VCR is a fascinating Twitch page, which has the tagline "Watch TV and Stay Indoors." Three nights a week, the Forgotten VCR host plays cult movies and esoteric video footage—"all my favorite things: kaiju, pro-wrestling, movie trailers, kung fu, music videos, giant robots, skateboarding, puroresu, instructional tapes, commercials, anime, and obscure video from the 80s and 90s."[16] In an interview with *PC Gamer*, Forgotten VCR's host, who insists on remaining anonymous, said he's a university professor by day and by night he shares these "mixtapes" from the collection of bootleg VHS tapes that he's been accumulating since he was in high school. He uses the revenue generated from his Twitch stream to bid on obscure tapes from Malaysia and Thailand in Yahoo Auctions.[17] When I last watched, he played a set of American and Japanese commercials for video cameras and VHS recorders from the 1980s and 1990s, which were full of mesmerizing colours and graphics. Another favourite Twitch destination of mine is Old Timey Computer Show, a 24-hour stream of vintage programs on digital technology, personal computers, and computer graphics with synthesizer jingles, neon green grids, retro GUIs, and 8-bit typefaces that now invoke nostalgia. Many of the videos that appear on Old Timey Computer Show have long been available on YouTube and the Wayback Machine, but the charm of the stream is its consistency. I'll tune in for ambient background noise and visuals, and, just as I think I'm getting tired of it, something delightful will surface, like an elderly guest on *Computer Chronicles*—a show that used to air on PBS from 1983 to 2002—who demonstrates how she used the programming language BASIC to chart her knitting. These broadcasts remind me of opportunities that have been missed. Computers have always had consequences, but, twenty years ago, there was still the possibility that the internet wouldn't result in hopeless situations like Torr's.

As it happens, Twitch was founded by a livestreamer—one who sometimes slept on camera. This individual started his account largely to get the attention of VCs and the burgeoning tech industry. In the late aughts, Justin Kan was a noticeable and ubiquitous presence at Bay Area start-up happy hours and conferences like South by Southwest. He would wear a camera that was attached to a baseball cap and carry a backpack with a laptop inside that would broadcast his everyday adventures over Sprint's 3G mobile network. The setup was heavy but necessary: he launched the project before iPhones became available in 2007, and even then, the iPhone didn't have a video camera until 2009.[18] Justin.tv was released concurrently with the reality TV craze that brought us *The Hills*, *The Bachelor*, *American Idol*, *The Amazing Race*, *Top Chef*, and *The Real Housewives of Orange County*. Like Ana Voog, Kan received national media attention for the novelty of his lifecasting project. Justin Kan was the first user of what would become a

16 The Forgotten VCR Twitch page can be found at https://www.twitch.tv/forgotten_vcr.

17 W. Fenlon, "This streamer turns '80s found footage into wildly entertaining weekly mixtapes," *PC Gamer*, 27 October 2020, https://www.pcgamer.com/this-streamer-turns-80s-found-footage-into-wildly-entertaining-weekly-mixtapes.

18 While fact checking this, I came across a 2012 *Engadget* blog post in which the writer lists all the applications and products that he used to livestream an event at his wife's synagogue. He concludes, "Yes, the sound quality's not great, you've got no zoom, and there are plenty of other issues. But in a pinch, this is the sort of setup that lets you stream an event with only wireless bandwidth and your iPhone—and if that's not living in the future, I don't know what is." M. Rose, "My cheap, simple livestreaming rig: iPhone, Ustream, Zagg and Clingo," *Engadget*, 26 September 2012, https://www.engadget.com/2012-09-26-my-cheap-simple-livestreaming-rig-iphone-ustream-zagg-and-cl.html.

platform known as Justin.tv; the product of a start-up he founded with Emmett Shear, Michael Seibel, and Kyle Vogt. It was an open platform on which anyone could stream their lives, just as Kan had done for the eight months prior to its release. But even when live-streaming equipment became less cumbersome, Justin.tv never quite found a core community of people broadcasting their lives as he had done—its most devoted users livestreamed themselves playing videogames. In 2011, Kan and his co-founders spun out a vertical for these users, which they named Twitch.

The success of Twitch has come full circle as users splintered off from livestreaming games to lifecasting—the type of content that Justin.tv had been created to host. But just as the internet for which Ana Voog created content is different from the one on which Torr broadcasts, Twitch is also the product of an internet that is different from the internet on which Justin.tv hosted lifecasts. Amazon directly owns Twitch, and indirectly it powers much of the internet. The cloud infrastructure and server farm, Amazon Web Service (AWS) was launched in 2006, just a year before Kan's start-up. Now, AWS dominates the web as it is the backbone for tens of millions of websites like Zoom, Netflix, and Airbnb, and the webpages for countless schools, municipalities, and organizations, not to mention Twitch. Just last year, it was reported that Twitch hosts 91% of all livestreaming content—and that content is Amazon's too.[19] Its stake in the company is growing more and more visible. In February of 2021, Amazon began playing anti-union ads on Twitch, the platform it owns, to counter an organizing drive at its Bessemer, Alabama warehouse.[20] The quirky archival livestreams and fishbowl cams on Twitch seem less wholesome when they are interstitially interrupted for Twitch viewers in Alabama with glossy clips from people on camera saying, "I always wanted to work at Amazon. Vote no for the union."

The world wide web, once decentralized not only in its protocols but in its ownership as well, has been consumed by corporate power. It is not possible to sleep as peacefully on camera as Ana Voog and her companions once did. There's always an interloper —and not just an unknown viewer. The dream of the internet has become a nightmare.

19 Thomas Wilde, "Streaming report: Twitch inherits Mixer's streamers, now has 91% of all content produced," *GeekWire*, 7 October 2020, https://www.geekwire.com/2020/streaming-report-twitch-inherits-mixers-streamers-now-91-content-produced.

20 Lauren Kaori Gurley, "Amazon Sends 'Vote NO' Instructions to Unionizing Employees, Tells Them to Use New Mailbox," *VICE*, 24 February 2021, https://www.vice.com/en/article/3anw9k/amazon-sends-vote-no-instructions-to-unionizing-employees-tells-them-to-use-new-mailbox.

Paul Graham, *Television Portrait (Jack, Bradford)*, 1988

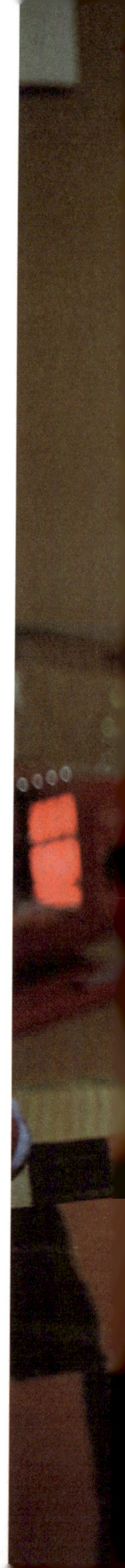

Paul Graham, *Television Portrait (Ryo, Tokyo)*, 1994

Paul Graham, *Television Portrait (Cathy, London)*, 1989

Sumayya Vally

A Public Space in Which to Access the Digital Commons

Traditionally, the role of architecture has been to confine or control space, shaping social experience and relations through static forms. Our architectural vocabulary and forms largely belong to a past era of static space and have not hybridized or morphed to accommodate and inspire changing spatial conditions, to include the shifting, fluid, and amorphous digital, or the history of peoples for whom movement, not stasis, is the predominant experience.

Design expressions for identity and political freedoms and of the digital commons dance allegorically alongside each other. The digital commons holds possibilities for finding architectures for both migration and subverting control, forms of representation alongside themes of diaspora and hybridity, and all that which is fluid, shifting, undefined, continuously redefining, evolving, and mutating.

1 In urban design terminology, we think of "private" and "public," "inside" and "outside" as static qualities,

2 but our contemporary spatial experiences in the digital public realm belong to a different kind of order: shifting, intangible, scale-less, infinite, not bounded by gravity, geography, or time.

3 Convention: the history of conventions is intrinsically and unavoidably linked to histories of colonization, slavery and "legalized" exploitations of land, resources, and people.

4 New conventions must be forged:

5 physical, digital, and augmented,

6 while listening to the echoes of those who have sought to do this before us, and fearlessly crafting futures in the cracks of the present.

7 All territories are bound.

8 In certain forms, the state's conventions are the sites that give form to architectures of inclusion and exclusion, where futures are decided, molded, and made.

9 Their forms can be manipulated to carve spaces for dialogue between peoples, cultures, ideas, and ambitions; where politics, the present, and futures are discussed and declared; and through which relations are built, tested, and performed.

10 By definition, هجرة (hijra) refers to "immigrating," "passing," or "coming." It is a word with both Latin and Arabic roots. Historically, it was used to describe Prophet Muhammad's flight from Mecca to Medina to escape persecution.

11 Included in its etymology are the words for "departure," "exodus," and "journey."

12 Interestingly, in Urdu, the term has also come to mean "fluidity of identity" or a "third identity," particularly in relation to gender and culture.

13 In this definition, the body is understood to be a literal site of transition,

14 a vessel through which culture and identity journey and in which both are housed.

15 Late 2010: The Arab Spring, a series of anti-government protests, uprisings, and armed rebellions that spread across the Middle East.

16 The revolution spreads swiftly on social media throughout the region, as new protests appeared in response to success stories that had been shared between and across geographies.

17 The use of social media platforms more than doubles in Arab countries during the protests.

18 23 March 2016: An artificial intelligence chatbot, Tay, is released by Microsoft Corporation via Twitter,

19 causing subsequent controversy when the bot begins to post offensive and inflammatory racist, sexist, and homophobic tweets to its Twitter account. Microsoft shuts down the service only sixteen hours after launching it.

20 June 2020: the most precarious economic and political crisis in Lebanon's history.

21 July 2020: a famine worse than that of 1918.

22 August 2020: the third largest explosion in world history.

23 Port: a space of crossing, of transition, of crossover. A highly programmed space, akin to an airport, where slippages of control, territory, and access have consequences that far exceed the port's actual geography.

24 In the so-called developing world, one has only to track the proliferation of trade- and duty-free economic zones that have sprung up around land, air, and water ports to understand their importance to the fiscal growth of any given nation.

25 The port refers to land, air, water, and cyber scapes; may explore edge conditions, trade relations, and cultural exchanges; and can be situated between past and present, between home and away, between the here and the now, between natural and supernatural, and

26 between crossings and controls (of species, of things, and of conditions).

27 Augment: to make greater, larger, or more complete; or of a musical interval: made one half step greater than major or perfect;

28 to claim, reconfigure, correct, fuse.[1]

29 Sangomas diagnose, prescribe, and perform rituals to heal people physically, mentally, emotionally, and spiritually.

30 Johannesburg, 2020: “Connect with your ancestors” advertisements for Facebook and Whatsapp consultations and treatments with sangomas and traditional healers.

31 Divination: healing physical, emotional, and spiritual illnesses directing birth or death rituals, finding lost cattle, protecting warriors, counteracting witchcraft, and narrating the history, cosmology, and myths of their traditions.

32 Traditional healers are consulted by more than sixty percent of South Africans.

33 Claim heritages, reconfigure, and uncover histories; fuse places, times, geopolitics, and geopoetics.

34 Perhaps, in this project, an African and Arab (Summer) Sun rises over the digital square, and communities of women, diasporic groups, Arabs and non-Arabs, BIPOCs, gender-fluid people, multi-religious, -literate, and -abled people, and others are there to greet it.

1 "Augment," Dictionary.com, https://www.dictionary.com/browse/augment.

Below:
HIG TRAFFIC SYSTEMS
+LIGHTLINE, 2017

Right:
KLEMENS SCHILLINGER
OFFLINE LAMP, 2017
SUBSTITUTE PHONE, 2017

As people spend more time looking down at their phones while walking in public spaces, there has been an increase in pedestrian accidents with motorists. The Dutch town of Bodegraven's pilot project +Lightline embeds a series of LED light strips in the sidewalks at intersections, which alternate between projecting green and red light in correspondence with pedestrian signals. Instead of attempting to curb or alter this new pedestrian habit of looking down through a series of public service announcements and campaigns, +Lightline accepts smartphones as part of the built environment.

Now that smartphones have become ubiquitous, there is a growing societal concern over digital dependency with handheld devices. Substitute Phone and Offline Lamp act as intermediary devices by placating a person's urge to constantly reach for or touch their phones. Substitute Phone is a "dummy phone" that accepts certain gestures that are used to operate smart devices, such as swiping, scrolling, and pinching, to help the user abstain from the often-involuntary impulse to touch their cellphone. In contrast, Offline Lamp employs a logic of exchange: by placing a smartphone into the drawer at the lamp's base and closing it, the lamp's light is activated. While the lamp offers light, that light is turned off as soon as a user checks their phone for updates.

The +Lightline in Bodegraven, lit up to alert pedestrians to oncoming traffic. Photograph: Edwin Bruining

The Offline Lamp, which only turns on when a smartphone is stored in its base. Photograph: Leonard Hilzensauer

Substitute Phone's stone beads mimic the feeling of scrolling and swiping. Photograph: Leonard Hilzensauer

Agency

Are you a conscious consumer? Do you use your city as a space for collective action?

 Lucas Foglia, *A Natural Order (Natalie Carrying Firewood, Wildroots Homestead, North Carolina)*, 2006

SPIRIT
FAther'S IN the
Orwell
1984
Animal
Farm
(He Who CON
-OIL CONTROLs the
WORLD
(FLOOD
of the

Lucas Foglia, *A Natural Order (Homeschooling Chalkboard, Tennessee)*, 2008

Lucas Foglia, *A Natural Order (Rita and Cora Aiming, Tennessee)*, 2007

UNSENSE
100 HOMES, BRAINPORT SMART DISTRICT, 2018

As the effects of capitalism have become nearly impossible to escape, some individuals have turned to self-sufficient communities to cultivate a sense of self-determination. As a flexible grid designed in response to the needs and demands of its eventual inhabitants, Brainport Smart District is a circular, sustainable community being developed in the Helmond municipality of the Netherlands. With 100 Homes, part of the larger Brainport project, the ambition is for the community to be autonomous and self-sustaining in nearly all respects, from energy generation to food production and water management. Though in many ways similar to the aspirations for the intentional-living communities formed in North America during the 1970s, the Brainport Smart District has a twenty-first century slant: residents will jointly manage their user data, which is tracked by the built environment and meant to be used to optimize the district to suit its inhabitants. The project is premised on the idea that digital tools can be used to create a feedback loop between inhabitation and habitat, ultimately allowing for society and the built environment to change in pace with one another.

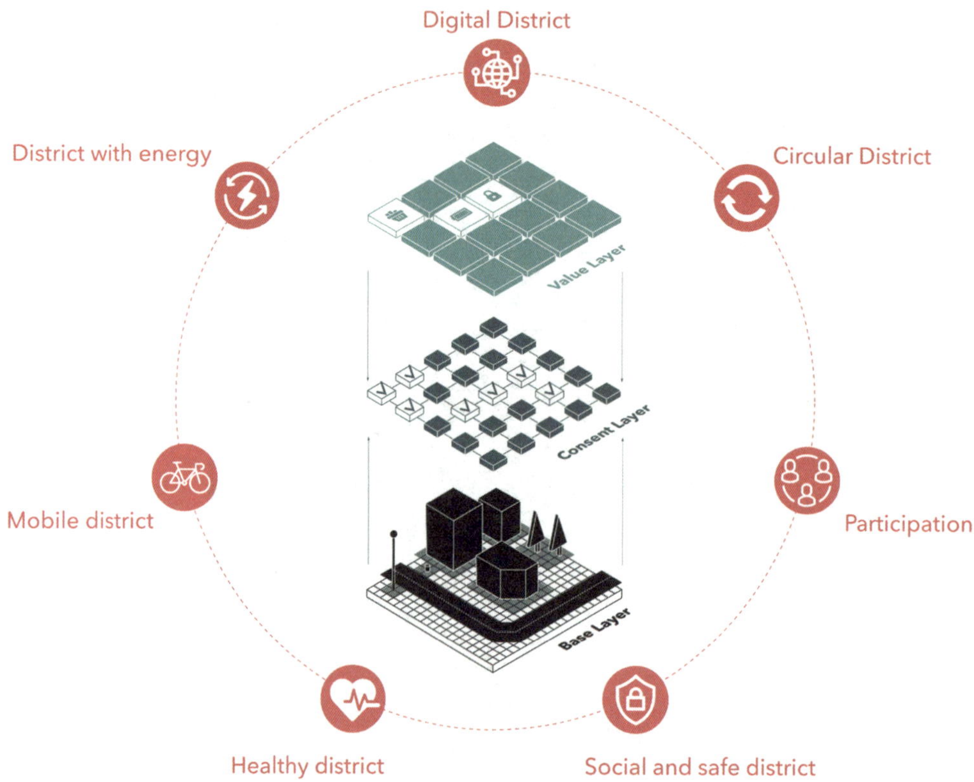

Diagram of the integrated logic of 100 Homes, where residents, rather than tech companies, own their data

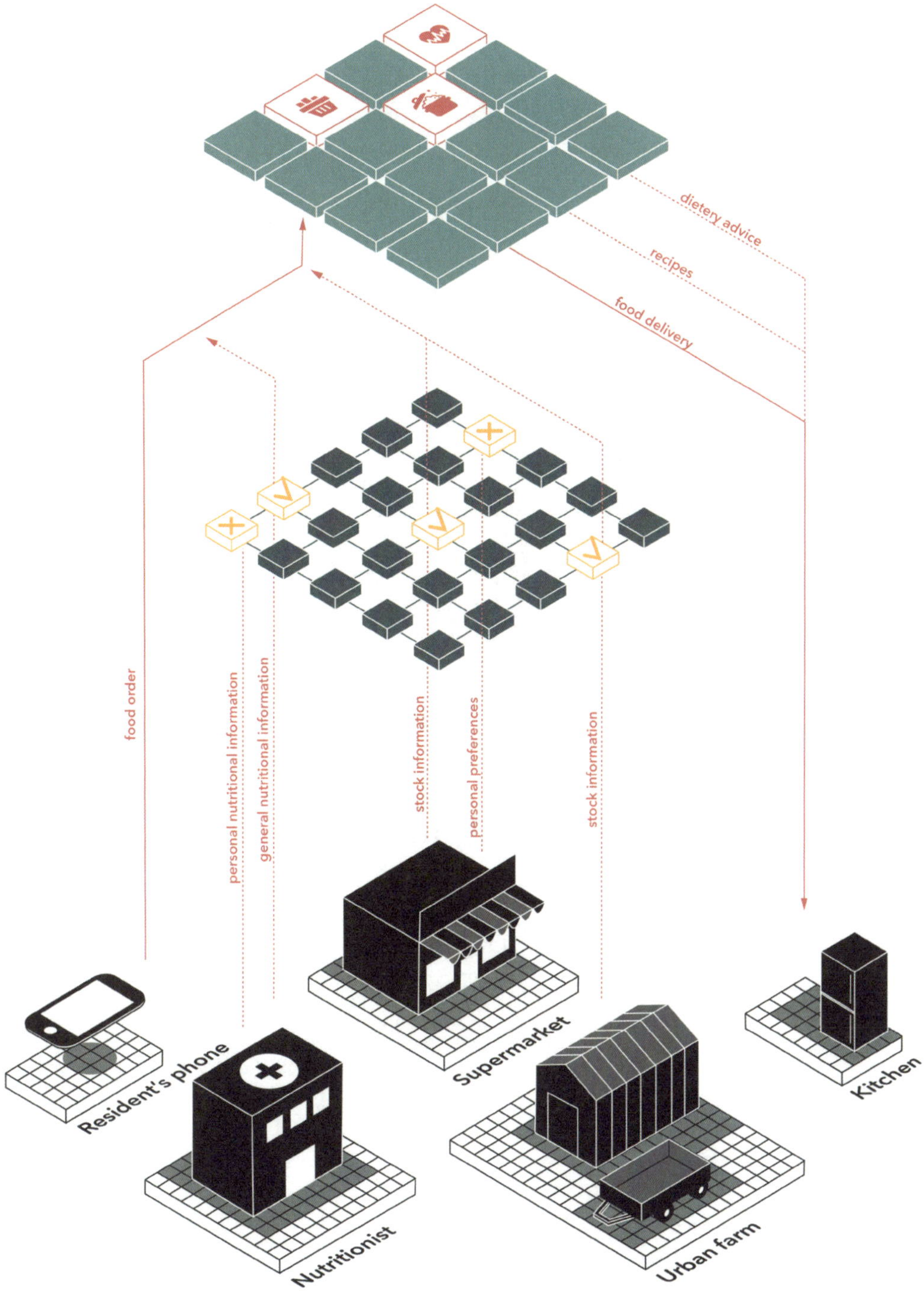

Diagram depicting the ways in which data on needs and consumption habits is collected from residents, and in turn used to shape their neighbourhood

Glass straws present a sustainable alternative to single-use plastic. Photograph: Matthieu Brouillard, CCA

While studying olive ridley sea turtles on the coast of Costa Rica in 2015, a team of scientists noticed a plastic straw lodged in the nostril of a male turtle. They filmed the somewhat graphic process of extracting the straw from the turtle's nose with a pair of pliers, and marine conservation biologist Christine Figgener uploaded the video to YouTube. The eight-minute video began circulating online and made its starring sea turtle, Ridley, an emblem for the cause to ban plastic straws. The video continued to gain momentum, coming to a head in 2018 as social media influencers and celebrities pledged to stop using plastic straws, while many restaurants, cafes, bars, and hotels outlawed them altogether. As bans on single-use plastics are implemented by more and more legislative bodies, the resulting solution has been the production of reusable alternatives, with glass straws emerging as a popular choice.

Oat milk has gained popularity as consumers seek out animal-friendly alternatives to dairy milk. Photograph: Matthieu Brouillard, CCA

As environmental consciousness becomes an increasingly present feature in mainstream culture, the milk with which one takes their coffee has become a basis on which to judge individual morality. The focus seems to have shifted from health concerns related to milk consumption, which led to the introduction of organic milk; to the comfort of the cows that produce the milk, which resulted in an increased value on grass-fed and pasture-raised cows; and finally, to animal welfare concerns which have steered consumers toward non-dairy alternatives such as soy, nut, and oat milks. However, the moral choice of dairy or non-dairy is unstable, as new considerations and criticisms of non-dairy alternatives arise. Recent understandings of the large quantities of water required to produce nut milk have caused hesitation among some consumers, while one of the most popular oat milk producers, Oatly, has accepted investments from the Blackstone Group, a company that directly contributes to the destruction of the Amazon rainforest and global deforestation.

Block Bird's by The Future Market offers a transparent supply chain line of chicken, using blockchain to record all data about the product. Image courtesy of Mike Lee, The Future Market, New York.

With ever-complexifying supply chains that serve to further obscure where commodities originate from, how they are produced, and how they are distributed, consumers are typically left to make purchasing decisions based on minimal information, much of which is obscure and difficult to verify the accuracy of. The Future Market's concept product, Block Bird's, seeks to create transparency in food logistics by employing Blockchain to authenticate production information for consumers. The journey that a Block Bird's chicken takes from "egg to grocery store" is not only tracked and documented, it is plainly printed on the product's packaging. This novel degree of transparency is meant to empower the consumer to be able to make purchases that align with their values and also to incentivize ethical production and distribution methods by giving them visibility.

Trash jars, used to hold consumers accountable for their personal waste, have become popular among those who aim to live a zero-waste lifestyle. Photograph: Matthieu Brouillard, CCA

The mason jar is perhaps the most recognizable icon of a sustainable lifestyle—simultaneously symbolizing take-away smoothies, dry goods bought in bulk, and homemade soup packed for an office lunch. Its more recent use as a receptacle in which to collect one's trash further entrenches it as a symbol of an environmentally friendly lifestyle, or more specifically, a zero-waste lifestyle. The zero-waste movement was named and popularized by blogger-turned-author Bea Johnson who, in 2009, decided to drastically reduce her family of four's consumption of disposable products and document the process on her blog. By year's end, the amount of non-compostable and non-recyclable trash that the Johnsons produced fit into a single quart-sized mason jar—compared to the four pounds of trash that the average American produces each day. The image Bea posted to her blog of her "trash jar" quickly became the metric by which the zero-waste lifestyle was quantified. Rather than a receptacle or even a measuring device, the trash jar is aspirational—its contents only account for the trash that one personally disposes of, failing to measure any of the waste that is produced by others who render products or services for zero-waste consumption. Reducing one's annual trash production to fit a single mason jar is certainly an environmental good, but a good that does not necessarily have an effect beyond one's own household and conscience.

Title: Portlandia
Season/Episode: S01E01
Year: 2011
Network: IFC
Country: USA

Portlandia is a collection of sketches, put together by Fred Armisen and Carrie Brownstein, with biting humour and a kitsch aesthetic. It is a mysterious and multi-faceted series: satire bordering on parody of the hipster-ia of the early 2000s, and its obsessions and attempts to find alternative lifestyles. The socio-cultural community that is the central object of the series was also its viewership when it first aired, to whom it offers a deformed mirror image. Today, the series presents the opportunity to critically observe what we no longer want to be and what we could have become.

A Space With No Trash Collection

> It is not so much by the things that each day are manufactured, sold, bought that you can measure Leonia's opulence, but rather by the things that each day are thrown out to make room for the new. So you begin to wonder if Leonia's true passion is really, as they say, the enjoyment of new and different things, and not, instead, the joy of expelling, discarding, cleansing itself of a recurrent impurity. The fact is that street cleaners are welcomed like angels, and their task of removing the residue of yesterday's existence is surrounded by a respectful silence, like a ritual that inspires devotion, perhaps only because once things have been cast off nobody wants to have to think about them further.[1]

For trash collection services to cease, a radical shift in mindset and behaviour is necessary to understand that same trash in place as raw matter and raw resource[2] to be redistributed, reused, and recoupled. As a counterpoint to the reliance on street cleaners in Leonia, what are the spatial and cultural implications if trash collection halts and the possibility of discard becomes obsolete? Can new collectivities form around an ontology and an economy that values everything as a resource? What is the transformative potentiality of the things around us that we live with? What are their afterlives and by-products?

As trash services stop, some municipalities roll out policies that include material usage bans of plastic bags and Styrofoam, while others focus on infrastructural innovations such as building systems with integrated pneumatic tubes to facilitate material recycling. But it is not the centralized and technological management that facilitates a cultural shift to this mode of thought, it is creative collective thinking that produces behavioural, aesthetic, and even "ethical"[3] innovations that overturn individualistic capitalist habits and desires.

To sift, scavenge, salvage, repair, compost, reuse, glean, barter, recirculate: these become the new terms of living. The insatiable cycle of consumption and capital-oriented growth make way for alternative forms of labour; care; and maintenance of things, communities, and places. A reprioritization of ecology occurs, without sanitizing it, as material is kept in place and can no longer be unevenly distributed elsewhere, stored out of sight.

At the same time, the revaluation of waste introduces a culture of fixing and tinkering of those things that would otherwise be thrown away. New lives are given to broken, torn, and shattered objects in repair workshops and upcycling labs that become part gallery, part store, and part educational outlet. Sometimes the act of repair is casual, but, for some, repair increasingly becomes a refined art form, borrowing from the *kintsugi* technique of mending broken ceramics with powdered gold. Instead of disposing of objects when they are no longer shiny and new, breakage and repair become part of the history of those things and fissures and modifications are celebrated. Indeed, these methods and modes of living spread from ways of re-making things to ways of re-making and reusing buildings, as new architectural types arise amidst vacancies and shifting social demands. "Spolia" takes on a renewed meaning for homes and these new types, from refined *kintsugi* techniques of repair and binding to maximalist bricolage.

1 Italo Calvino, "Continuous Cities," in *Invisible Cities*, trans. William Weaver (London: Vintage Books, 1974), 102.

2 Following Georges Bataille's notion of an abundance of resources rather than a scarcity of them as described in Allan Stoekl, "Orgiastic Recycling," in *Bataille's Peak* (Minneapolis: University of Minnesota Press, 2007), 115–149.

3 Myra J. Jird, "Waste, Landfills and an Environmental Ethics of Vulnerability," *Ethics and the Environment* 18, no. 1 (Spring 2013): 115.

Domesticity is no longer relegated to the single-family house or the single apartment unit. Inhabitants become part of larger metabolic cycles with their neighbours and they begin to rely on one another—one person's compost becomes another person's fertilizer, which helps to grow another person's vegetables; one child's outgrown high-tops are swapped for another child's rainboots; one person's old magazines transform into another person's art canvas, and so it goes—much like an industrial ecology that translates one industry's outputs into another industry's inputs. A domestic ecology—a home ecology—is formed.

This home ecology produces an equilibrium of sorts that opens the door to a slew of new and supplementary domestic types within apartment buildings, districts, and residential neighbourhoods. Spaces previously for trash (sidewalks, bins, trash-compactor rooms, basements, garages) along with sites for consumption of the new (clothing and grocery stores, shopping malls, and the like) are reclaimed by inhabitants. Both formal and informal new economies and forms of labour are instigated as old habits of consumption and discard cease.

Individualized packaging of consumable goods, particularly food and cleaning supplies, become outdated, and, instead, people gather and shop in bulk with their neighbours and for their neighbourhoods. Bulk storage at the scales of the house, the building, and the district replace the scale of the cabinet and the pantry—the gathering of ingredients and preparation of meals becomes a shared endeavour. Types that disrupt the supply chain to create more direct relationships between suppliers and inhabitants produce a decentralization of local food distribution and recycling hubs, reducing packaging, organic waste, and diversion mishaps. Spatial formats of swap meets, barter floors, and flea markets alongside a virtual LISTSERV introduce new physical marketplaces and sites of exchange. Homes borrow and hybridize agricultural storage types at the district and domestic scales, such as the grain silo, to keep and distribute bulk goods. For the distribution of essential liquids, such as fresh drinking water and milks, local refilleries that are part gas station and part return to the wells of the town commons, open to abolish single-use containers.

In the cultivation of this attitude toward both reducing trash and trash having an intrinsic value, ways and means of living shift in a variety of ways. Some inhabitants gravitate toward an ultralight life—a streamlining and reduction of things and rituals,[4] some inhabitants are liberated from the permanence of things and embrace the possibility of a life in flux with a constantly changing spatial reconfiguration and curation of things within their homes; some inhabitants double down on the commitment to their domestic spaces and objects, embracing maintenance, repair, and history. Others absorb the cultural changes in ways that are not so easily apparent, in the adoption of small shifts in daily habits and behaviours, from how they brush their teeth, to how they pour their cereal into their bowls, to what they see upon looking out of their bedroom windows.

4 Intentional Estates Agency (Tei Carpenter, Jesse LeCavalier, Dan Taeyoung, and Chris Woebken), "Some Degrowth Portfolios," *Pidgin*, no. 26 (2019): 190–213.

CLIMATE
STRIKE
PROTECT
WATER, CLIMATE
COMMUNITIES

Bryan Thomas, *Climate Strike NYC*, 2019

Bryan Thomas, *Climate Strike NYC*, 2019

THE HOMO DEPOT

UNITED IN
OUTRAGE
THE RESISTANCE MARCH
RISE AND RESIST
RISEANDRESIST.ORG
Monday, September 23 • 5:30 PM • Bryant Park to Washington Square Park

Bryan Thomas, *Climate Strike NYC*, 2019

Boxes with sad faces reminiscent of the Amazon logo left outside of the company's founder and CEO Jeff Bezos' New York City penthouse by protestors, 2020. Source: Bloomberg

Introduced by Amazon in 2015 to celebrate the twentieth anniversary of the company's founding, Prime Day has since become an annual international "shopping holiday"—second in sales only to Cyber Monday. With a business model that underprices products to the point of taking losses on sales, on Prime Day Amazon offers further reductions to prices that have already enabled the company to monopolize most retail categories. Amazon's success relies on providing the lowest prices and quickest delivery times to its consumers, but this convenience comes at a cost—a cost that is abstracted through the company's online interface and logistics network in which the consumer is not typically required to interact with Amazon employees (or even another human being). Building over the course of several years, this cost was revealed to be paid by the company's employees—the site from which the company extracts the most profit. After Amazon announced that its 2019 Prime Day would be a two-day event for which it would promise one-day shipping, rather than the already incredibly fast two-day timeline, warehouse workers in several countries went on strike and organized protests to demand better working conditions. In solidarity with those workers, calls to boycott that year's Amazon Prime Day circulated via social media tagged #BoycottAmazon. While the posts were shared and tweeted broadly and seemingly received mass support online, that year's sale was the largest shopping event in the company's history, with over 175 million discounted items sold. By design, not a single consumer had to cross a picket line to take advantage of the sale, they simply had to click.

A gilet jaune, now understood in France as a symbol of resistance after a series of protests which began in 2018. Photograph: Matthieu Brouillard, CCA

The *gilets jaunes* [yellow vests] that motorists in the EU are required to have in their vehicles at all times took on a new significance in 2018, when they became the official uniform (and namesake) of a movement for economic justice. The movement began in reaction to French President Emmanuel Macron's plan to raise the tax on fuel—a green tax that Macron explained was imperative in the fight against climate change, but that was expected to disproportionately affect drivers in rural towns and peri-urban areas of France who were already having to drive longer distances for lesser wages, while struggling to keep up with the rapidly increasing costs of living. This initial point of contention evolved into a more general and ongoing concern that those making decisions are urban elites who are disconnected from the working class and those located outside of urban centres. As the symbol of a wider anti-government movement, the garment's high visibility clearly signals a plea from its wearers to be seen by those in power.

KOTTI & CO., ESTUDIO TEDDY CRUZ + FONNA FORMAN
GECEKONDU, 2012, 2015

The lack of affordable housing in most major cities is not only a considerable problem but, in certain ways, has come to be the defining feature of urban living. While architects are typically enlisted to build more housing and, occasionally, to build "different" housing or to build housing "differently," the Gecekondu is, instead, an architectural project that points to the systemic conditions that have led to the current housing crisis. Inspired by demonstrations like the occupation of Tahrir Square in Cairo and the global Occupy movement, Gecekondu—which comes from the Turkish for "being built overnight"—is a structure of wooden pallets and lightweight metal bars that was erected the night of 25 May 2012 on the last remaining sliver of public land in front of Berlin's privately owned Kottbusser Tor. Upon being built, the Gecekondu's walls were immediately plastered with multilingual information leaflets, posters, banners, and resources for local residents affected by gentrification and housing unaffordability. The Gecekondu contributes to creating housing equity not by building housing, but by creating a space in which resources can be distributed and issues of housing scarcity, rent, and urban development policy can be freely discussed. The implementation of the Gecekondu in Berlin has led to subsequent iterations of the project, referred to as the Retrofit Gecekondu, which focus on the Gecekondu principles to create more adaptable infrastructures within wider contexts of immigration and marginalization.

The Gecekondu Retrofit, which united Kotti & Co. with Estudio Teddy Cruz and Fonna Forman, offers a flexible structure to house community services, 2015

KOTTI & CO., ESTUDIO TEDDY CRUZ
+ FONNA FORMAN
GECEKONDU, 2012, 2015

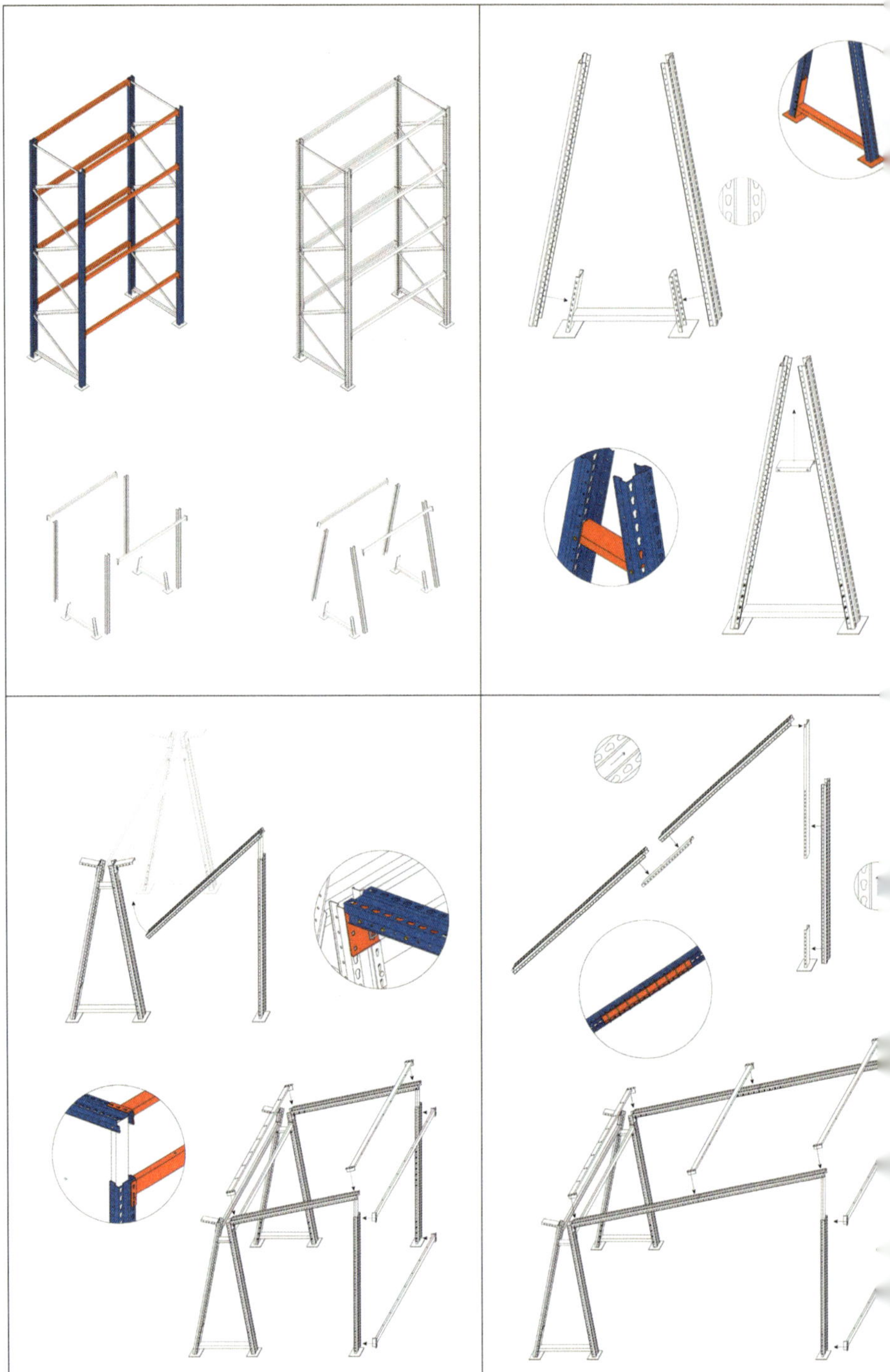

Assembly drawing depicting various iterations of the Gecekondu Retrofit, 2015

Title: She's Gotta Have It
Season/Episode: S01E01
Year: 2017
Network: Netflix
Country: USA

Created by Spike Lee as an update to—or creative extension of—his 1986 film *She's Gotta Have It*, this series follows the daily life of Nola Darling as she navigates three romantic relationships in Fort Greene in Brooklyn. Darling's interactions in her neighbourhood accumulate into a collective diary of a predominantly Black community, bound both socially and geographically. The series documents issues that this community faces: discrimination, assimilation, systemic racism, gentrification, cultural appropriation, and identity politics—themes the director also addressed in 1989, with *Do the Right Thing*.

CROOKLYN
CROOKLYN

Mario Gooden

A Space for Removed Monuments

Monuments, Memorials, and Purgatory

In the essay "Of Other Spaces" published in the spring 1986 issue of *Diacritics*, French philosopher Michel Foucault defines the concept of heterotopia as akin to a counter-site of contestation and inversion. According to Foucault, a heterotopia is paradoxically a real place, but it exists outside of all places. Existing between the conceptual and the physical location in space, a heterotopia is not dependent upon a building typology or form, but rather it exists in relationship to a condition among a set of relationships such as crisis, trauma, deviance, contradiction, accretion, aberration, exclusion, and compensatory subjugation—that is the subjugation of others as a form of recompense for a self-perceived deficiency.[1] While Foucault ruminates that certain kinds of colonies functioned in this manner such as Jesuit missions in South America, where the daily existence of the colonizers and even much more so for the colonized Indigenous population was regulated at every turn, there should be no question during the current moment of global social revolution that the construction of race and its attendant racism contemporary to the European colonial project has a deleterious effect and exposes that the European is also raced. For the European position of superiority as articulated in the dialectic in Hegel's *The Philosophy of History* is dependent upon assigning a position of inferiority to non-Europeans: Negros, Asians, and Indigenous peoples. Furthermore, as author Toni Morrison explained in a 1993 interview, "Don't you understand, that the people who do this thing, who practice racism, are bereft? There is something distorted about the psyche. ... It's is a profound neurosis ... it feels crazy, [because] it is crazy."[2]

In addition to the colony, the cemetery serves as another heterotopia for consideration. As Foucault explains, in Western culture, the cemetery has always fundamentally existed. Originating in the centre of the city, adjacent to or surrounding a church, the cemetery also existed in the form of tombs beneath the church or within the church itself. At the end of the eighteenth century as Western civilization grew less assured of its belief structures, the cemetery migrated outside the border of cities, as emphasis shifted away from the soul to that of the dead body and its association with illness. In a certain manner, the cemetery not only became a heterotopia but also a purgatorial location between death and an afterlife. Recently, in the United States, cemeteries have increasingly become new sites for the removed confederate monuments to Civil War figures that were erected in city centres and town squares in the late nineteenth and early twentieth centuries as a reaffirmation of white supremacy and infliction of trauma to Black Americans extending to colonial era enslavement. While some such monuments had previously been located in cemeteries, the heterotopic ambivalence of these sites somewhere between "Paradiso" and "Inferno" is a recognition of these monuments and their protagonists between former glory and current damnation. Rejected by formidable institutions, local and national museums such as the Smithsonian Institution, the cemetery is a counter-site, a non-typology, and an anti-building for these artefacts.

Other contested monuments and memorials to colonial figures across the United States, Canada, Britain, and the African continent have been removed, shrouded in tarps or other forms of concealment, and relocated to temporary and sometimes secretive storage locations. The decolonization of public space through the removal of these artefacts to provisional warehouses is also another example

1 Michel Foucault, "Of Other Spaces," *Diacritics* 16, no. 1 (Spring, 1986): 24–27.
2 Toni Morrison, interview by Charlie Rose, *Charlie Rose*, 7 May 1993, video, https://charlierose.com/videos/18778.

of a heterotopic purgatory. Although the warehouse is a site of accretion and the accumulation of time similar to Foucault's description of the museum or library, it lacks the cultural and epistemological foundation that serves the development of society. It owes its condition to the supply chain of neoliberal capitalism that consumes, transforms, and excretes various kinds of byproducts.

The question of what type of architectural space is suitable to eventually house, preserve, and access these monuments is a question of society's values and how it comes to terms with its history. While on the eve of the fiftieth anniversary of the Nazi takeover of Germany there were historical exhibits, theatre and art productions, publications, and public discussions, there were no displays of monuments or memorials to the Nazi era in Germany, because they do not exist. The unofficial slogan for Germany's 1983 recognition of its Nazi era was "Collective Guilt? No! Collective Responsibility? Yes!"[3]

Forty-five years earlier, on 11 November 1938, the architect Giuseppe Terragni presented his design for the Danteum to Mussolini at the Palazzo Venezia in Rome, shortly after Mussolini had signed the "Pact of Steel" with Hitler and the Nazis. The Danteum was designed as a "celebration of the words of Dante, considered a primary source for Mussolini's creations" and other similar nationalist monuments to glorify the arts as a function of State ideology.[4] Conforming to Dante's *Divine Comedy*, the Danteum contained three main spaces: Inferno, Purgatorio, and Paradiso. Terragni's design for purgatory contains seven square terraces derived from overlapping proportions and dimensions of where the roof mirrors the floor and contains seven square openings to the sky. As the space of penitence in Dante's *Divine Comedy*, it is a space of liminality caught between the reflexive conditions of ground and sky and the play of geometric (in)determinacy. Although it was never built, perhaps Terragni's design is the site for the contemplation of disputed monuments and memorials—a space of the in-between and "the realm of conscious and unconscious speculation and questioning—the zone where things concrete and ideas are intermingled, taken apart and reassembled—where memory, values, and intentions collide."[5]

3 Susan Neiman, "There Are No Nostalgic Nazi Memorials," *The Atlantic*, 14 September 2019, https://www.theatlantic.com/ideas/archive/2019/09/germany-has-no-nazi-memorials/597937.

4 Thomas L. Schumacher, *Surface and Symbol: Giuseppe Terragni and the Architecture of Italian Rationalism* (New York City: Princeton Architectural Press, 1991), 193–194.

5 Fred Koetter, "Notes on the In-Between," *Harvard Architecture Review* 1 (1980): 69.

Designed specifically to allow for the quick and collective compilation of resources and information, shared Google Docs have become an important form of communication, due in no small part to their ability to be both anonymous and public. With the release of Google Sheets, information could be further abstracted as organized sortable data within a spreadsheet. These applications allow for the creation of a stable URL that directs to a living document which can easily be edited and updated. The compilation of these sheets, originally conceived as accounting tools, have become a way to instigate accountability toward various parties through the collection of shared data. While social media platforms have been effective tools for publicizing information and building momentum for movements, Google Docs and Sheets allow for the ability to be unidentifiable while sharing. This alleviates some of the fear of possible consequences that may follow coming forward publicly, such as the possible loss of employment or future employment opportunities—a fear that is mitigated with the Museum Salary Transparency Google Sheet, in which those who work in cultural institutions around the world share how much money they make. Though one's identity is anonymous to others accessing and adding to the public Google Sheet, as a company, Google tracks all of its users' activity across all of its products—whether logged into their Google accounts or not.

	Studio Name	Black (B) or Indigenous (I) Owned	Women (W) or Non-Binary (NB) Owned	Location	Type of Work
1	2dots Space	B		Accra, Ghana	Design
2	3D Design Studio: A I + P, Ltd.	B	Prefer not to answer	Chicago, Illinois	Architecture, Branding, Interior Design
3	4RM+ULA	B		St. Paul, MN	Architecture
4	A+A+A		W	New York, NY	Advocacy, Architecture, Design, Interior Design
5	AAmp Studio	B	W	Toronto, Canada Maine Los Angeles, CA	Architecture, Design, Branding
6	AÇA		W	San Francisco, California	Architecture, Design
7	ACDO	Prefer not to answer	Prefer not to answer	Toronto, Canada	Interior Design
8	ACID, LLC			Los Angeles, CA Vancouver, Canada	Design
9	AD—WO	B	W	Providence, Rhode Island	Architecture, Art, Design
10	Adjaye Associates	B	Prefer not to answer	New York, NY	Architecture, Interior Design, Landscape Architecture
11	Aeism Agency	B		Paris, France London, UK Dublin, Ireland	Design
12	AFARAI	B	W	Amsterdam, The Netherlands	Architecture, Design, Research
13	AFROMINIMA	B		Lagos, Nigeria	Industrial Design, Product Design
14	Afterparti	B	Prefer not to answer	London, UK	Advocacy, Architecture, Association, Editorial, Research
15	Agency—Agency		W	NYC, NY Toronto, Canada	Architecture
16	Aileen Kwun		W	New York City, NY	Consulting, Editorial, Research, Design criticism, Journalism

BIPOC Studios spreadsheet, which compiles BIPOC-owned design studios into a collective resource

In 2006, activist Tarana Burke coined the phrase "Me Too" in a post she made to her MySpace page to help people who had experienced sexual violence. While Burke's post brought many of her followers together, when Alyssa Milano adopted the same phrase to hashtag her 2017 tweet about having been sexually assaulted and urging others to share their own stories of sexual abuse and harassment using the same hashtag, it started a global movement. Within hours of Milano's post, #MeToo was translated into other languages—#BalanceToPorc, #QuellaVoltaChe, #YoTambien—and within just ten days of the post, nearly two million people had come forward with their own stories. Though at the time it seemed like these stories were being taken seriously for the first time and that change was finally afoot, it was only in 2020 that one of the men who had been called out, American film producer Harvey Weinstein, was formally convicted—a case that may not have even gone to trial had it not been for *The New York Times*' and *The New Yorker*'s exposés detailing decades of allegations against the film producer.

#MeToo
#BalanceTonPorc
#QuellaVoltaChe
#YoTambien

#metoo

Jen Schradie

Digital Spaces: Online Safety and Offline Structures in France and the U.S.

When one thinks of child labour laws, the workplaces that are conjured up may include imagery of pollution-spewing factories or sweltering farm fields. But online spaces filled with YouTubers and TikTokers are the sites that France has been regulating under these terms with abandon. In 2020, the French legislature passed a law regulating child influencers with the aim of protecting their labour rights: ensuring that they are not working too much and that their pay is protected. France is not just regulating digital spaces with these child labour laws; recently, French President Emmanuel Macron announced, over Twitter, that the country would start regulating internet content itself against "terrorism." He tweeted, "Internet est un espace de liberté, nos réseaux sociaux aussi. Mais cette liberté n'existe que s'il y a une sécurité ..."[1]

1 In English: "The Internet is a space of freedom, our social networks too. But this freedom only exists if there is security ..." [author's translation].

This is not the first time that France has legislated the safety of online spaces. In 2014, the French parliament passed a law against online harassment as part of a broader law on gender equality. Two years later, a "Digital Republic Law" was passed in France that had forty-eight articles protecting digital spaces, with a focus on privacy. Another law to limit disinformation was passed in 2018, and, then in 2020, the French parliament passed sweeping legislation to criminalize online hate speech, including the promotion of racism, religious attacks, as well as child pornography.

This regulation of internet spaces to make them "safe" is in stark contrast to the largely unfettered digital landscape in the United States, where the internet freedom that Macron mentions is culturally and politically enshrined. Despite Facebook's founder and CEO Mark Zuckerberg being brought before American congressional committees, and the company periodically announcing self-regulating policies on everything from fake news to violent posts, the effect of the proverbial fox guarding the henhouse has been minimal at best.

Whether with child influencers and fake news or with online harassment and cancel culture, digital spaces seem to be landmines of uncertainty and insecurity. With the acceleration of digital technology as integral to everyday living and working, the safety of these internet spaces is becoming increasingly vital. In this essay, I trace the historical trajectory of digital spaces to show how online communities have been shaped by societal structures, in the contexts of France and the United States. As two so-called Western capitalist democracies, France and the U.S. may seem similar on the surface, but they not only have different regulations around digital technology, they also have distinct histories of contextualizing digital spaces and in relation to how egalitarian and safe these spaces feel.

Early conceptualizations of what we now call the internet were based on systematic information sharing. One could go back as far as eighteenth-century France to early encyclopedia writers, such as Denis Diderot, who was instrumental in writing and editing "factual" information that was published in a novel way that directly challenged the power of the church. Though he briefly landed in jail for his anti-church writings and came from a petite bourgeoisie family, his education and his writing thrust him into the world of royal elites, who financially backed his *Encyclopédie*. His project was also supported by *des Lumiéres* (French Enlightenment philosophers), who directly enriched the thinking behind the French Revolution. Diderot represents what would later become the Enlightenment period of the internet—a period characterized by the idea that collective information sharing could overthrow the yoke of powerful institutions.

More than one hundred and fifty years later, another innovator, this time in the United States, pushed the envelope forward for digital space. From a modest upbringing, Vannevar Bush, an American scientist and inventor of early analog computers, eventually became embedded in the military (and nuclear) industrial complex of the era. Bush wrote a foundational article in 1945 called "As We May Think," in which he calls for a "memex," with linked information in a "private file and library ... in which an individual stores all his books, records, and communications, and which is mechanized so that it may be consulted with exceeding speed and flexibility."[2]

Though Diderot and Bush lived two hundred years apart from one another, they were both challenging the preconceived notions of knowledge and knowledge-making, and they were both obsessed with compiling and organizing information in such a way that it could systematically reach the greatest number of people possible. Both Diderot and Bush were also building information communities—precursors to today's digital spaces. They wanted the respective information communities that they were propagating to be wider than they had ever been previously. And though history books are rife with stories of individuals, rather than institutions, inventing and innovating, neither Diderot nor Bush were floating alone in creative spaces. They both understood that societal structures, whether political, economic, or cultural, are key to the creation of information flows.

But who was included in the communities that Diderot and Bush were cultivating? Diderot's encyclopedia was a big step forward in cultivating inclusivity, but books were the purview of the small minority in France who were literate, and Bush's audience was similarly made up of intellectual (and military) elites. Though they were both pushing the envelope and aiming to broaden access to information, they were also both part of the enveloping power structures of their respective times.

When we think of online communities now and of how safe and secure they may or may not feel, it is important to think of the broader contexts that create them, in addition to thinking about who can best exploit them. Part of that broader context is understanding that many of the people (like Bush, for example) who have been the most noted for advancing what we now understand as digital spaces are white men with academic, government, or military backing. And though a growing number of people are acknowledging the important role that women have played in the history of computing, the critical computing work that women did was still situated in male-dominated spaces that were rife with hierarchy and bureaucracy.[3] This was certainly the case for many steps

2 Vannevar Bush, "As We May Think," *The Atlantic*, July 1945, https://www.theatlantic.com/magazine/archive/1945/07/as-we-may-think/303881.

3 See for example, Mar Hicks, *Programmed Inequality: How Britain Discarded Women Technologists and Lost Its Edge in Computing* (Cambridge, MA: The MIT Press, 2017).

in the building of information sharing communities in the 1960s, from the showcasing of IBM computers at the 1964 World's Fair to the inaugural launch of the first internet connection in 1969—the result of ARPANET, a program funded by the American military.

One of the key architects of ARPANET, Larry Roberts, once described the connectedness and sharing that would be made possible by digital spaces as "[a] network will foster the 'community' use of computers. Cooperative programming will be stimulated, and in particular fields or disciplines it will be possible to achieve 'critical mass' of talent by allowing geographically separated people to work effectively in interaction with a system."[4] Despite the World's Fair reaching out to the general population, Roberts' vision missed the mark as to what these online communities would be in their nascent stages. In 1969, the internet was far from mirroring what was happening all over the United States with another massive project that had been taking shape in the few decades prior to the World's Fair: the linking of cities with the construction of highways. And though, in the future, the internet would be described using imagery of the infrastructure network—it often being referred to it as an "information superhighway"—at the time, ARPANET was not yet linking people in their homes via their desktop computers. Rather, it was connecting just a few people at research centres in cities across the U.S. to one another. Already at its launch, ARPANET was not creating egalitarian spaces.

In effect, rather than individuals (digital innovators) building digital spaces for networked individuals (citizens) to participate in digital spaces, it was and continues to be communities of people (digital innovators) embedded within structures (scientific and government institutions) building structures (digital systems) that are used by people within structures (different demographics and local institutions). In short, people in structures build structures used by people in structures, to borrow some phrasing from Pierre Bourdieu. It follows that even though these new digital systems were challenging the power of other communication systems, much like Diderot's *Encyclopédie*, the scientists who created them were still embedded in power structures of their own (universities, military think tanks, and the like), as were the mostly white male communities of people who were then able to use these systems (other academics and military scientists for the most part). While it is true that any innovation is initially used by other innovators and early adopters, this fact is too oft an excuse for the exclusionary ways in which systems are developed. The resulting public sphere, or in this case the resulting digital public space, is governed by rules that are created by those in power and resources are not always made available to everyone. With promise to network horizontally, the development and diffusion of the internet was thought to change this dynamic.

4 Larry Roberts, "Multiple computer networks and intercomputer communication," *Proceedings of the First ACM Symposium on Operating System Principles* (January 1967), 3.1–3.6.

The digital community of the 1970s was marked by the blossoming of email communication. In fact, emails accounted for the vast majority of traffic on ARPANET, and yet they were still generally only sent and received by people with the same profiles as ARPANET's inventors. Even though the networking itself was seemingly horizontal, its definite underlying structure is made evident in considering who was accessing it over that decade: mostly military-funded researchers and academics across a select number of university campuses. Granted, there was indeed a lot of work being done by corporations and university researchers behind the scenes to try to bring these technologies to more people. For instance, government-funded French academic researchers in collaboration with the tech firm R2E specifically developed the first computer, Micral, to have a micro-processor that could be mass-produced. Other French innovators with ties to government research agencies, such as Louis Pouzin, created datagrams and CYCLADES, which were instrumental for what would later become the protocol for the next decade's world wide web. And while the U.S. and France were certainly not the only countries developing internet technologies, the developments being made in both countries were embedded in academic and government institutions, though they would soon diverge from this shared path.

In the 1980s, there were efforts to try to expand the base of the digital community away from its institutional roots. In the U.S., as Fred Turner exhaustively notes in his 2006 book, *From Counterculture to Cyberculture*, the communal living and anti-authoritarian culture in Northern California shaped the online communities that sprouted on the Whole Earth 'Lectronic Link (the WELL)—one of the best known internet forums for discussions of that era and one whose founders were college-educated white men who were influenced by anti-institutional hippy culture.[5] While the U.S. had the open WELL, France had the state-run Minitel. On the surface, these two systems seem very different. France's Minitel was an early form of what would eventually become the world wide web. It was extremely advanced for the 1980s: people could use the system, which came pre-loaded on desktop computers that were just slightly larger than the earliest Macintosh computers, to do their banking, perform searches, play games, and much more. Minitel had two key features that are not widely known: first, rather than a closed system, it allowed its network and, therefore, its users to connect to other related networked systems online, and, second, it also had online forums, including some for internet dating, all of which were used as digital community spaces. These spaces were not only egalitarian in that they were available to all French telephone subscribers, they were also playful spaces that also appeared to be safe spaces.[6]

5 Other internet forums of the time were Usenet groups, all of which had various threads devoted to topics of interest, from politics to pets. Though, conceptually, these groups were not much different from what we now know as Facebook groups, at the time, these digital communities were connecting people within and between France and the United States, as well as people from other connected countries, which was seen as truly revolutionary.

6 This open-closed comparison is also overly simplistic given the government involvement in ARPANET and French Unixian activists who were organizing for an open French internet for electronic democracy. See, Camille Paloque-Berges, *Mapping A French Internet Experience: A Decade Of Unix Networks Cooperation (1983–1993)* (London, UK: Routledge, 2017); and Julien Mailland and Kevin Driscoll, *Minitel: Welcome to the Internet* (Cambridge, MA: The MIT Press), 14.

By the end of the 1980s, the userships of both the Minitel and the WELL were expanding. They grew to be even larger with the 1989 launch of the protocols for the world wide web and publicly available web browsers. Still, it was primarily people with college educations and those with the financial resources to acquire these new tools that were able to use them.

At the same time, the symbolic nature of the Berlin Wall coming down was a literal incarnation of the famous Apple commercial in which a woman uses a sledgehammer to smash a screen on which an authoritarian leader is speaking to stone-faced followers—a literal nod to George Orwell's *1984*. The idea that Apple was promoting was that digital technology was going to democratize and horizontalize information and communication. The problem was that tech companies, like Apple and other big-tech firms in Silicon Valley, would eventually take over these digital spaces, propping the wall that Apple claimed to have taken down in 1983 back up.

The 1990s marked an era of diffusion, albeit uneven diffusion. While not adopted at the rates at which they are today, digital spaces were no longer just the purview of the early innovators and adopters, though the needle still tilted in their direction. Yet American policymakers, including President Clinton, began sounding the alarm on the digital divide with calls for more "Digital Opportunity."[7] Researchers began tracking online access, although at this point, the question as to whether or not you had a computer and an internet connection was a binary one, largely based on socioeconomic differences. Nonetheless, this question was more typically asked in the U.S. than in France, where the Minitel was still widely available. Despite some efforts, the Minitel never expanded its reach outside of France and remained a nationwide system.

In the U.S., rather than just a handful of institutions, computer companies, academics, and the military, the 1990s brought an explosion of people who were trying to stick their fingers in the honey pot of digital tech. This dot-com boom, from which Silicon Valley earned its international reputation, was a strange brew of utopian leftist and horizontal ideals with hyper capitalism, as websites built on very little substance captured millions in venture capital. In the late 1990s, Silicon Valley was like the Wild West: if lavish dot-com launch parties are any indication, those that struck gold on Wall Street were creating a hierarchy that would eventually turn into Big Tech. Those startup founders who could get angel investments and then hit it big with an initial public offering (IPO) were predominantly white, male, and college-educated, despite the myth that any college dropout could innovate their way into the tech world. The California-based companies that were taking hold at

7 "From Digital Divide to Digital Opportunity," The White House (archive), https://clintonwhitehouse4.archives.gov/WH/New/digitaldivide/index.html.

this time would eventually end up controlling not only American digital spaces and their users, but global ones, as well.

Newsgroups and discussion forums were still important spaces for digital community building and information sharing at this time, but the 1990s were all about websites, which implied a digression in the quest for more person-to-person connection. America Online (AOL), for instance, was a dominant email and web portal that was a one-stop-shop for communicating and shopping, as well as the company tracking these movements for data profits. Ironically, at the time, AOL was mocked by many in Silicon Valley for being such a closed shop, but, now, most tech companies are moving in the same direction, though it is a direction that is seemingly in contrast to the purported value of openness held by the counterculture.[8] The digital spaces that resulted from the 1990s actually served a somewhat more demographically representative user base but, in the U.S., they were deployed with a tight corporate grip. On the other side of the ocean, the Minitel was still thriving—but it would not continue to do so for much longer.

While there were utopian hopes for online democratic communities decades earlier, it was in the mid-2000s that the enthusiasm for digital spaces exponentially grew. This enthusiasm was particularly rooted in platforms that made it easier not only to share text but also photos and videos—a function that had previously required setting up a website. With faster and better visual connections via platforms such as Facebook, YouTube, and Twitter, online communities and digital spaces suddenly became simultaneously more intimate and more expansive. The proliferation of social media platforms expanded the use of static one-to-many websites to more instantaneous and interactive many-to-many platforms. Most of the online sharing that was done in these spaces was among personal networks. It wasn't until the next decade that the reach of this sharing would multiply and provide more distinct online communities, as with Facebook groups, for instance. While adoption rates increased, digital inequality rates on social media persisted.[9]

As Silicon Valley's social media platforms continued to grow around the world, in France, the 2010s brought the death of the Minitel. As the worldwide network was overtaking it, usage had been waning.

This period was also notable for online spaces globally: there was both a dramatic rise and fall in the belief and trust in digital technologies, particularly in their ability to foster online communities that could serve as loci for collective action. But the commonly held utopian belief that digital technologies enable more egalitarian democratic involvement than was possible in the pre-digital era

8 It is worth noting that some companies, like Facebook and Weibo, have been operating on a model similar to AOL's from their outsets.

9 Jen Schradie, "The Digital Production Gap: The Digital Divide and Web 2.0 Collide," *Poetics* 39, no. 2 (April 2011): 145–168.

because of the rapid and direct communication features of digital technologies has persisted.

Digital platforms were not only spaces in which to talk about politics but spaces in which to actually *do* politics. People were certainly doing other things on these social media platforms, but those that often got the most notoriety were those using the platforms for digital activism. But claims about the power of online collective action and its new architectural possibilities were derived from visible outliers: social movements who were using Facebook, for example, as communication tools for organizing and protest, or Twitter, in its earlier days, for quickly communicating police locations or informing the public (including journalists) what was happening in real time.

In fact, at the dawn of the 2010s, the so-called Arab Spring ushered in celebratory cries of "Twitter Revolution" and "Facebook Revolution." In 2011, the Indignados movement took hold in Spain and as Occupy Wall Street encampments were being set up all across the U.S., and both of these movements embraced the use of social media for organizing, often bypassing traditional organizational communication channels. It wasn't until 2015 that France had a smaller version of these anti-institutional movements called Nuit debout, which employed Twitter and Facebook as key sources of communicating, as well as mimicking the offline General Assemblies and participatory hand gestures used in both the Spanish and American movements four years earlier. In 2018, the Gilets jaunes movement took off in France. Rather than the Nuit debout movement of far-left and college-educated activists centred in cities and towns, the Gilets jaunes movement had a broader cross-section of participants, including member of the working-class, and was initially centred in very small villages, where the blocking of traffic circles was its signature tactic.

Because the Gilets jaunes movement couldn't be connected to a single trade union, political party, or national organization, many assumed that the internet could explain the emergence and diffusion of the protest movement. In fact, the Gilets jaunes movement is celebrated as exemplary of the claims that Facebook can ignite spontaneous revolution and that it provides a safe and critical community space—in this case, a safe space for community organizing. Many point to various digital sparks, such as the videos that a technologically savvy musician who lives in northwestern France created and posted on Facebook early on to encourage people to protest, which eventually went viral. Both scholars and journalists have argued that digital technology, rather than organizations, drive modern social movements and cultivate online communities, but this is a misguided reading.

Even in the Gilets jaunes movement, digital technology's role in fostering political participation has taken a dark turn: from Donald Trump's toxic tweets to Brexit's online cesspool. In 2018, the role that outfits like Cambridge Analytica and that Facebook itself played in fomenting far-right movements came to light. Soon after, the French Minister for Europe and Foreign Affairs, Jean-Yves Le Drian, announced an investigation into fake news and Russian interference in France's 2017 presidential election. What was once thought of as a digital army of white knights out to save the day was all of a sudden being understood as a horde of bots and hacks orchestrated by authoritarian institutions. And yet, many still want to put faith in the internet, over institutions, to shape digital communities.

But both digital utopianism and digital dystopianism fail to acknowledge people on the ground and their existing in-person networks, as well as the fact that populist movements that seem to arise out of nowhere are not new to the digital era. We don't call the French Revolution a letter movement and we don't refer to the American civil rights movement as a mimeograph revolution. Without a doubt, the spread of information during a time of upheaval is certainly faster with the internet, and the Gilets jaunes movement was no exception. But what would qualify the movement as a digital one? The internet is a communications tool—an efficient one, but it's still just a tool. For the Gilets jaunes, organizing risky traffic protests (in that what they were doing was illegal and could result in arrest) still required on-the-ground networks of people who had a baseline of trust to work together.

Yet the internet is a tool that was initially designed according to the idea that sharing information, especially publicly, bears little risk. While the sharing of information tends to be low risk, social movements tend to be particularly risky for participants, especially if they are targeting state power, as was the case for the Gilets jaunes. And, yet, in France, as long as protests remain nonviolent (which most of the Gilets jaunes protests did) there is often little in terms of negative repercussions for protesters. For instance, French labour laws are strong and largely prevent workers from being fired for political organizing. However, in certain areas of the U.S., particularly in the rural South, Black working-class activists have expressed fear that posting about their activism online could get them fired.[10] Layered on top of these forms of repression is a deep and wide digital divide.

This fear factor is prevalent among other marginalized communities, whether other people of colour, women, or anyone who is in the wrong side of a power imbalance. This is the irony: these spaces that are supposedly meant to provide people with a platform to

10 Jen Schradie, *The Revolution That Wasn't: How Digital Activism Favors Conservatives* (Cambridge, MA: Harvard University Press, 2019), 56–60.

overcome power imbalances often end up being unsafe for the very people who would presumably benefit from having them the most. I found that across thirty-four social movements, those that had middle- and upper-class members had much higher levels of digital engagement than those that had members from low-income and working-class backgrounds.[11] A recent study has even found that for Black Americans, posting about racism and issues like Black Lives Matter can have detrimental effects on job prospects.[12]

For those who are oppressed in society, online spaces like Black Twitter have become a refuge, much like other forms of media and physical spaces have been in the past.[13] However, as these spaces are often public spaces where people in power can quickly take over, they can be difficult to maintain as safe spaces and can easily become minefields of trolls—racist, sexist, or otherwise. What was once supposed to be a digital paradise where the masking of identities would erase all gender and racial barriers, has ended up not only reproducing but often exacerbating discrimination and harassment online.

The utopian digital bubble was decidedly punctured, though, in the mid-2010s with Gamergate and with Edward Snowden's revelations about the attack on people's individual privacy. The safety of online spaces has been threatened more severely in the U.S. than in France, which has been much stricter about protecting the privacy of individuals—both at a national level, as well as part of the European Union. Not only does the broader Europe-wide General Data Protection Regulation from 2016 force websites to ask permission for personal data collection, but France itself passed similar legislation the same year with even more stringent privacy protections.

At the same time, individual awareness of online privacy, rather than just government regulation, permeates the French social media experience. For instance, unlike American schools, where parents frequently communicate with one another online using contact information that is shared by the school, this practice is considered an invasion of privacy in France. In addition, it appears to be much more common for French people to use pseudonyms on platforms like Facebook than in the United States, as is the case in many European countries, some of which even had to go to court with Facebook to protect the right to use nicknames. Aside from the obvious language differences, American Facebook is not the same as French Facebook, as are the two countries' digital spaces different.

This over fifty-year digital history and policy explains why the experience of online social space is distinctive not only for each person based on their identity but is also different in a patterned way

11 Jen Schradie, "The Digital Activism Gap: How Class and Costs Shape Online Collective Action," *Social Problems* 65, no. 1 (February 2018): 51–74.

12 Howard S., Kennedy K., and Tejeda F., "Social Media Posts About Racism Leads to Evaluative Backlash for Black Job Applicants," *Social Media + Society* (October 2020).

13 Meredith Clark, "Black Twitter: Building Connection through Cultural Conversation," in *Hashtag Publics: The Power and Politics of Discursive Networks*, ed. Nathan Rambukkana (New York City: Peter Lang Publishing Inc., 2015), 205–218.

for each user, based on the country in which they live. As Langdon Winner points out, technology itself has politics but more than that, in terms of how they come to the "digital table," the end users do as well.[14] For people who don't have the structural backing to tackle the white-male-dominated digital public space, this support can be found in the form of communities—online or offline—or it can be found in the form of more regulated platforms, like those in France. While hate speech, for example, still exists in France, there are laws in place to prevent online instances from seeping into everyday information spaces. The end result is that people in France tend to be more wary of online spaces in the first place and, once there, there are more protections in place.

And this is the irony at the root of digital spaces. Despite the clichés that decentralized American technology is somehow more democratic than centralized French technology, there is power in having digital safety nets, whether put in place as means to overcome the digital divide or to protect against online harassment. The classed, gendered, and raced institutions that created many of today's predominant digital spaces seem to be open and free, but it is, paradoxically, their algorithmic and profit-driven openness that puts the most vulnerable at risk and makes digital communities unsafe and precarious.[15]

We are still left with the information sharing utopia that Diderot envisioned—even with the digital version of his *Encyclopédie*, Wikipedia, which, though seemingly neutral, is rife with the massive dominance of white men both in the content it includes and in its community of moderators. The inequities reproduced in digital spaces will not be resolved within or by any individual platform, despite its best efforts, while profit-seeking corporations do not have an incentive to even try. It will take people organizing and forcing its institutions, especially governments, to resolve social inequalities offline in order to create safer spaces online. A truly enlightened digital space will only be safe when its creation is not just more egalitarian but the societal structures around it are, as well.

14 Langdon Winner, "Do Artifacts Have Politics?" *Daedalus* 109, no. 1 (1980): 121–136.

15 Sociologist Jo Freeman termed this paradox "the tyranny of structurelessness in Jo Freeman, "The Tyranny of Structurelessness," *The Second Wave* 2, no. 1 (1972): 2.

Title: Mr. Robot
Season/Episode: S01E04
Year: 2015
Network: USA Network
Country: USA

Sometimes a television series manages to capture a social emergency so vividly that it becomes symbolic of it. This is the case with *Mr. Robot*, a show in which Elliot, a hacker with social anxiety, and his diabolical mentor, Mr. Robot, along with the society, uphold their manifesto to liberate the masses from debt. Elliot and his accomplices act as contemporary Robin Hoods or Guy Fawkeses, but with one difference: they are not always right, they do not always know what the right thing to do is, and they make mistakes. They are at once human beings and heroes.

COOP HIMMELB(L)AU
CHBL JAMMER COAT, 2014

Though the idea of being unknowingly tracked while in the public sphere or online may be cause for concern, many are aware that their smart devices track their movements and online activities—a fact that they knowingly reconcile in favor of the convenience these devices afford. Accessories such as the CHBL Jammer Coat make this negotiation easier by allowing the wearer to carry their devices on their person while blocking all radio signals to them by way of the coat's material—a textile with metal woven through it. Only when the device is removed from its compartment in the coat, presumably to actively be used, can it track the whereabouts of its user.

Photograph: Markus Pillhofer

NORTHEASTERN UNIVERSITY, MIT, AND IBM
AI SPOOFING T-SHIRT, 2019

While regulations are slowly being introduced to protect the privacy of internet users, the artificial intelligence that is becoming more commonly used to surveil people in physical spaces is proving more difficult to regulate and, in some cases, is being deployed by regulatory bodies themselves. With facial recognition technology becoming increasingly accurate, individuals who wish to remain anonymous while in public are turning to wearables that exploit artificial intelligence's limited understanding of the human form. The AI spoofing t-shirt uses a colourful, kaleidoscopic pattern to essentially make its wearer invisible to surveillance operated by a widely used object detector called Yolov2. Though this type of artificial intelligence impinges on individual privacy, it is employed in other situations, such as by self-driving cars, in which it is relied on to ensure everyone's safety—at least the safety of everyone it can identify as a person.

Photograph: Matthieu Brouillard, CCA

A Space for the Invisibilization of Power

1. Making trans-scalar power invisible

In a rendering for the design of 432 Park Avenue, a man wearing a top hat and a velvet frock coat sits on an MR20 chair, looking at the sky through what seems to be a levitating piece of glass, through which the whole view is filtered to look like an oil painting. This rendering conceptualizes the entire design of 432 Park Avenue, the tower that set the standard for a new generation of supertall, high-end apartment buildings.[1] Its construction resulted in a vertical repetition of what its rendering had already announced.

Its construction also meant something for architecture's evolution. It transformed the primary architectural experience—that of looking onto a landscape from a safe and comfortable armchair—into a form of post-Anthropocene possession, a new type of trans-scalar architectural power and social divide. In the words of Phillip Crupi, a CGI expert, the way renderings of interiors digitally manufacture clearness is meant to "produce the feeling of a simultaneous visual ownership of both the interior and the exterior."[2] This is only possible through the coordination of design forms that have, to date, been perceived as independent: namely, interior, bodily, material, environmental, and socio-territorial design. 432 Park Avenue's window demonstrates how architectural detailing is intrinsically a technique for societal rearticulation. It also shows that inequity is the result of architectural inventiveness.

The supertall tower's frameless and seemingly candid square window is only an effective means of socio-territorial control because it is literally invisible. Overall, it succeeds in proving how inhabiting is now no longer something that can be situated in a single architectural location or at the scale of a building alone but rather must be situated as a process constructed in transitioning across multiple scales and materialities.

Politically, this distributed and transitioning architecture is not only the enactment of power but is also the site where power is now being challenged. The many ways in which this architectural effort is headed for failure shows the cracks where dissident forms of architecture are now emerging.

2. Clearness as territorial divide

All eighteen high-end supertall towers being constructed in New York City in 2020 have something in common. They are all cladded in ultra-clear glass (UCG), which lacks the greenish tone that ferric oxide gives ordinary glass. UCG is a low-emission glass fabricated out of a very rare silica that can only be found in a handful of locations around the world, including the St. Peter Sandstone Formation in Ottawa, Illinois, the traditional lands of the Kaskaskia people. UCG provides a neutral base that increases the effectiveness of radiation-shielding coatings, allowing designers to edit the way exteriors are seen from high-end interiors through glass filters, turning daily life into an Instagram-like experience. The skies seem bluer, creating an illusion that the air around the buildings is cleaner than it actually is. UCG inscribes high-end interiors into a milieu seemingly detached from environmental struggles. It is an architectural device that creates environmental deproblematization. Google's and Apple's headquarters, high-end apartment buildings, high-tech labs, and medical facilities are all cladded in UCG.

1 "Supertall" is the term used to designate towers that are taller than 289 metres.
2 Phillip Crupi, interview by Jesse McCormick (Office for Political Innovation), June 2019.

Contemporary power is encapsulated in UCG, as much as it is produced and maintained through UCG. Producing UCG necessarily involves the removal of iron oxide, a process which requires doubling the amount of energy used during traditional glass production processes. Seventy-three percent of the energy fueling UCG production comes from natural gas extracted by fracking, which directly contributes to the pollution of 30,000 miles of aquifers in Susquehanna Valley, Pennsylvania. Visual environmental deproblematization is in fact coordinated by the offsetting of New York City's carbon footprint to Pennsylvania.[3]

3. Architectural detailing as socio-territorial design

When magnified, one can see the roundness of the low-iron silica grains, which makes the geological formations that result from their aggregation porous and permeable. They allow water, minerals, air, and gases to flow through them and accumulate. This characteristic of silica gives it the capacity to nurture life in its geological state. Plants, insects, and animals find their habitats in the wet flows that the porous rocks breed. These low-iron silica rock formations were the ecosystems in which Kaskaskia communities stewarded the durable co-existence of various species on their traditional lands. This type of silica's specific roundness and formability are also the reasons why it is used in hydraulic fracking to fill the veins that are drilled open and to help channel gas up to the ground's surface where it can be collected.

That the act of looking through a low-iron silica-made frameless window is at all comfortable shows how deeply contemporary materiality and architectural detailing are forms of socio-territorial design. It is through this form of control that high-end regimes establish forms of centralized interspecies domains that disrupt possible alliances between humans and other-than-humans based on mutual care for one another. Windows are socio-territorial battlegrounds and participating in these battles is what inhabiting now consists of.

3 This movement of pollutants was made as part of Michael Bloomberg's 2012 Clean Heat Project.

Do you own, rent, or subscribe to your housing? How many people are you willing to share a kitchen with?

DANIELLE BRANDON

HAIR stylist

$12,324.00

IN MY EARLY 20S I GOT A CREDIT CARD TO "build credit". They somehow gave me a $6,000 limit. At the time i never had money to pay bills & eat. So i decided to buy a little new clothes. Why not? Soon that avalanched until i could not pay off my dept at the end of the month. Dental bills, car repair, plane tickets at times groceries & gas were put on the card. No matter how i try to chip away i can never seem to get out from under it. Even though i live a frugal life.

Brittany M. Powell, *The Debt Project (Debt Portrait #1, San Francisco, CA)*, 2013

Martin Olive

Executive Director - Vapor Room Cooperative

$930,716.54

I was audited by the IRS for opening a medical cannabis dispensary in 2004 & 2005. The IRS applied an obscure IRS provision - 280E which disallowed me from deducting cannabis "cost of goods" as a standard business deduction. Subsequently, I am forced to pay the full income tax plus interest & penalties. Added to that huge tax burden, I suffered a brain aneurysm & had surgery plus 10 days in ICU without health coverage!

Brittany M. Powell, *The Debt Project (Debt Portrait #8, Oakland, CA)*, 2013

MIKE

ARCHITECTURAL DESIGNER

$160,000

MASTERS DEGREE (4) YEARS

REAL ESTATE DEAL

UNEMPLOYMENT

 Brittany M. Powell, *The Debt Project (Debt Portrait #10, San Francisco, CA)*, 2013

Though the housing crisis has long been framed as the result of a housing shortage, it can equally be interpreted as a problem of distribution. Envisioning an alternative way of allocating housing, Doma buys properties and redistributes them to its members, who make market-rent payments to live in the spaces and build equity shares in Doma's property holdings. Though smart contracts bind members to terms set by the housing platform, they are intended to allow members to maintain a degree of flexibility in their housing accommodations, made possible by a network of diverse property types across the globe. The concept allows for the best of both renting and buying, combining the flexibility of renting and the security of building equity through ownership.

A platform for equitable housing

doma.city

One of many PodShare co-living spaces in California. Photograph: PodShare

Subscription-based rental platforms claim to offer solutions to the lack of affordable housing or the difficulty in securing office space through short-term co-living and co-working arrangements. Access to these spaces is typically attainable without the financial commitments of a standard lease agreement, with the flexibility to relocate to other properties within a given platform's network. While these platforms have relatively similar target markets, each one caters to a particular niche of young professionals. PodShare repositions hostel accommodations, providing bunk beds branded as "pods" in an open environment designed to maximize "social collision." The company, whose pods are located across California, promotes an affordable co-living model in which housing is reduced to a service—no different than music streaming or meal kits—to be consumed through daily, weekly, or monthly subscription plans.

ÉDOUARD FRANÇOIS
LA HAUTEUR POUR TOUS, 2011–2018

In his book *La hauteur pour tous*, Édouard François offers a building scheme in which individuals live across the entire height of a high-rise building. This distribution is accomplished through the pairing of units on lower floors and with unspectacular views with terraces on higher floors with unobstructed views, creating cross-assigned spaces for tenants. In addition to potentially creating new kinds of homes, this proposed vertical living concept grants all inhabitants equal access to the view from the top. Usually, this elevated outlook is a perk available only to those with the means to rent or purchase a penthouse suite. Redistributing the view and the spatial privilege of living at a height has the potential to be more than just a symbolic reorganization, as it undermines the creation of luxury units at higher floors and, hence, the creation of a socioeconomic-based segregation within high-rise residential buildings.

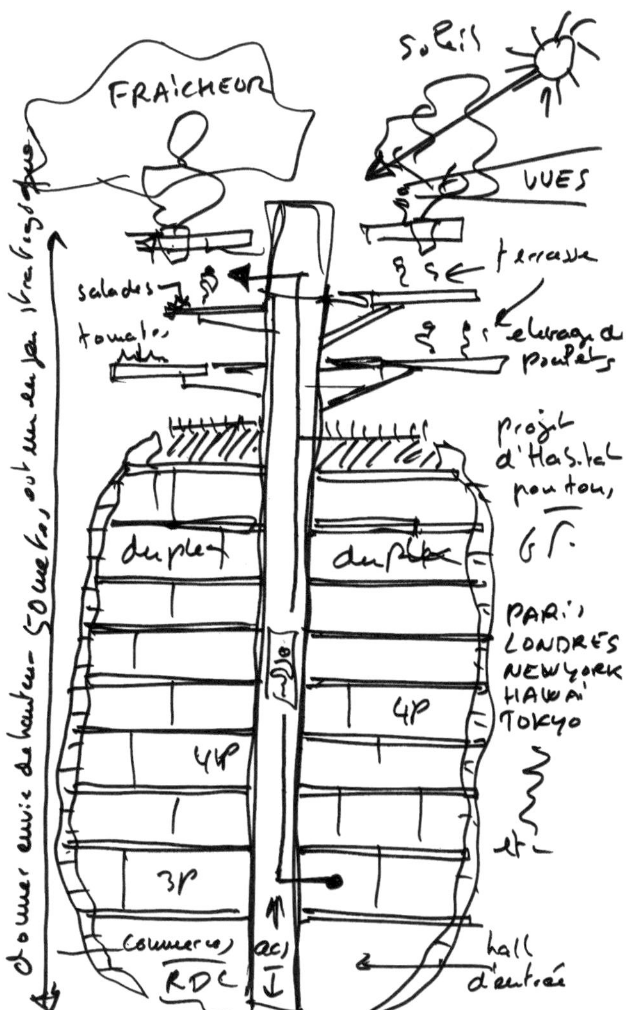

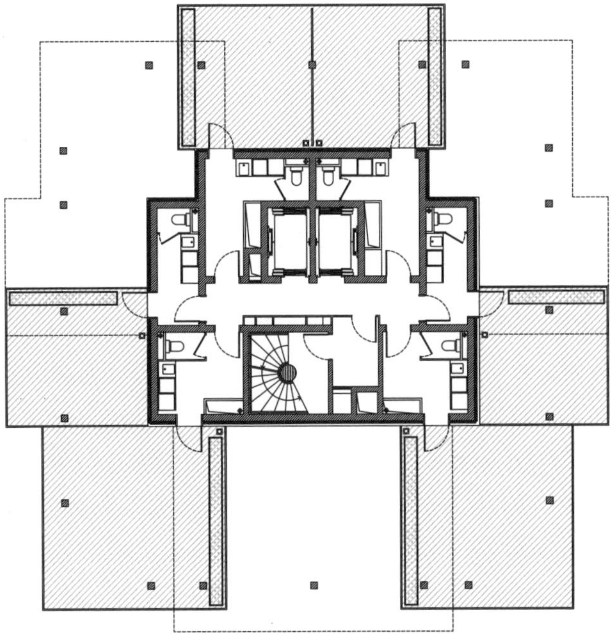

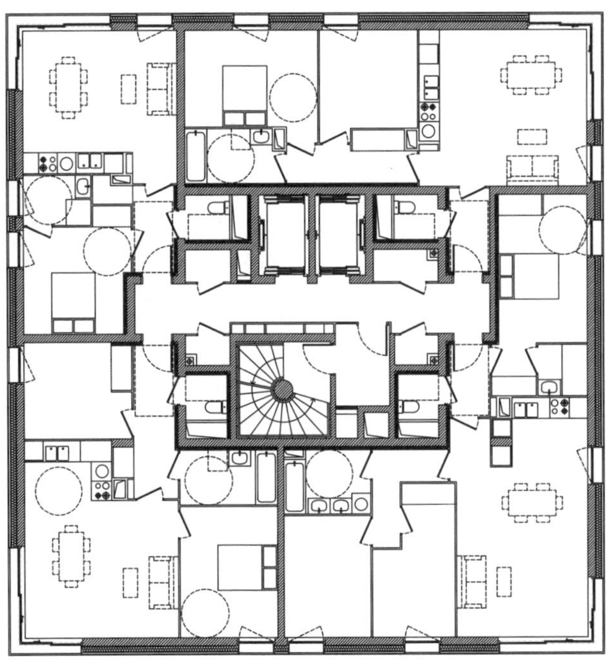

Floor plans of a tower in Grenoble, France, whose spatial organization emphasizes a redistribution of apartment views and balconies, creating a more equitable allocation of living spaces throughout the height of the building

JACK SELF
THE INGOT, 2016

The cause for low rates of homeownership amongst the generation that followed the Baby Boomers is often cited as the fact that incomes have not risen proportionally with the cost of housing. Conceived of in response to a housing market that negotiates primarily between time, space, and money, the Ingot is a gold-plated residential high-rise that towers over London's skyline at a staggering 350 metres. Though the tower's materiality and height seem to signal that it was designed for a high-income demographic, its design is actually a critical commentary on unbridled real estate speculation and ever-escalating property values in urban areas, and was conceived of to house low-income, precarious workers. The project manipulates the mechanisms of debt and subverts the tools of real estate speculation, using an algorithm to create value that is used to subsidize rents. Making use of a bond, the Ingot redirects the influx of capital investments in real estate to those who are usually most vulnerable to being displaced or unable to access housing in the first place. The project turns the logic that supports the neoliberal housing market against itself to redistribute accumulated capital.

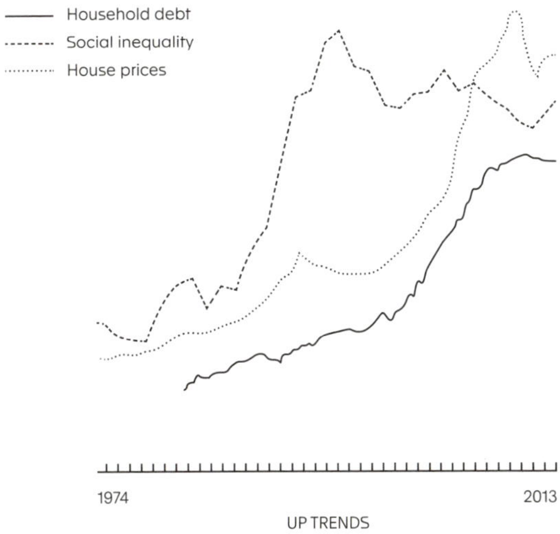

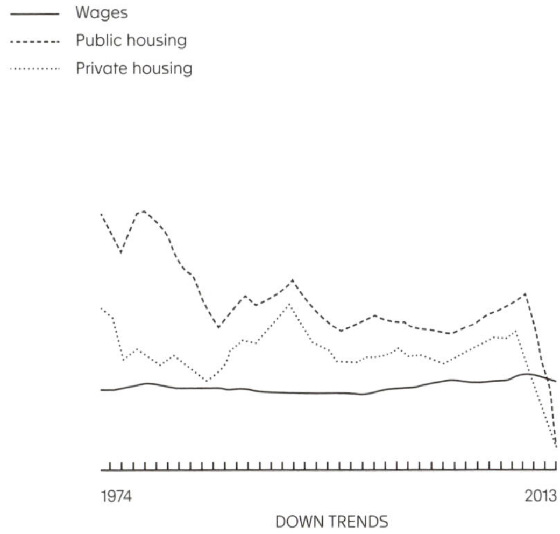

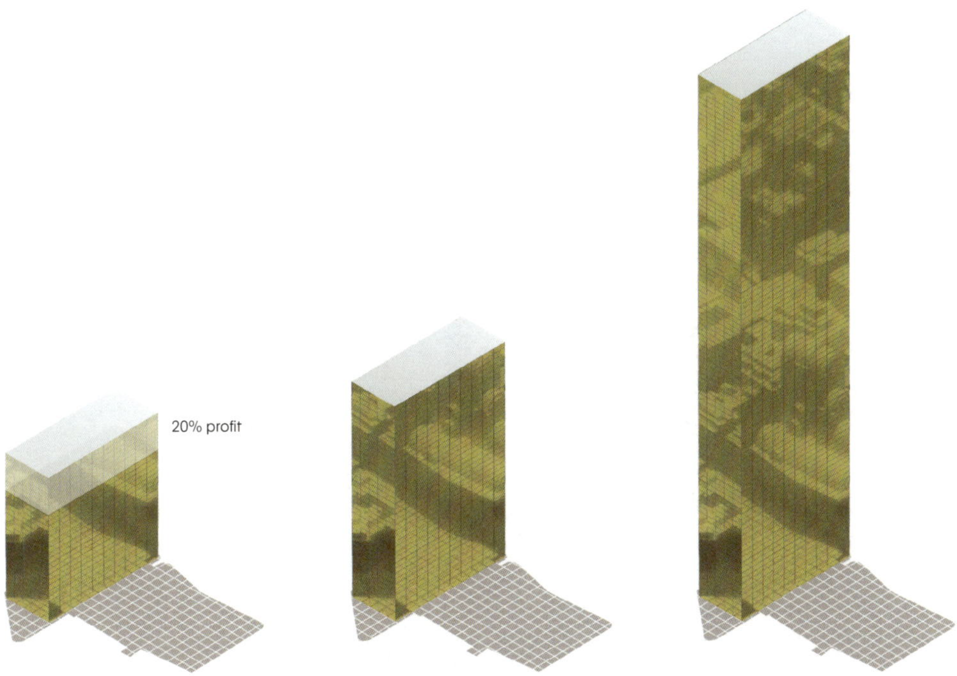

Developer's Model
Height: 90m
100% Market Rate
Cost: £182.219m
Value: £218.662m

Affordable Model
Height: 106m
Bond Term: 25yrs
ROI: 6%
s106: 0%
72% Market Rate
72m2pcm: £2092
Rentable m²: 85,896

The Ingot Model
Height: 356m
Bond Term: 50yrs
ROI: 5.5%
s106: 15%
46% Market Rate
72m2pcm: £1352
Rentable m²: 287,496

DOGMA AND NEW ACADEMY
PROMISED LAND, 2018

Late capitalism has transformed virtually all architectural design practice and building construction into a real estate venture. Promised Land aims to reconfigure residential building construction and operation into a cooperative practice that fosters collective dwelling. Brussels, London, and Helsinki each serve as sites for a different housing model, each of which consider policy, labour, and real estate as part of the design process in an effort to rethink the privatization of land and the notion of housing as a commodity. Based on a community land trust model, the Belgian prototype is an elastic and evolving framework for all the aspects of building, from construction to ownership, in order to accommodate fluid living arrangements. The Communal House is a model for a building cooperative in London that employs a self-building, taken on by a tight-knit group of self-organized individuals and families who want to share costs of land and construction and, eventually, the building. The project envisioned for Helsinki, which was conceived of in collaboration with the Y-Foundation, follows the Finnish housing-first approach that provides housing to people experiencing homelessness, who then contribute labour to build the homes—labour which subsidizes future rental payments. Though the three models are each based on diverse concepts, they all aim to create housing that can resist real estate speculation, and in doing so reclaim housing as a human right.

Brussels, Rue Demosthene, facade toward the inner courtyard

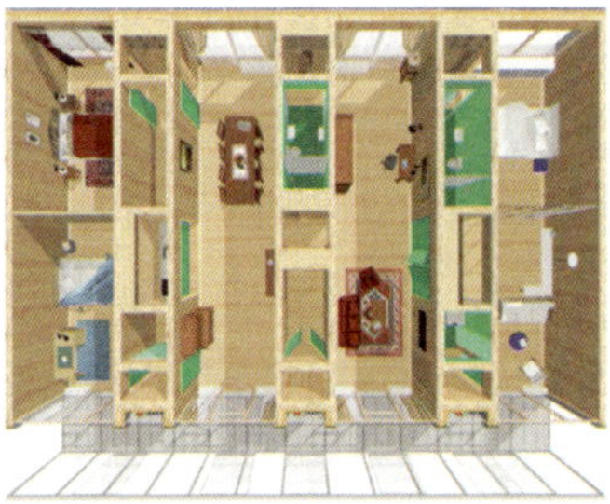

Brussels, four room apartment and one room

COMMUNITY LAND TRUST BRUSSELS — SOCIAL AND FINANCIAL STRUCTURE

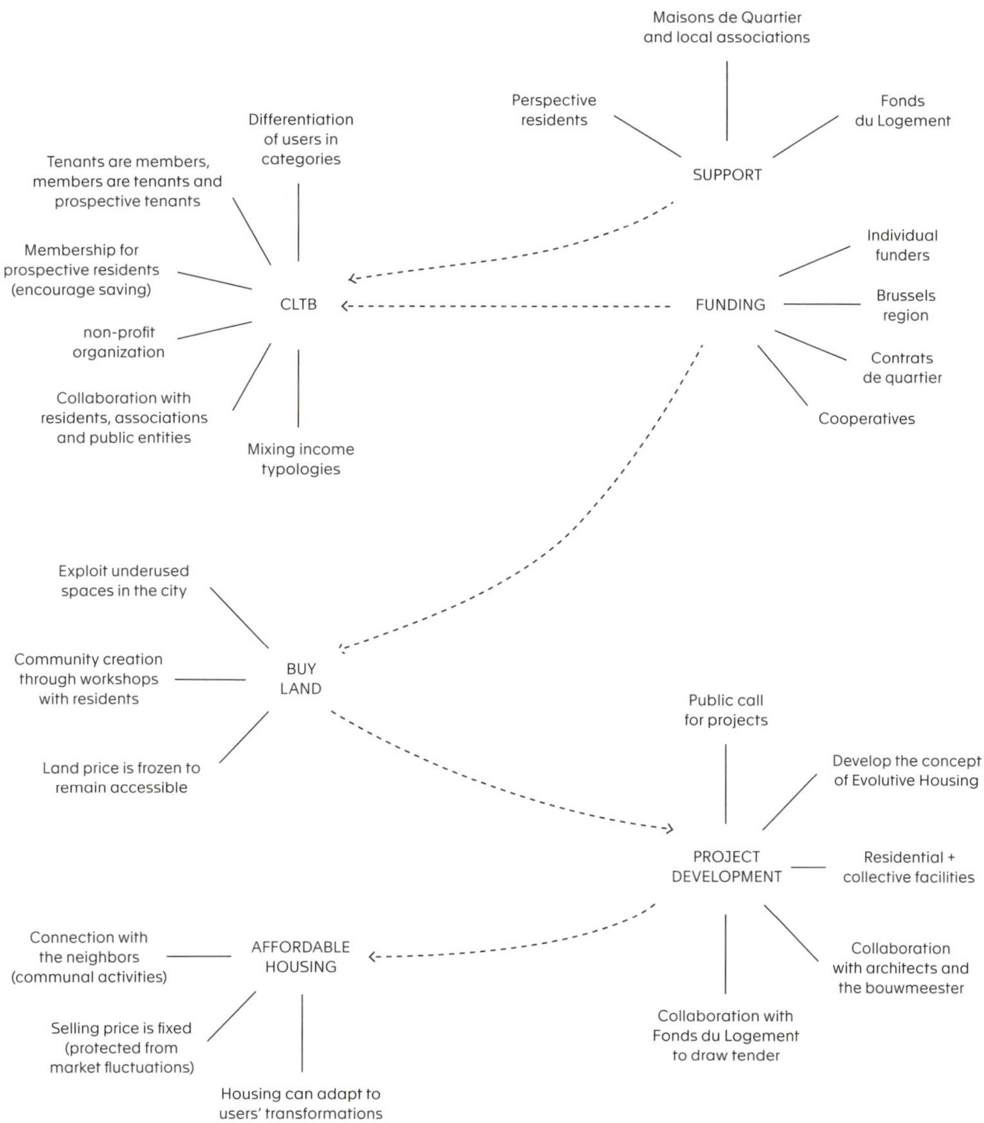

SUN CO-OP — SOCIAL AND FINANCIAL STRUCTURE

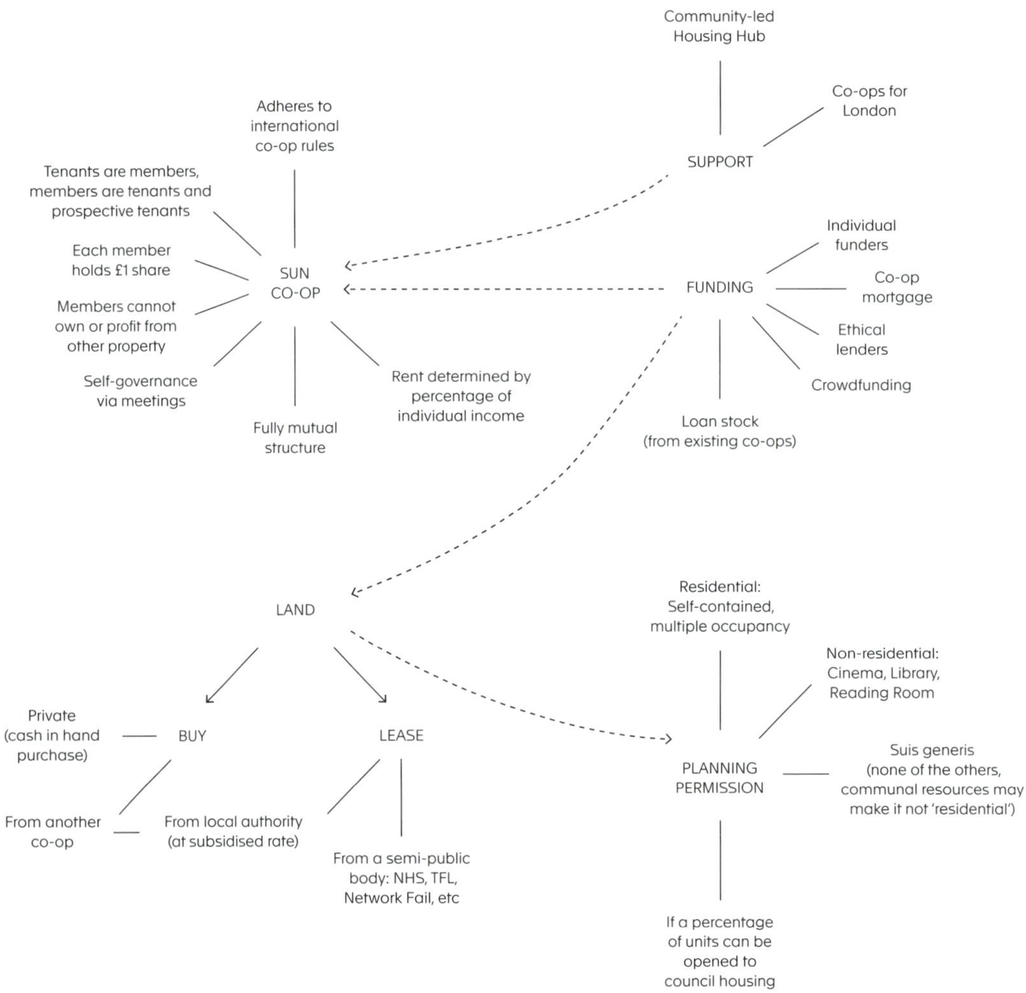

London, three room apartment

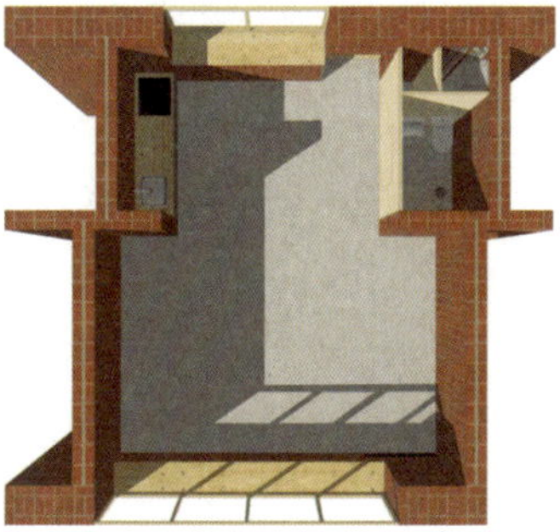

Helsinki, shed 'prototype' building, where workers build, eat, and live together

BYSANTTI — SOCIAL AND FINANCIAL STRUTURE

Y-FOUNDATION

Y-Foundation acquires the site into its land trust from the City of Helsinki, and rents it to the real estate corporation (R.E.C) at a below-market rate.

Y-Foundation invests into R.E.C. by buying 15 units into its housing stock for standard rate in statebacked housing, 3600 €/m²: 2 160 000 €

Construction materials: 1 290 000 €

Construction services: 3 000 000 €

Builders' daily allowances: 1 500 000 €

BYSANTTI Real Estate Corporation (REC):

50% Y-FOUNDATION | 50% LABOUR COOP

NEW ACADEMY LABOR COOPERATIVE

New Academy establishes a real estate corporation (R.E.C) that owns the new building.

Young Builders join the cooperative and make work contracts with the R.E.C.

15 Young Builders from the cooperative make a labour investment into the project:

33 000 hours of site work

New Academy: *Design and development of project and venture*

Each builder: *57 weeks of construction* *40 hrs work week* *35 €/day allowance* *18 000 bricks/builder*

R.E.C is owed 50/50 by the labor cooperative and Y-Foundation. The young builders have right-of-use to 15 units, the other 15 are rented out by the Y-Foundation. In case a builder decides to live elsewhere, their unit will be rented out by Y-Foundation and the builder will receive a monthly allowance from the rented unit.

As the R.E.C is debt-free (it only hold obligations to its labor investees), it can be used by the cooperative as collateral to fund construction phases of other ventures, expanding the cooperative's non-commercial housing portfolio.

Each year, the number of people who lose their homes and are unable to access housing grows, escalating into a homelessness crisis in many cities. Those without housing who have access to a vehicle often use it as a dwelling space, but most municipalities do not allow individuals to sleep in their cars in public parking, leaving vehicle dwellers vulnerable. Acknowledging the impact of these regulations on people who use their cars for shelter, the New Beginnings Counselling Center initiated a Safe Parking Program in Santa Barbara in 2004, asking parking lot owners and operators to allow individuals and families who live in their cars to park in their lots overnight. In addition to providing a safe and legal place to sleep, New Beginnings also offers amenities and social services at these sites. The success of the program has been replicated in cities across California.

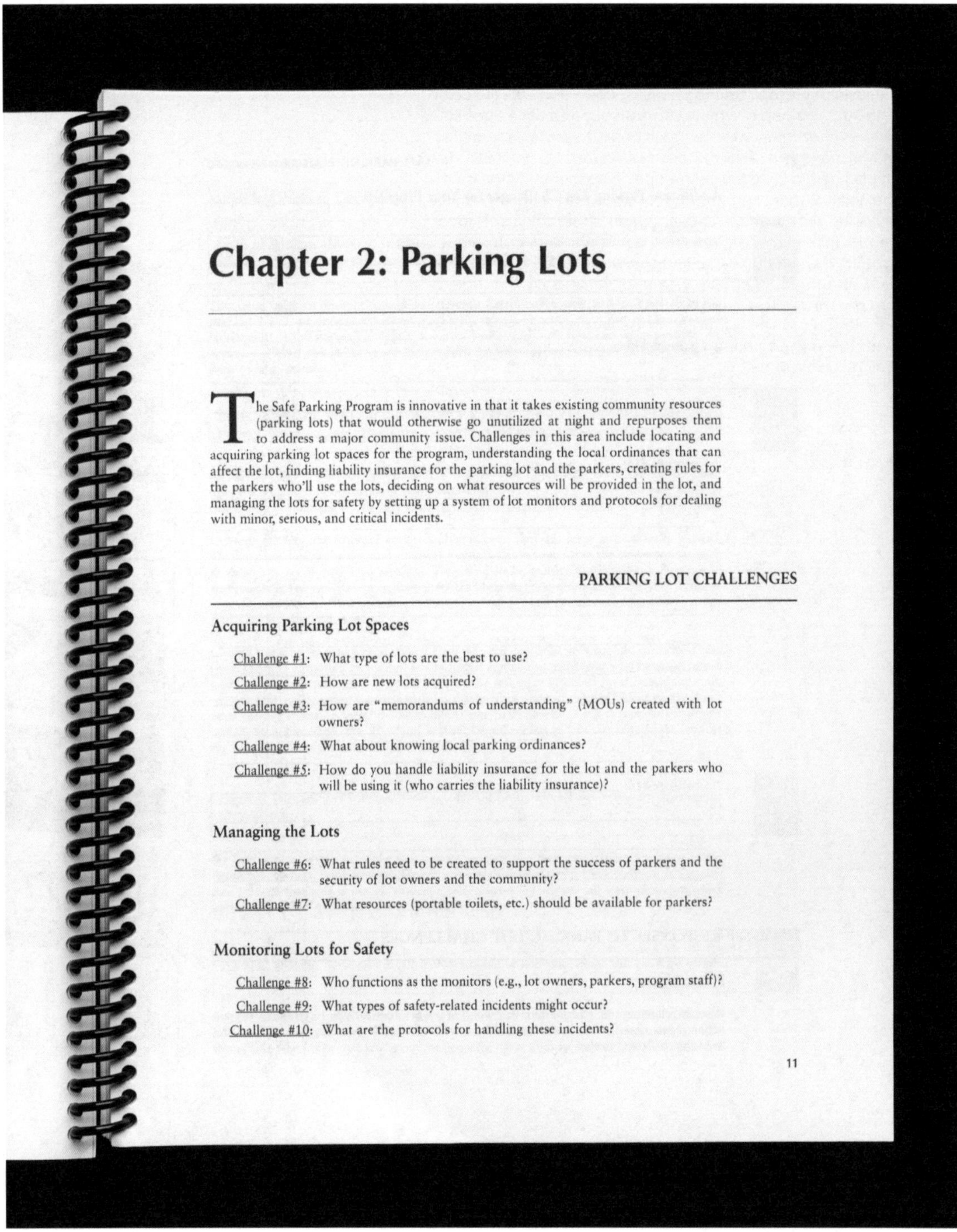

Chapter 2: Parking Lots

The Safe Parking Program is innovative in that it takes existing community resources (parking lots) that would otherwise go unutilized at night and repurposes them to address a major community issue. Challenges in this area include locating and acquiring parking lot spaces for the program, understanding the local ordinances that can affect the lot, finding liability insurance for the parking lot and the parkers, creating rules for the parkers who'll use the lots, deciding on what resources will be provided in the lot, and managing the lots for safety by setting up a system of lot monitors and protocols for dealing with minor, serious, and critical incidents.

PARKING LOT CHALLENGES

Acquiring Parking Lot Spaces

Challenge #1: What type of lots are the best to use?

Challenge #2: How are new lots acquired?

Challenge #3: How are "memorandums of understanding" (MOUs) created with lot owners?

Challenge #4: What about knowing local parking ordinances?

Challenge #5: How do you handle liability insurance for the lot and the parkers who will be using it (who carries the liability insurance)?

Managing the Lots

Challenge #6: What rules need to be created to support the success of parkers and the security of lot owners and the community?

Challenge #7: What resources (portable toilets, etc.) should be available for parkers?

Monitoring Lots for Safety

Challenge #8: Who functions as the monitors (e.g., lot owners, parkers, program staff)?

Challenge #9: What types of safety-related incidents might occur?

Challenge #10: What are the protocols for handling these incidents?

11

Safe Parking Program Manual, Santa Barbara New Beginnings Counseling Center

ASSEMBLE AND STILLE STRASSE
STILLE STRASSE, 2012–2015

Senior citizens are amongst the most at-risk of poverty, making them particularly susceptible to escalating housing costs and cuts to social programs. In 2012, a group of elderly citizens squatted Stille Straße 10, a multi-generational community centre in Berlin, to protest the municipality's intent to close it. After 112 days of squatting, however, the municipality agreed to keep the centre open. Subsequently, the members of the Stille Straße community collaborated with the multidisciplinary collective Assemble to envision an affordable communal housing model for seniors. The resulting concept offers both autonomy and community through a hybrid ownership model, in which one half of each apartment is privately owned, while the other half is rented from the co-op. This arrangement is reflected in the design, which is analogous to the relationship between a house and its garage, with the owned space providing privacy and the rented space offering socialization.

Axonometric drawing depicting the "moved-in" condition of Stille Strasse, with privately-owned units separated from spaces rented from the co-op by a soundproof wall

HOW MANY PEOPLE ARE YOU WILLING TO SHARE A KITCHEN WITH?

Title: Crashing
Season/Episode: S01E01
Year: 2016
Network: Channel 4
Country: UK

Property guardians are people who are allowed to live in otherwise unoccupied former commercial, public, and historic properties which have been set up to facilitate co-habitation at low rental costs, in exchange for acting as house-sitters, protecting the site and warding off squatters from taking up residence. In London, the status of property guardians is regulated by law. A group of young adults with this status co-living in an abandoned hospital are the subject of *Crashing*. Though these property guardians have found a place to stay for the time being, they know it is not a permanent solution. There's laughter, but it has a bitter edge: it is, after all, a dramedy.

SAM CHERMAYEFF OFFICE
ANTHROPOCENE LLC, 2020

Anthropocene LLC is a multi-family vacation home located in The Rockaways that caters to urbanites looking to experience communal living without interrupting their daily lives. Typical domestic functions are arranged in a motel-like scheme that situates private bedrooms and bathrooms in one programmatic bar for each household, while the communal kitchen, dining, living, and recreation spaces are grouped in a separate cluster. The floor plan is intended to be flexible enough to house many guests in multiple configurations, while also maximizing space for shared amenities. As many of its guests are likely to reside in normative private homes, the vacation home offers an opportunity to try out sharing domestic space, which could serve as a gateway to incorporate communal practices into their quotidian living situations.

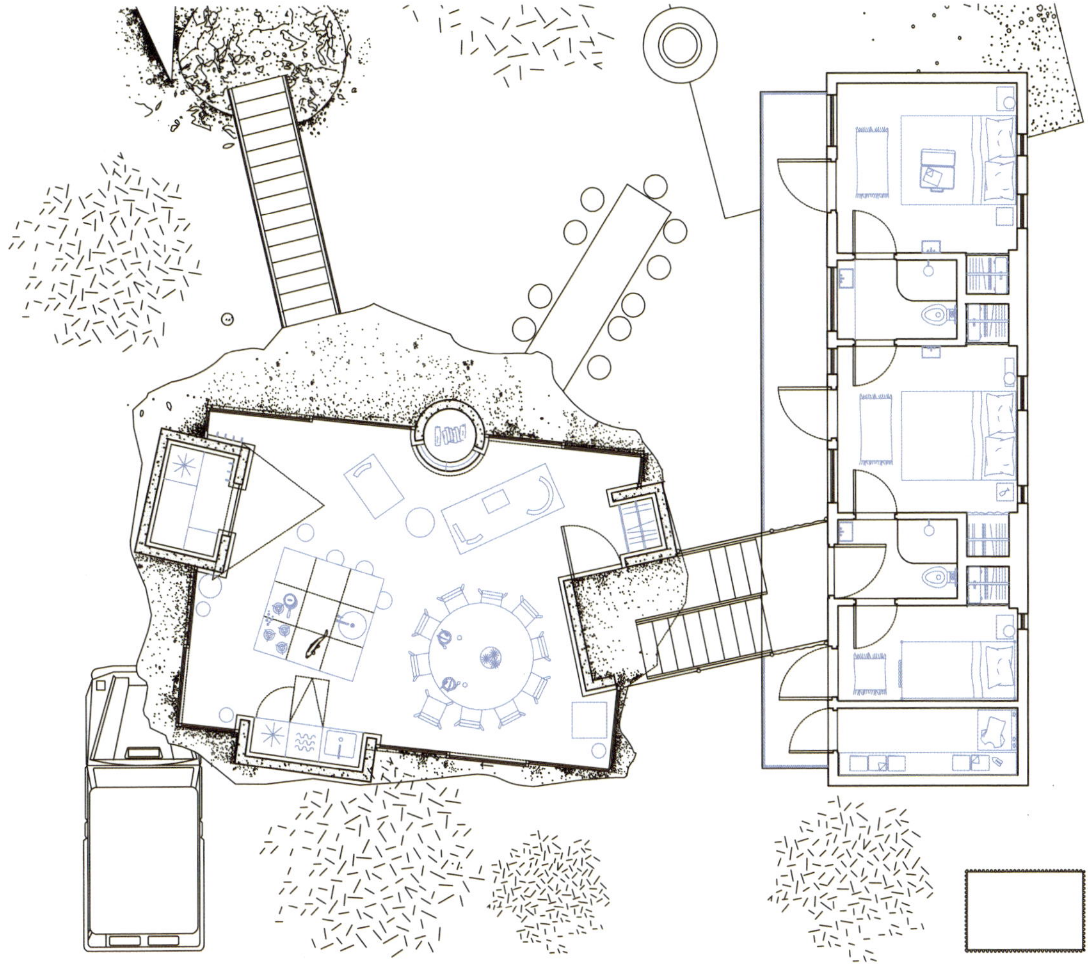

Plan and model showing the separation of bedrooms from a big kitchen-dining-living area

JUNE14 MEYER-GROHBRÜGGE & CHERMAYEFF
KURFÜRSTENSTRASSE, 2012

The densification of urban space has led architects to search for new models of cohabitation that encourage life, work, and community to coalesce. Driven by the desire to live openly, the six intersecting towers that make up Kurfürstenstrasse in Berlin include floor slabs that overlap at key points, creating intersecting vertical and horizontal volumes and breaking down the boundaries between units. The towers are comprised of twenty multi-bedroom condominiums, three commercial spaces, and one studio apartment. Although the structure offers a sense of continuity, each unit has a completely distinct character, and interstitial spaces between units are left open such that they can be shared. The architectural form simultaneously allows residents to lead an individualistic lifestyle and to share spaces with a community of like-minded people, though the building itself does not require that inhabitants live communally.

Here is the flat of Lars

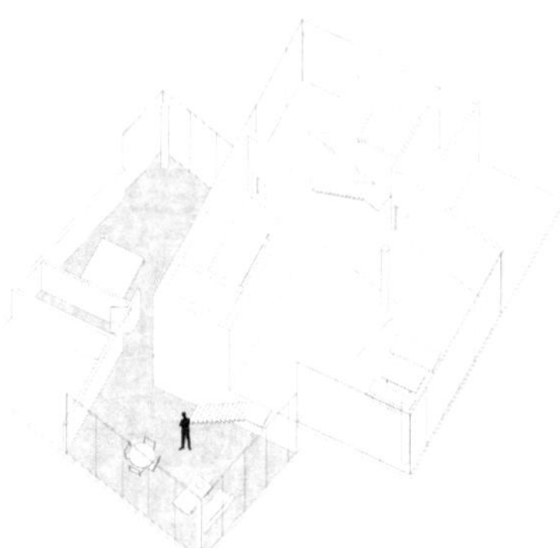

Here is the flat of
Sam & Johanna

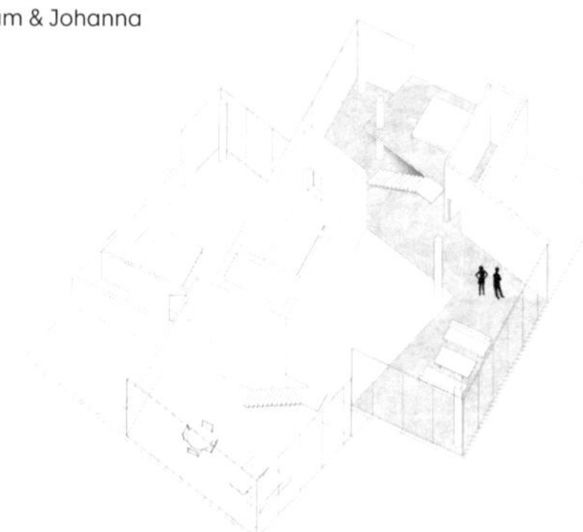

Or can be a kitchen for Lars

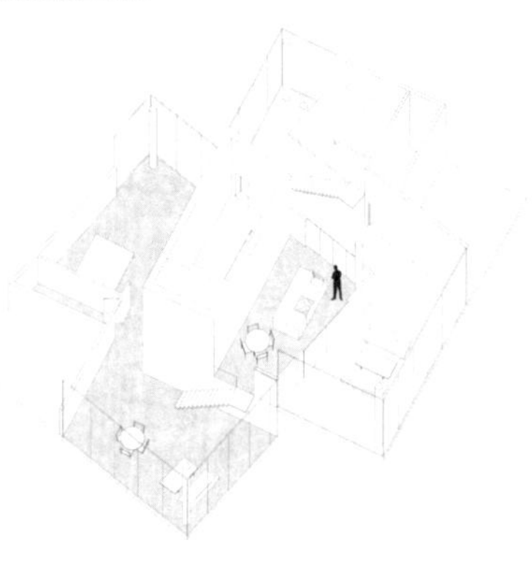

Or can be an open space for
all of them

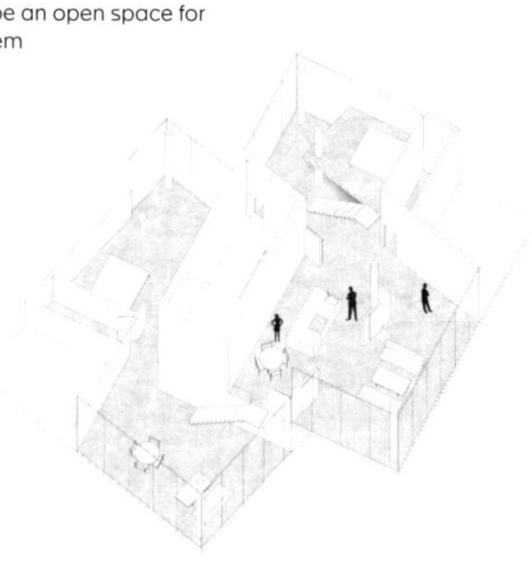

And here is a shared space between the two flats

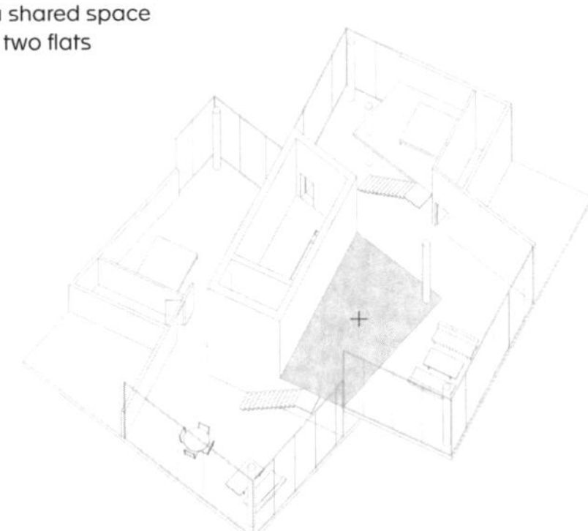

The space can be a kitchen for Sam & Johanna

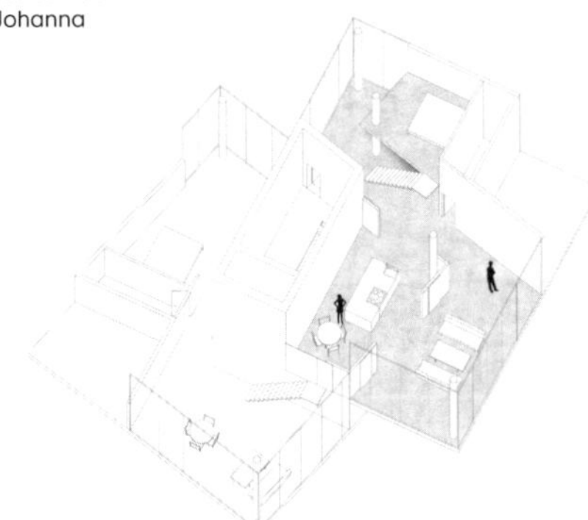

What is happening in these two flats,

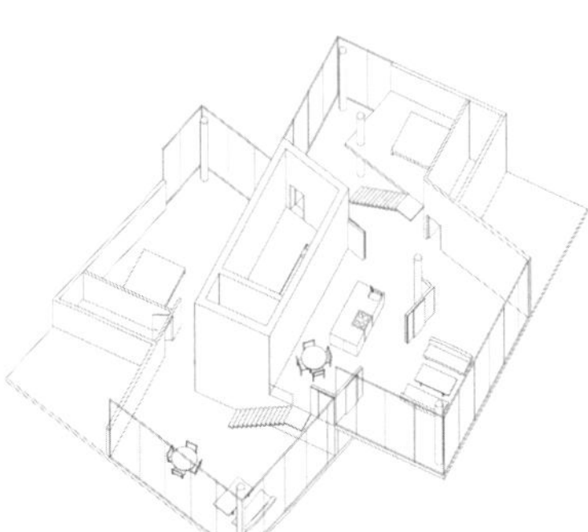

can happen somewhere else in the building

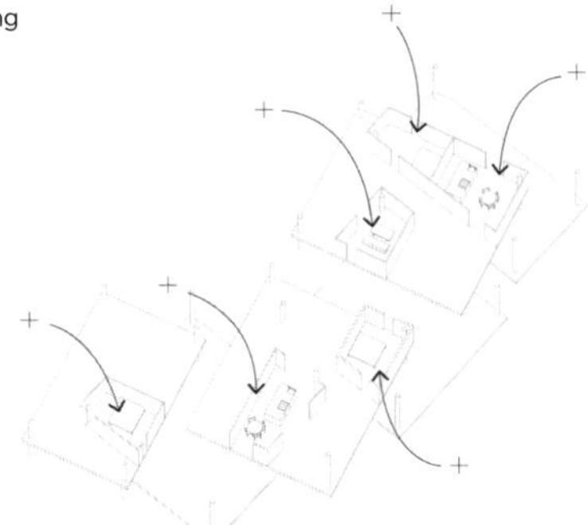

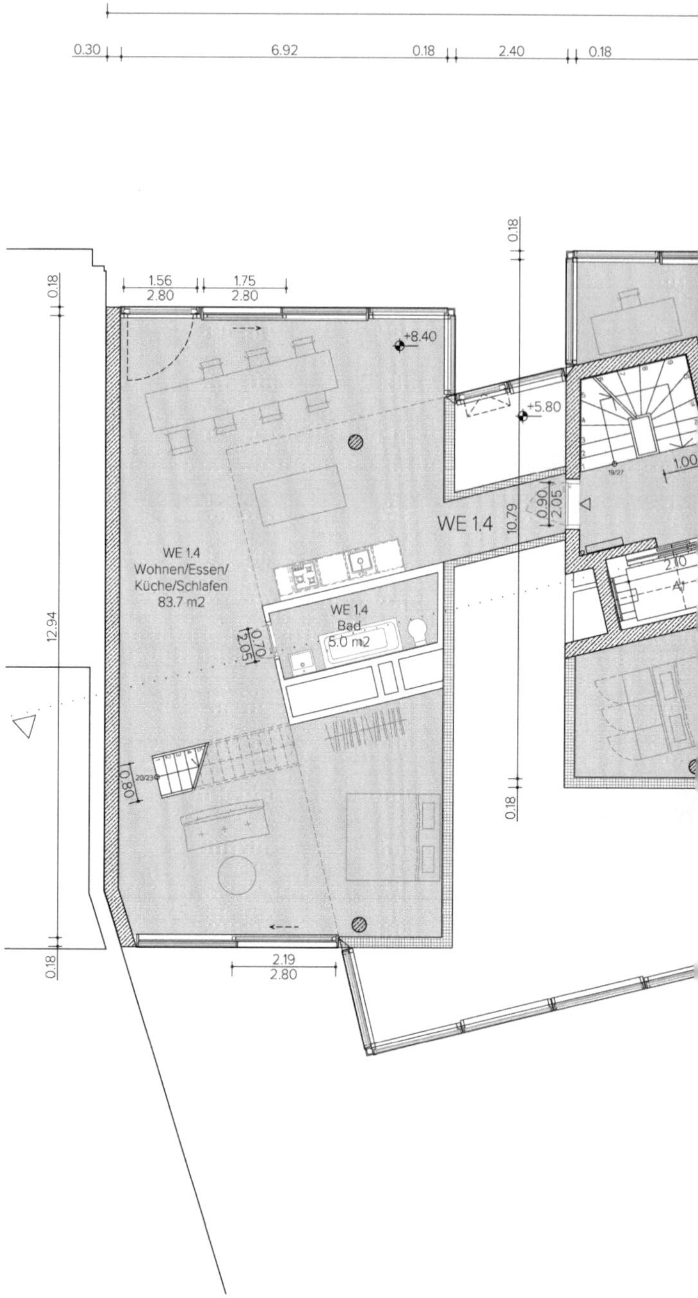

Kurfürstenstrasse Building Group, plan

WE 3.4
Bad
5.1 m2
WE 3.4
Abstellraum
7.2 m2
WE 4.3
Bad
5.6 m2
WE 4.3
Schlafen
11.5 m2
WE 4.3
Schlafen
17.6 m2
WE 4.3
(BF)
WE 4.3
Bad
6.1 m2
WE 5.4
Wohnen/Essen/
Küche/Schlafen
63.9 m2
WE 5.4
(BF)
WE 5.4
Bad
6.7 m2
WE 6.3
Schlafen
16.1 m2
Luftraum
Luftraum

Though the densification of suburbs has long been discussed as a means of making them more environmentally sustainable and diverse, House with a Missing Middle proposes the densification of a suburban residential type as a means of making these areas attractive to a younger demographic. Kellyville, a suburb of Sydney, is expecting an influx of new residents due to a recently completed subway station, specifically young professionals who will be looking for housing that accommodates a diverse array of household arrangements. House with a Missing Middle anticipates the needs of this new demographic by transforming a mansion designed for a nuclear family into a multi-residence manor to include either four three-bedroom townhouses or eight one-bedroom units—allowing eight to twelve individuals to be housed on a plot that would typically only accommodate around four. The house's "missing middle" refers to the space that would have been allocated as a living room in a conventional single-family home, but in this new scheme is a green courtyard—allowing for social interactions between residents and introducing an envrionmental infrastructure to the suburbs.

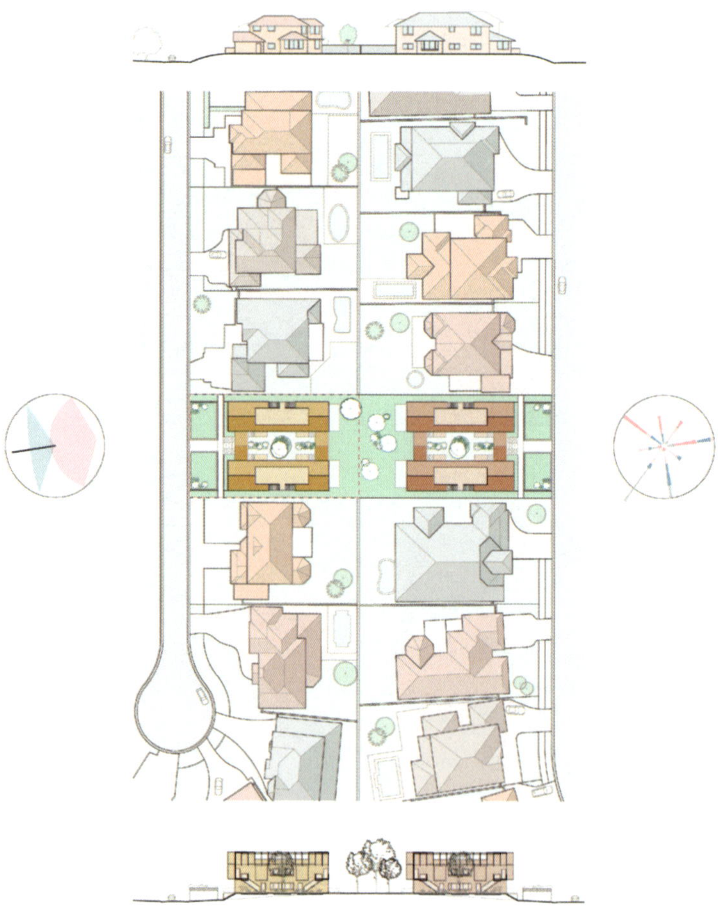

Site plan, elevation, and perspective of multi-residence compound
inserted in a neighbourhood of single-family homes

What will you do if you live to 100? Do you know how you were conceived?

Nadia Sablin, *Aunties*, 2008–2014

Nadia Sablin, *Aunties*, 2008–2014

Nadia Sablin, *Aunties*, 2008–2014

POLLARD THOMAS EDWARDS
NEW GROUND CO-HOUSING, 2010–2016

As women on average have higher life expectancies than men, women in heteronormative relationships are more likely to face the prospect of living alone in old age and the feelings of loneliness and isolation that tend to follow. Aiming to evade this possible reality, a group of elderly women in the United Kingdom came together to create a cooperative housing project, designed specifically for seniors. The group was involved throughout the entire design process, resulting in a building complex that resembles a series of cottage-style row houses organized around a green courtyard. Shared facilities like

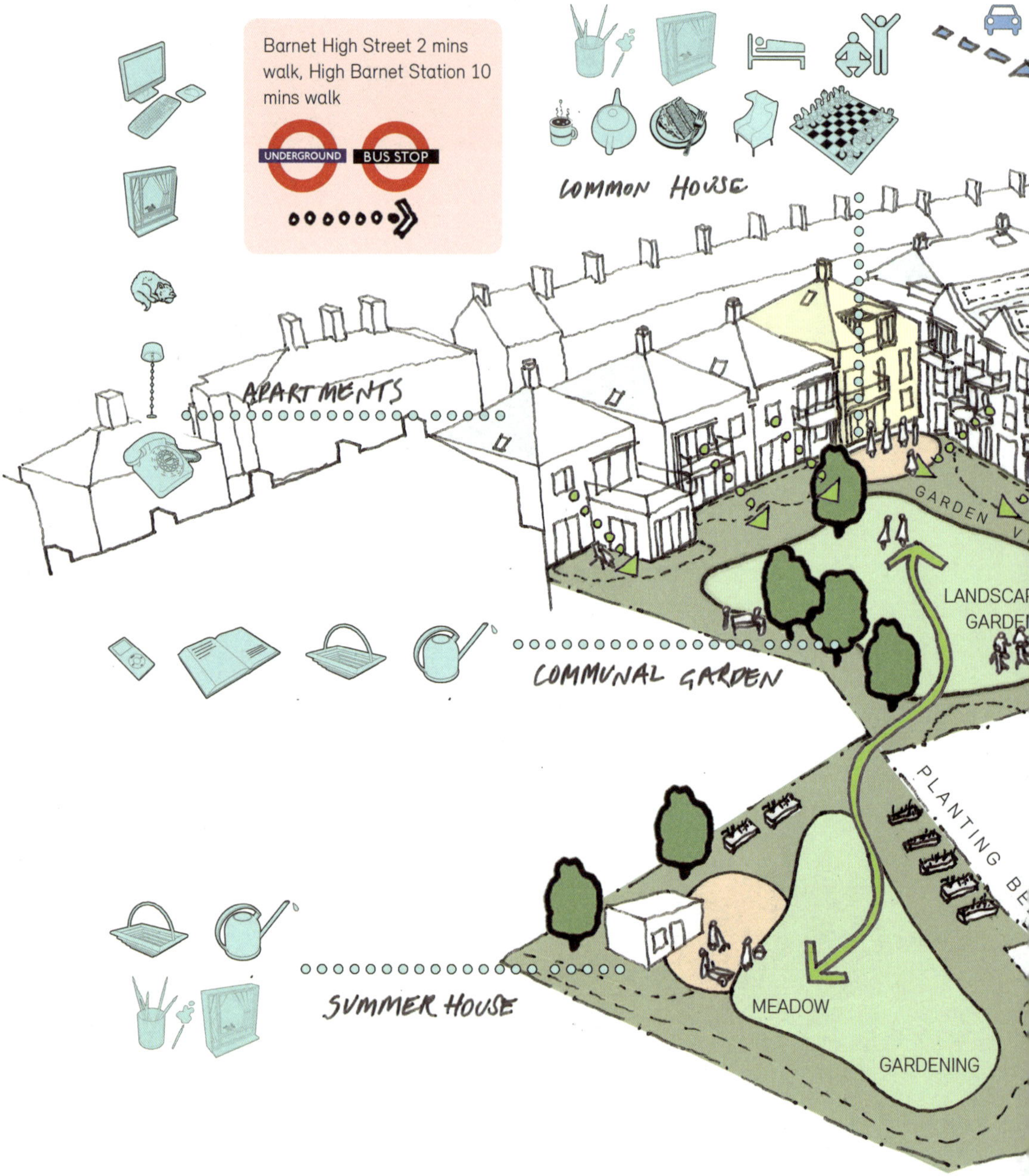

guest bedrooms and a launderette are dispersed throughout the building, and the weekly ritual of communal meals brings all twenty-six inhabitants together to break bread at a shared table. The cooperative's residents are diverse in terms of socioeconomic class, race, and ethnicity, and inhabitants have access to diverse ownership options, from owning to renting. Though there are many differences between them, all of New Ground's residents are women who are at least fifty-five years old.

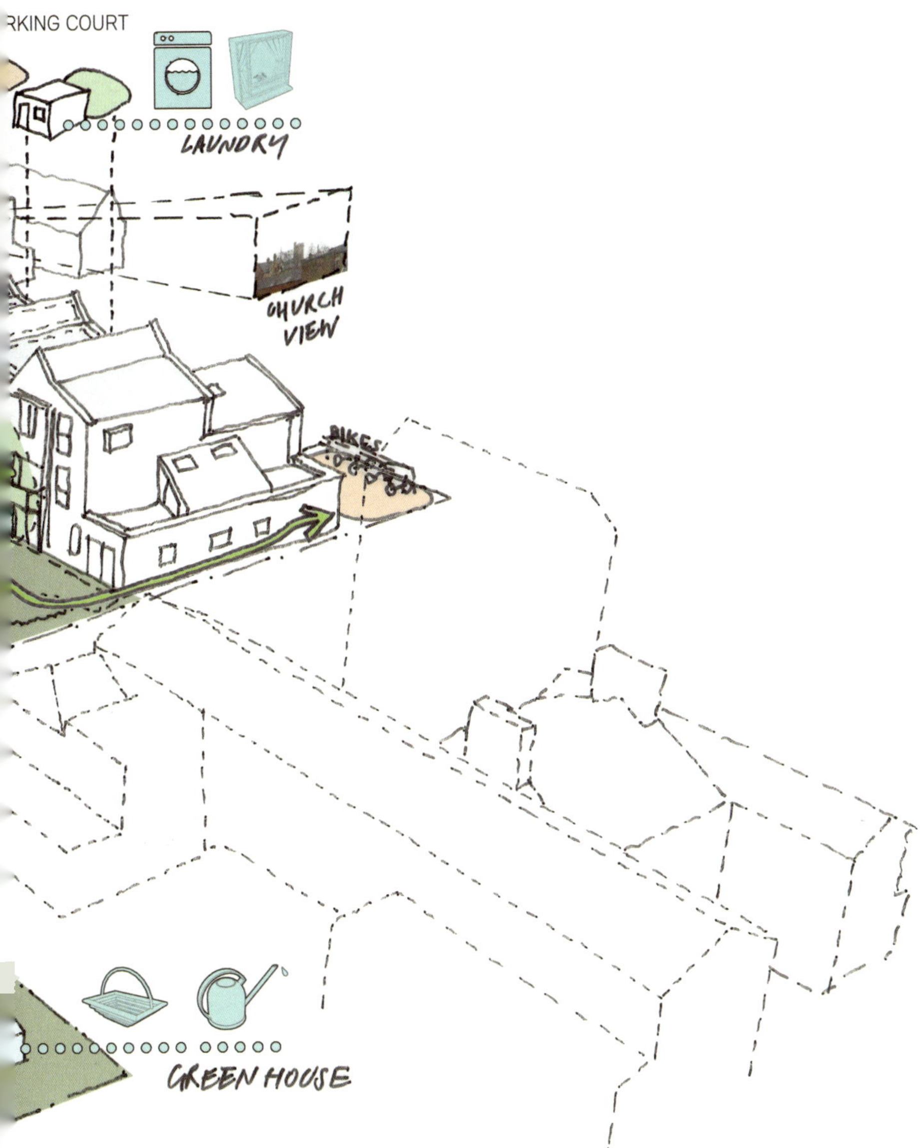

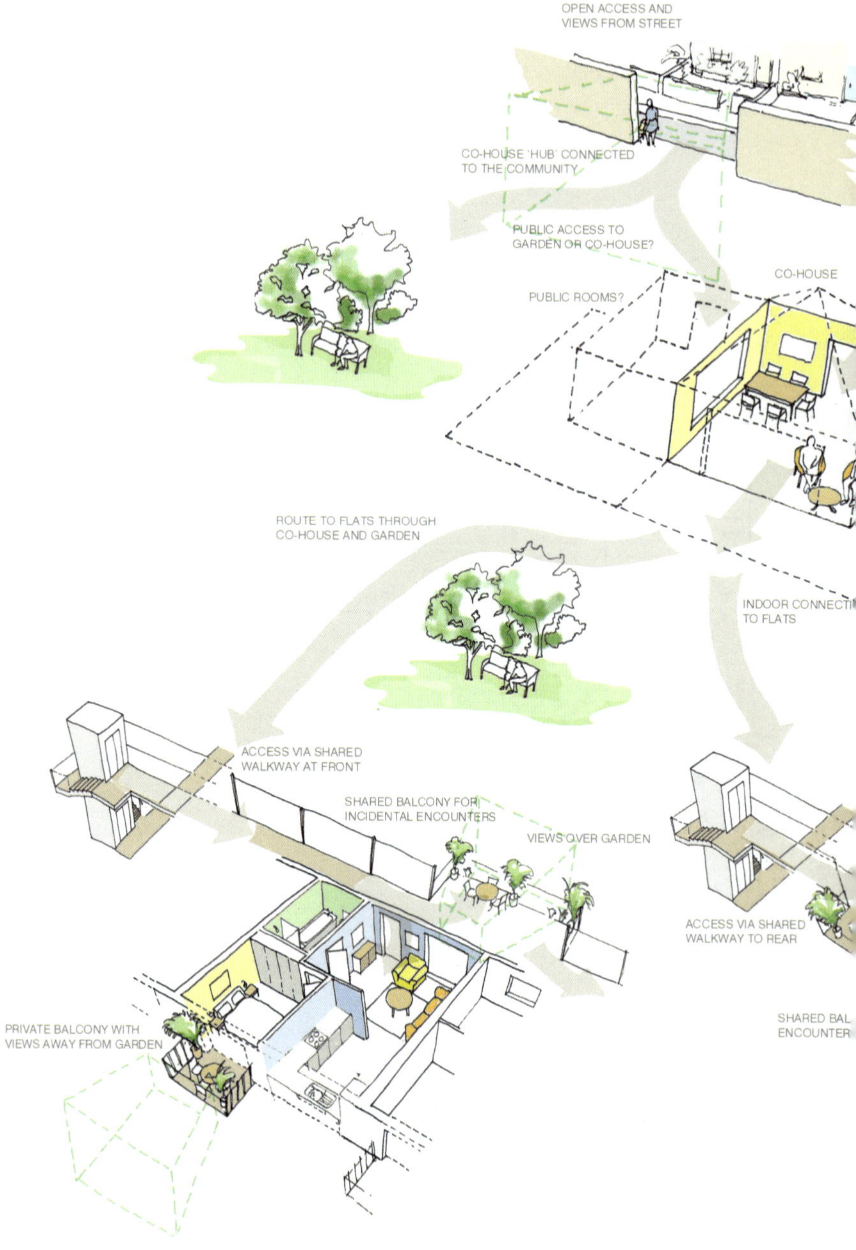

New Ground Co-Housing's organizational logic is such that personal and communal spaces are dispersed, encouraging incidental encounters and connected views while still maintaining basic levels of privacy for residents

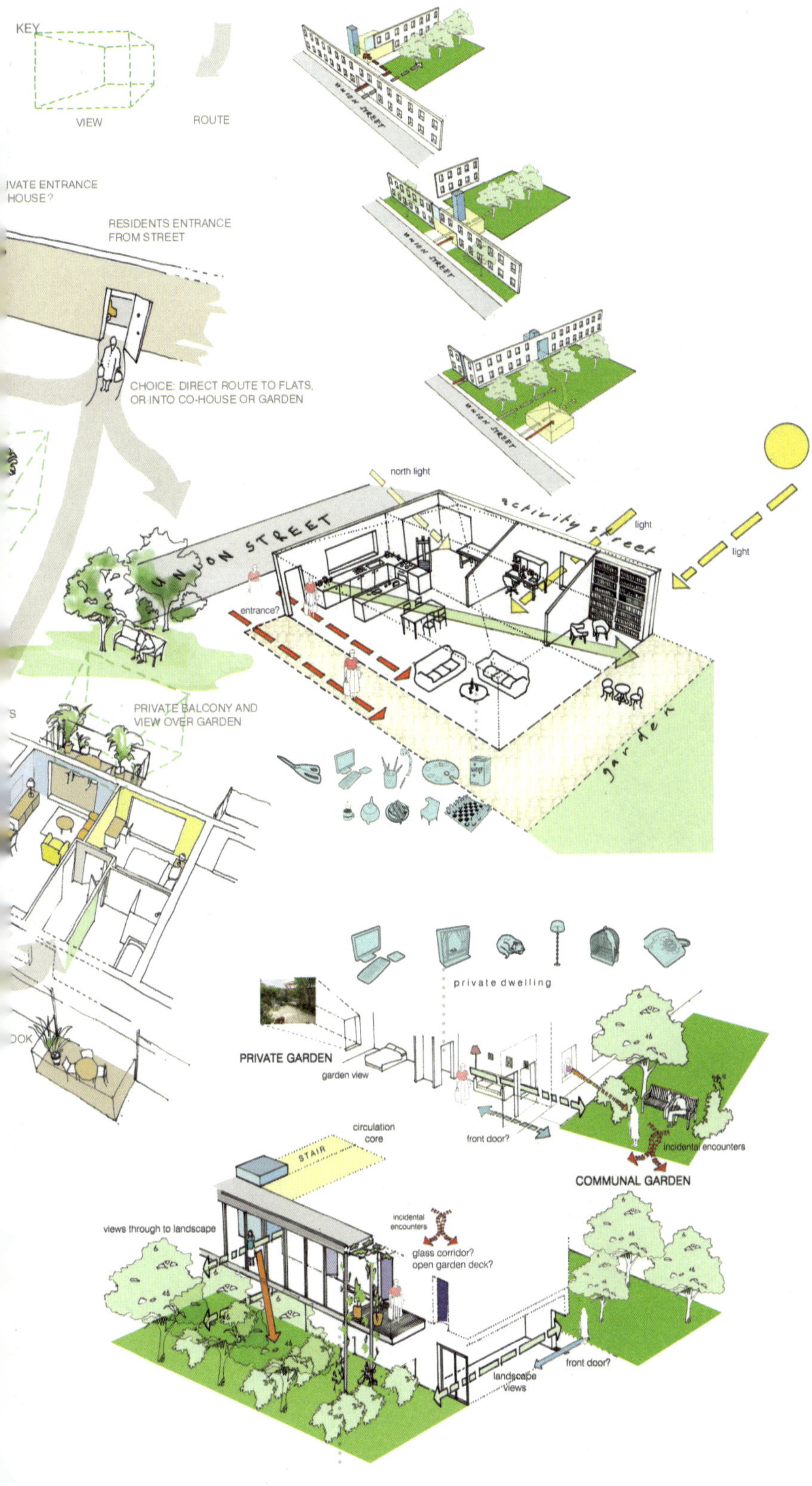
KEY
VIEW
ROUTE
UNION STREET
IVATE ENTRANCE
HOUSE?
RESIDENTS ENTRANCE
FROM STREET
CHOICE: DIRECT ROUTE TO FLATS,
OR INTO CO-HOUSE OR GARDEN
north light
activity street
light
light
UNION STREET
entrance?
garden
PRIVATE BALCONY AND
VIEW OVER GARDEN
private dwelling
PRIVATE GARDEN
garden view
front door?
incidental encounters
COMMUNAL GARDEN
circulation
core
STAIR
views through to landscape
incidental
encounters
glass corridor?
open garden deck?
landscape
views
front door?

Title: Grace and Frankie
Season/Episode: S04E10
Year: 2018
Network: Netflix
Country: USA

Grace and Frankie are two women in their seventies who had to completely rethink their lives after both their husbands came out and got married to one another. From the creator of *Friends*, Marta Kauffman, and starring the iconic Jane Fonda and Lily Tomlin, the show embodies a dominant storyline in contemporary television: life beginning anew in seniordom—in this case, a new life, perhaps, catalyzed by starting a line of sex toys.

i am
harriet

Ann Neumann

Where the Old People Dance: The Crisis in American Public Housing

When Hurricane Sandy flooded the sleepy Brooklyn neighbourhood of Red Hook, the seniors' centre at 6 Wolcott Street filled up like a bathtub. Below street level and tucked into the side of a red brick public housing complex, the facility was completely destroyed, leaving the one hundred seniors who relied on the centre for a hot breakfast and lunch every day, with nowhere to go.[1] But the Red Hook Senior Center provided its vibrant regulars with another vital nourishment: community.

1 "One Year After Sandy, Red Hook Senior Center Struggles To Find A Home," *Fox News*, 11 January 2017, https://www.foxnews.com/world/one-year-after-sandy-red-hook-senior-center-struggles-to-find-a-home; and Heather Chin, "RACIES Red Hook Senior Citizens Program will relocate permanently," *Brookyln Reporter*, 30 May 2013, https://brooklynreporter.com/2013/05/raices-red-hook-senior-citizens-program-will-relocate-permanently.

Almost all of the seniors were occupants of the Red Hook Houses (Red Hook East and Red Hook West), the largest housing projects in Brooklyn and the second largest in the city, with 2,891 apartment units.[2] Many of the residents of the Red Hook Houses had been neighbours for generations and, like any close-knit community, had a highly-developed system for keeping an eye out for each other. Sandy tested these bonds. The high waters of the hurricane shut off power in all of the project's buildings, the electrical and boiler systems of which were in basements. Community leaders and tenants quickly mobilized a network of support. The Red Hook Initiative, a ten-year-old non-profit organization that had not lost power, became a hub for residents of the houses who needed to charge their phones, get food, and receive necessary services like basic first aid.[3] The seniors were able to provide each other with an additional layer of support: they were never forgotten or left alone.

Yet the community's needs in the wake of Sandy were ongoing. More than a month after the hurricane struck, *New York Daily News* reported that "4,015 residents there were still without heat and hot water and 2,125 were without power. [22] of the project's 32 buildings were either without heat and hot water or power."[4]

Soon plans were made to temporarily house the seniors' centre in the nearby Joseph Miccio Community Center. By way of a set of stairs or a slow elevator, the seniors took over Miccio's basement galley kitchen and a few adjoining rooms (one was filled with a very busy pool table)—largely unattractive, industrial, and low-ceilinged. Soon, tables filled the main room, leaving a narrow aisle down the middle that directed attention to the kitchen, and the walls were covered with flyers, paper flowers, streamers, and photos of the posing seniors. Parties—to celebrate any holiday, from Father's Day to Veteran's Day—were held either in the packed lunchroom or upstairs on Miccio's basketball courts, the athletic drills of youth supplanted by a DJ and elderly men and women, in hats and skirts, making moves on the dance floor.

Until the afternoon in 2013 when I first walked down the stairs to Miccio's basement—the pluck and swagger of Latin music overwhelming me—my primary interaction with seniors had been over ten years as a hospice volunteer, most often in the homes of middle-class and upper-middle-class New Yorkers. The greatest challenges for these declining elders, isolated in their city homes, were keeping loneliness at bay and finding good in-home health aides.[5]

More than seventy-six percent of Americans over the age of fifty own their homes.[6] Homeownership provides this community with

2 New York City Housing Authority, *NYCHA 2020 Fact Sheet* (New York City, NYCHA, March 2020), https://www1.nyc.gov/assets/nycha/downloads/pdf/NYCHA-Fact-Sheet_2020_Final.pdf, 2.

3 Red Hook Initiative, *Red Hook Initiative: A Community Response to Hurricane Sandy* (New York City: Red Hook Initiative, 2013), https://rhicenter.org/wp-content/uploads/2019/11/RHI-Hurricane-Report-6_2013.pdf, 2.

4 Greg B. Smith, "NYCHA head tells tenants who are still without power that they'll get a credit for their troubles —in January," *New York Daily News*, 12 November 2012, https://www.nydailynews.com/new-york/nycha-head-powerless-residents-hang-article-1.1200964.

5 Unlike the problem of loneliness, landing a good, twenty-four-hour-per-day home health aide—the going rate for which in New York City is at least US$13 per hour—can be solved with cash.

6 Joint Center for Housing Studies of Harvard University, *Housing America's Older Adults*, (Cambridge, MA: Joint Center for Housing Studies of Harvard University, 2018), https://www.jchs.harvard.edu/sites/default/files/Harvard_JCHS_Housing_Americas_Older_Adults_2018_1.pdf, 2.

financial stability when their monthly income is limited by retirement, and a home is an important asset that can be leveraged to pay for health care and even institutionalization in later years when care needs increase. Studies have shown, too, that moving homes can negatively impact the mental and physical health of elders, and homeownership tends to decrease the number of such moves that seniors may experience.[7] But for those who do not own their homes—in the United States, the vast majority of whom are people of colour—monthly rent can quickly eat into the fixed incomes of many elders (which is, on average, half that of elder homeowners). Since 2013, the black-white homeownership gap among older households in the United States has stood at a full twenty-four percent—the highest rate since record keeping began in 1976.[8] Though this disparity between elder homeowners and elder renters is persistent, government planning and services are designed for elder homeowners, and the assumption that the majority of elders owns homes then penalizes elders who do not.

During my years as a hospice volunteer, I saw one side of this disparity starkly, the side of predominantly white homeowners. Time-capsule apartments on the Upper West Side with parquet floors, Eames curtains, and tastefully framed art were memoirs of lives lived well. But the tidy homes were too quiet: children and grandchildren were far flung, seldom visiting, and old friends and colleagues had died. I would read newspapers to them, ask them questions, and we would discuss politics. These were lonely people, slowly retreating from the world, desperate for company to enliven their last few interminable weeks or days. Loneliness, after smoking and obesity, is one of the leading preventable health risks among seniors.[9] I had come to Miccio to offer my skill—bringing the world to isolated elders—but it was immediately clear to me that in the packed little room where men and women sat at humble jumbled tables, laughing, poking fun, working on word-finds and crossword puzzles, and listening to music, I was not the salvational entertainment.

Maria Sanchez is the program director of the seniors' centre, which is one of fourteen facilities in part run by the Spanish Speaking Elderly Council-RACIES, which, "[provides] its members with information, education, services and programs that will help them live positive, healthy and independent lifestyles."[10] Sanchez is skilled at filling out Medicare and Medicaid forms, housing applications, and Social Security forms, as well as consulting with utility companies and settling disputes over card-table games of dominos. She handed me a blood pressure cuff and sent me into the crowded lunchroom. I wrapped the padded black-Velcro sleeve around one wrinkled arm after another. Poof, poof, poof, hiss. I recognized some of the faces from the neighbourhood—I had

7 Ann Neumann, "Transfer Trauma: America's Seniors Suffer as Care System Pushes Them Between Sites," *The Guardian*, 28 May 2020, https://www.theguardian.com/us-news/2020/may/27/elder-care-us-nursing-homes-transfer-trauma.

8 Joint Center for Housing Studies of Harvard University, *Housing America's Older Adults*, 3.

9 "Loneliness and Social Isolation Linked to Serious Health Conditions," Centers for Disease Control and Prevention, 26 May 2020, https://www.cdc.gov/aging/publications/features/lonely-older-adults.html.

10 "RACIES Senior Centers," RACIES, https://www.raices.us/senior-centers; and Senator Valmanette Montgomery, "Senator Montgomery celebrates the opening of the new Red Hook Neighborhood Senior Center," The New York State Senate, 18 December 2017, https://www.nysenate.gov/newsroom/articles/velmanette-montgomery/senator-montgomery-celebrates-opening-new-red-hook.

been living in Red Hook for a dozen years—but I wasn't a neighbour in this setting. I was official-looking only because I was a middle-aged white woman—the only white person in the building—carrying an official-looking medical device. I saw so clearly then how very little I knew about the community that I had ostensibly come to help. The vital lesson that the Red Hook seniors would teach me was how important resilient homes and communities are to the health of seniors—and therefore to public health.

***

Housing is healthcare. One encounter with someone panhandling on a street corner will tell you that human life suffers when it is lived for extended periods out of doors. The impending aging boom will coincide with other factors, like the inaccessibility of healthcare and pharmaceuticals, the decline in the number of jobs with a living wage, and the increasing cost of living, particularly the cost of housing. These factors, over the next few decades, will combine to devastate the lives of American elders to a degree that we have not seen in generations.

Social and fiscal trends, political and environmental events, and disruptions to so-called normative life courses can deeply impact health outcomes even decades later. The incidence of longer life expectancies, for instance, has begun to flood the country's inadequate and unprepared long-term care resources, resulting in a shortage of gerontologists and other health practitioners. A more granular example: the health of nursing home residents has been jeopardized by the long-term care industry's dogged reliance on under-paid women of colour, many of whom work multiple jobs to survive—likely contributing to the spread of COVID-19 throughout American nursing home facilities. The pandemic itself will likely alter the health and life expectancy of all those lucky enough to survive it, in America and abroad.

Scholars have found that the health and well-being of those born during the latter half of the Baby Boom has been directly affected by those who preceded them. The financial depressions of the 1970s, during this demographic group's formative years, set the stage for later disparities; by the 1980s, this group found themselves in their twenties and facing heightened job competition due to a glut of workers and resulting in wage deflation, which made well-paying jobs hard to come by, particularly for individuals who didn't have the opportunity to complete post-secondary school training. This age cohort experienced unemployment at greater rates than any demographic group born at any time before or since. And as a result, many have experienced periodic homelessness throughout their life spans.[11]

11 Dennis Culhane, Dan Treglia, Thomas Byrne, Stephen Metraux, Randall Kuhn, Kelly Doran, Eileen Johns, and Maryanne Schretzman, *The Emerging Crisis of Aged Homelessness: Could Housing Solutions Be Funded by Avoidance of Excess Shelter, Hospital, and Nursing Home Costs?* (Philadelphia: University of Pennsylvania, 2019), https://www.aisp.upenn.edu/wp-content/uploads/2019/01/Emerging-Crisis-of-Aged-Homelessness-1.pdf.

Now, that generation is aging and dying prematurely: "Research has shown that they experience geriatric medical conditions such as cognitive decline and decreased mobility at rates that are on par with those among their housed counterparts who are 20 years older."[12] As this cohort reaches its senior years, those experiencing homelessness will continue to increase, from 2,600 in New York City in 2017 to a projected 6,900 in 2030. Across the country, the total number of seniors experiencing homelessness is expected to triple.

Other data also point to the impending financial precarity of seniors. As Fernanda Santos wrote for *The New York Times* in September 2020, "nearly one in 10 households that includes someone age 65 or older ... doesn't have money to buy enough food."[13] And despite possessing an increased number of chronic and preexisting health conditions, many of these elders continue to work.[14]

This growing homeless elder demographic will cause the costs of healthcare to increase across the board, from social-service use to hospital and nursing-home stays. The combined shelter and healthcare costs for this population in New York City alone will exceed $450 million by 2030. Surely, the researchers conclude, investing some of this projected expense in housing now would offset the devastating effects on people's lives and reduce costs to the city in the long run.[15]

Yet, cities across the country have failed to reign in the real-estate industry at the same time as they have overseen expanded defunding of public housing, particularly at the federal level.[16] "If nothing changes," Santos writes, "an additional 2.4 million of the poorest senior citizens in the United States will have no access to affordable housing by 2038."[17]

In a 2017 article in *The New York Times Magazine*, Matthew Desmond, a sociology professor at Princeton, wrote, "Poverty and homelessness are political creations."[18] In the piece, Desmond argues that homeownership has been systemically privileged by the U.S. government—primarily through the extravagant mortgage-interest deduction entitlement program, which coincided with the whittling-away of budgets for Medicare, Social Security, and housing assistance. More often than not, this governmental prejudice against renters leaves low-income and already marginalized populations to fend for themselves.

***

Red Hook is a neighbourhood of more than eleven-thousand residents, nearly six thousand of whom live in the Red Hook Houses.[19]

12 Culhane et al., *The Emerging Crisis of Aged Homelessness*, 2.

13 Fernanda Santos, "Elderly and Homeless: America's Next Housing Crisis," *The New York Times Magazine*, 30 September 2020, https://www.nytimes.com/2020/09/30/magazine/homeless-seniors-elderly.html.

14 This data was compiled before the effects of the pandemic could be factored in.

15 Culhane et al., *The Emerging Crisis of Aged Homelessness*, 18.

16 "Memo to Members: President Trump Proposes Drastic Cuts to Affordable Housing Programs," National Low Income Housing Coalition, 11 March 2019, https://nlihc.org/resource/president-trump-proposes-drastic-cuts-affordable-housing-programs.

17 Santos, "Elderly and Homeless: America's Next Housing Crisis."

18 Matthew Desmond, "How Home Ownership Became the Engine of American Inequality," *The New York Times Magazine*, 9 May 2017, https://www.nytimes.com/2017/05/09/magazine/how-homeownership-became-the-engine-of-american-inequality.html.

19 Measure of America, *Well-Being in Red Hook, Brooklyn: Neighborhood Assets and Challenges* (New York City: Social Science Research Council, 2014), http://www.measureofamerica.org/wp-content/uploads/2014/10/RedHook-Fact-Sheet-2014-15.pdf.

The neighbourhood is a kind of peninsula, surrounded by water on three sides and cut off from the rest of Brooklyn by the elevated Brooklyn-Queens Expressway (a Robert Moses project). The area was settled by the Dutch in the 1630s and named *Roode Hoek* for its red soil and the jutting point of its shoreline.[20] A busy port, dock workers once made up a majority of the neighbourhood's labourers. The Red Hook Houses, completed in 1938, were a Federal Works Program project under the Franklin D. Roosevelt administration, although the city pitched in to pay for the nearby playgrounds. Rent was six dollars a month when they opened.[21]

"The country's largest public housing system was once a seemingly reliable option for the working poor," *The New York Times* wrote in 2018.[22] Mayor Fiorello H. LaGuardia introduced the projects as an upgrade to the city's tumbling down tenements after the Great Depression. Tenements were single-family structures that had been converted to accommodate multiple families during the mid- to late-1800s, when emigration from Europe and elsewhere to New York City was at an all-time high. The conditions in tenement buildings were notoriously cramped, out-of-date, poorly ventilated, and often unsafe. The newly introduced public housing projects were considered to be a progressive solution to the city's problem of overcrowding. Local manufacturers needed housing that was both nearby their shops and factories and also inexpensive enough that their labourers could afford rent on their modest salaries. The new housing projects were meant to allow the city to increase the number of people that could be safely and comfortably housed and to upgrade the amenities available to tenants. Until the late 1960s, however, most welfare recipients were "effectively barred" from the city's public housing projects by authority's screening of potential residents for "moral factors, including alcoholism, irregular work history, single motherhood and lack of furniture."[23]

For this reason, until at least the late 1950s, most residents of the housing built and operated by the New York City's Housing Authority (NYCHA) were white. But those demographics changed rapidly after 1968, when activists and the federal government successfully pushed for the acceptance of low-income populations and people of colour to receive public assistance. By the 1980s, the city's crime and drug problems were seemingly endemic in the projects.[24] The nation's war on drugs and mandatory minimum sentencing policies preyed on people of colour and stigmatized the residents of public housing in a whole new way.[25]

Today, rent in NYCHA units is capped at thirty percent of the resident family's income and the average rent is US$548 (for context, the average rent for a one-bedroom apartment in Brooklyn in May

20 Michelle Montalbano, "A (Not So) Brief History of Red Hook," Brooklyn Public Library, 10 September 2019, https://www.bklynlibrary.org/blog/2019/09/10/not-so-brief-history-red.

21 Dylan, "Red Hook Houses," Atlas Obscura, https://www.atlasobscura.com/places/red-hook-houses; and "Red Hook," NYC Community Board 6, Brooklyn, https://www1.nyc.gov/site/brooklyncb6/about/neighborhoods/red-hook.page.

22 Luis Ferré-Sadurní, "The Rise and Fall of New York Public Housing: An Oral History," *The New York Times*, 9 July 2018, https://www.nytimes.com/interactive/2018/06/25/nyregion/new-york-city-public-housing-history.html.

23 Ferré-Sadurní, "The Rise and Fall of New York Public Housing."

24 David E. Pitt, "At Night, Drugs Invade The Projects," *The New York Times*, 1 September 1988, https://www.nytimes.com/1988/09/01/nyregion/at-night-drugs-invade-the-projects.html.

25 "A Brief History of the Drug War," The Drug Policy Alliance, https://www.drugpolicy.org/issues/brief-history-drug-war.

of 2020 was US$2,700, making residence in the city a costly privilege). More than 177,000 families are on the waitlist for New York public housing, but the units they hope to get into are aging into disrepair. One hundred and seventy-five out of the three hundred and two NYCHA developments are fifty years or older. Twenty-two percent of NYCHA residents are over the age of sixty-two.[26]

***

The core of New York City's plan to meet the needs of its rapidly increasing number of elderly residents—a number that is projected to increase by forty percent by 2040—is the neoliberal leverage of public and private equity (and tax breaks) to encourage for- and non-profit developers to construct new housing, on both city and private land to infill existing NYCHA structures.[27] Infill schemes tend to treat open spaces on NYCHA's 2,486 acres of land as an unused and available resource, even though these open areas currently provide residents with outdoor space, parks, playgrounds, and parking. Once called "towers in the park," NYCHA's projects were designed to provide residents with ample open space, but the Crime Prevention Through Environmental Design (CPTED) program, initiated in the 1970s and 1980s as a response to the city's economic decline, disinvestment in public housing (which resulted in poor maintenance of these outdoor spaces and the buildings themselves), and rising crime rates, led NYCHA to create a network of metal fencing that subdivided the previously open spaces.[28] The fences signaled that these spaces were not for the benefit of NYCHA's residents and, subsequently, they came to be used less and less frequently; and now much of that open space is considered by the city (and it's private-developer allies) as a way to pay off NYCHA's mounting debts.

Under the current Senior Affordable Rental Apartments (SARA) plan, low-interest loans of up to US$75,000 per unit will be provided to developers for buildings with fifty units or more, including studio and single-bedroom units. Thirty percent of the units built under this initiative will be reserved for homeless elders. SARA, unsurprisingly, looks a lot like Mayor Bill de Blasio's other initiatives for affordable housing, including the NextGeneration NYCHA (or NextGen) plan, which over the ten years following its 2016 launch date carves out space for new low-income housing out of the open spaces between and around existing NYCHA projects across the city.[29] For instance, ground was broken on 10 September 2019 for the Betances Residences, creating a much-needed 152 units, forty-five of which will be dedicated to housing seniors who are at risk of experiencing homeless. The two eight-story buildings are being constructed via a partnership between the city and private entities and will be built on a plot of publicly-owned land

26 New York City Housing Authority, *NYCHA 2020 Fact Sheet*, 2.

27 NYC Department of Housing Preservation and Development, *Senior Affordable Rental Apartments (SARA) Program Term Sheets* (New York City: NYC Department of Housing Preservation and Development, 2014), https://www1.nyc.gov/assets/hpd/downloads/pdfs/services/snh-sara-term-sheet.pdf.

28 This too is the case at the Red Hook Houses, both East and West, where much of the lawn space has been made inaccessible by permanent metal fences. Gita Nandan and Elliott Maltby, "The Field Guide to Fences: How the barriers we use define our spaces and ourselves, from the mundane to the maddening," Next City, 2 January 2017, https://nextcity.org/features/view/nyc-field-guide-fences-public-space; and New York City Department of City Planning and the New York City Housing Authority, *Connected Communities Guidebook: A practical guide for community engagement, open space design, and building preservation and construction on NYCHA campuses*, (New York City: New York City Housing Authority, 2020), https://www1.nyc.gov/assets/nycha/downloads/pdf/Connected-Communities-Guidebook.pdf, 51.

29 New York City Housing Authority, *Report of the Financial Division on the Fiscal 2021 Preliminary Plan, 2020–2024 Adopted Operating Budget, 2020–2024 Adopted Captial Plan, Fiscal 2021 Preliminary Capital Budget, Fiscal 2021 Preliminary Capital Commitment Plan, and the Fiscal 2020 Preliminary Mayor's Management Report for the New York City Housing Authority*, (New York City: The Council of the City of New York, 13 March 2020), https://council.nyc.gov/budget/wp-content/uploads/sites/54/2020/03/NYCHA.pdf, 27.

that was previously an outdoor track and several basketball courts for the local community.[30]

de Blasio hopes that by leasing city property to developers and collecting rent from completed projects, the city can raise enough money to pay off NYCHA's operating deficit, which is projected to be seventy-five million dollars next year.[31]

For all the complexity and commitment that the city has imbued these projects with and for all the investment that they have compiled for them, affordable housing advocates have been emphatic that public-private partnerships don't solve the public housing dilemma. These efforts, instead, put less-regulated, profit-driven organizations in a position of power over low-income residents and the housing market as a whole and epitomize the city's abdication of responsibility for public housing. There are much simpler and more ethical ways to solve the crisis of affordable housing, it should be noted, particularly for low-income seniors: fund NYCHA; tax second homes in the city; tax corporations, like Apple, that have off-shored their wealth; raise taxes on high-income earners. But these solutions require ingenuity and a culture committed to equality.

There are successful international examples that New York City and the rest of the country could examine and emulate. As Liza Featherstone wrote in *The New York Times* in October of 2020, "eighty percent of Singapore's residents live in public housing, which consists not only of apartments but also of self-sustaining small communities with their own schools, hospitals, supermarkets and many other amenities. With the vast majority of the city-state in public housing, there is no stigma to it, and the system is popular."[32] In 1960, only a year after Singapore gained independence, the country codified its commitment to affordable housing by legislating that the government could acquire public lands at an affordable price. By focusing on dense high-rises that are surrounded by ample open space, by rewarding the projects to good contractors, and by literally building community into the residences—with the consistent inclusion of usable common spaces, courtyards, and common vestibules—the Singapore government was able to foster a culture of public housing that remains affordable and respects residents.[33]

Other countries that have effectively used public housing to mitigate gross inequity including Belgium, which has a two-tiered public housing system, with a social tier and an intermediate tier that are both provided and maintained by various types of organizations.[34] In Vienna, the culture of squatting, which grew to be particularly strong following World War I, fostered broad public

30 NYC Department of Housing Preservation, "Press Release: City, State, and Elected Officials Joined Breaking Ground and Project Partners to Celebrate the Groundbreaking of a New Passive House Supportive Senior Residence in the South Bronx," NYC Department of Housing Preservation, 10 September 2019, https://www1.nyc.gov/site/hpd/news/087-19/city-state-elected-officials-joined-breaking-ground-project-partners-celebrate-the#/0.

31 Brendan Cheney and Dana Rubinstein, "De Blasio unveils 10-year NYCHA plan," *Politico*, 19 May 2015, https://www.politico.com/states/new-york/city-hall/story/2015/05/de-blasio-unveils-10-year-nycha-plan-028912.

32 Liza Featherstone, "Against the White Picket Fence," *The New York Times*, 13 October 2020, https://www.nytimes.com/2020/10/13/books/review/brave-new-home-diana-lind.html?smid=fb-share&fbclid=IwAR3g_DvpLBD3IKbxQXI0jKn3eiamRqlh4bLuBKu6T8fuwbEwQM7RXKACgRA.

33 Abhas Jha, "'But what about Singapore?' Lessons from the best public housing in the world," World Bank Blogs, 31 January 2018, https://blogs.worldbank.org/sustainablecities/what-about-singapore-lessons-best-public-housing-program-world.

34 Niall Patrick Walsh, "Comparing Social Housing in Countries Around the World," ArchDaily, 17 January 2020, https://www.archdaily.com/932075/comparing-social-housing-in-countries-around-the-world.

support for low-income social housing; and today sixty percent of the Viennese population live in social housing. Although new residences are built and maintained through private-public partnerships, rent is capped at about twenty to twenty-five percent of the salaries of residents and the operators of Viennese housing projects are closely regulated and are required to house residents at a range of income levels.[35]

New York City has placed all of its bets on a private-public partnership model, despite (or because of) the incredible power of the real estate industry in the city. Real estate donations to legislators are notoriously difficult to track (because donations are atomized by project, each of which is its own private entity), but the leverage of property into political power—think of New York's Real Estate Board or Rent Stabilization Association—is a hallmark of the city.[36] The city's leaning on private entities to fix social ills is also politically expedient. It serves the right masters. Up against the political force of New York City's real estate industry, the quality of life for an eighty-year-old Black woman—when, say, measured by the reliability of her heater, the number of long-time friends who can drop off a bowl of soup in January, or the extra twenty dollars that she can spend on insulin shots instead of rent—is, sadly, so very easy to ignore.

***

"I'm young!" Carmen tells me one weekday morning. She is wearing a reflective vest over warm, dark-coloured clothes, only periodically making eye contact over her two face masks. She is preoccupied with looking out for approaching children. Carmen, who was born in Puerto Rico, works as a crossing guard at the corner of Van Brunt Street, Red Hook's main thoroughfare, and Wolcott Street, only a few blocks from the pre-Hurricane Sandy location of the seniors' centre. It is a job that she has held since 1997, and because of the seniority she has accrued over the twenty-three years in this position, she earns thirteen dollars per hour, and works two shifts each weekday during the school year—a few hours in the morning, when school begins, and a few hours in the afternoon, when it ends.

Carmen was one of the first people I met in the basement of the Miccio Center seven years ago. She is vibrant, always cracking jokes, often dressing in colourful outfits. Carmen is seventy-three years old and, after more than a decade living in the nearby Gowanus Houses, she has lived in a tiny studio apartment in Red Hook West for the past four years. Her husband died thirty-seven years ago, leaving her to raise their four children alone. Whenever Carmen has a problem with her apartment,

35 Josh Crites, "The Best City in the World for Public Housing," Housing Futures, 28 September 2017, https://housing-futures.org/2017/09/28/the-best-city-in-the-world-for-social-housing.

36 Jordan Laird, "The largest donors to New York candidates," *City and State New York*, 1 November 2018, https://www.cityandstateny.com/articles/politics/campaigns-elections/largest-political-donors-new-york-candidates.html; and Samuel Stein, "The Housing Crisis and the Rise of the Real Estate State," *New Labor Forum* 28, no. 3 (2019): 2.

she tries to fix it herself. "They don't do nothing," she says of NYCHA, "You can report a ticket, they don't come." Her home is small and desperately needs cosmetic repairs, but she has two things many seniors with limited income desperately need: food and a home with climate control. And she has the seniors' centre nearby; although it has been closed since March, due to the COVID-19 pandemic.

Though the centre is closed, Carmen can still call Maria Sanchez at the centre and request that her lunch and dinner be delivered, though she already receives Meals on Wheels that include foods she enjoys, like fish and shrimp. "Every Sunday it comes," Carmen recently told me, "meals for the entire week. If I'm not there, they leave it with the guy next door." Carmen has an air-conditioning unit in her apartment that helps her get through the heat of New York City summers and, in the winter, she has "a lot of heat," she tells me, "Oh god they cook you!"

Red Hook West, the building that Carmen lives in, is multigenerational, but fifty-six of NYCHA's three-hundred-and-two developments have at least one senior-dedicated building (none are in Red Hook).[37] Other NYCHA resources for seniors include a program that provides companions to seniors who need them and a program that services naturally occurring retirement communities (NORCs)—buildings in which inhabitants have aged together.[38]

When I ask Carmen where she would live if she had all the money in the world, she tells me, "in a mansion, with a maid and a butler and ... a chauffeur! I wouldn't take [public] transportation!" When I told her that I missed the crowd from the seniors' centre, she replied, "They have a lot of parties! I used to dance like crazy. I miss everybody, but I see them outside now."

***

Today, the Red Hook Neighborhood Senior Center is located in a renovated building that once housed a daycare centre. It is literally next door to the Miccio Community Center, the centre's temporary location after Hurricane Sandy. This last move came in December 2017, five years after the hurricane devastated the original Wolcott Street location. The new building is grander than either of the prior buildings: a long ramp stretches from left to right against the façade, easing access; two concrete bears, their heads hanging, flank the front door; inside, new paint, shades, and floors have brightened the structure that had been sitting empty since 2012; the kitchen and bathrooms have also been recently renovated.[39]

37 NYC Department for the Aging, *Alternatives in Senior Housing Brooklyn* (New York City: NYC Department for the Aging, 2017), https://www1.nyc.gov/assets/dfta/downloads/pdf/publications/HousingBrooklyn2017v2.pdf, 6.

38 "Senior Programs," NYC Housing Authority, https://www1.nyc.gov/site/nycha/residents/senior-programs.page.

39 Julianne Cuba, "Senior Center Destroyed by Sandy to Reopen in Red Hook," *Brooklyn Paper*, 19 December 2017, https://www.brooklynpaper.com/senior-center-destroyed-by-sandy-to-reopen-in-red-hook.

The scars of Hurricane Sandy are still evident in the neighbourhood. Mayor Bill de Blasio's administration was slow to unveil their Recovery and Resiliency program, which isn't projected to reach completion until 2023. Many buildings are still using temporary boilers, housed in trailers in parking lots and on sidewalks.

Post-Hurricane Sandy construction has brought its own problems. Sixty families were without gas for more than one-hundred days last year.[40] The open spaces between the Red Hook Houses buildings are torn up: "surrounded by 39 acres of metal fencing and mountains of soil with courtyards turned into mazes" and four-hundred-and-fifty trees have been uprooted. The prolonged chaotic state of the neighbourhood has prompted protests.[41] And by the time Hurricane Isaias predictably struck New York City in August 2020, only twenty-five of the city's two-hundred-and-fourteen previously damaged buildings had been retrofitted with generators.[42]

Beyond construction, privatization, and the incessant floods of climate change, other factors continue to complicate the lives of NYCHA's seniors during the COVID-19 pandemic, like rising crime rates and access to services outside Red Hook that require the use of public transportation. And while the pandemic has caused the usually tight rental market in the city to ease in some neighbourhoods, Red Hook has been largely unaffected, attracting young white families, seeking a lower population density and the charm of the community on the water.[43]

I called up Mrs. Frances Brown, the president of the Red Hook East Tenants Association, expecting to get an earful from her about the disruptions caused by the pandemic and the difficulties they have caused for seniors. Brown is sixty-six and a frank talker. In 1992, she moved into 167 Bush Street, a NYCHA building, only two-and-a-half blocks from the location of the new seniors' centre.

"Seniors have a lot to offer," she said, "We don't just want to be babysitters." She told me that she comes from the school of Shirley Chisholm, the first Black woman to be elected to the United States Congress in 1968: "Chisholm taught that you have to vote," Brown said, "you don't just sit around complaining." If there is something Brown disagrees with, Brown feels obligated to change it.

NYCHA's housing projects are far from perfect, and righting political objectives such that they best serve elderly residents will always be an uphill job, but, Mrs. Brown said, "It's not about where you live, it's how you live."

40 Anna Quinn, "Red Hook NYCHA Residents Went Without Gas for Months: Report," *Patch*, 11 June 2019, https://patch.com/new-york/gowanus/red-hook-nycha-residents-went-without-gas-months-report.

41 "Red Hook Houses residents demand NYCHA slow down construction project," *ABC 7*, 28 July 2020, https://abc7ny.com/nycha-red-hook-houses-brooklyn-redelveopment-redevelopment/6339039.

42 Kathleen Culliton, "Red Hook Houses Wait for Generators as Storms Pummel NYC," *Spectrum News NY1*, 13 August 2020, https://www.ny1.com/nyc/all-boroughs/news/2020/08/12/red-hook-houses-wait-for-generators-as-storms-pummel-nyc.

43 Nikhita Venugopal, "MAP: How Red Hook's White Population Surge Is Changing the Neighborhood," New York Visualized, 18 November 2016, https://www.dnainfo.com/new-york/20161118/red-hook/red-hook-demographics-white-population-real-estate.

Title: Mary Kills People
Season/Episode: S02E01
Year: 2017
Network: Global
Country: Canada

Mary kills people, indeed, but she is not a murderer. She is an emergency room doctor, and, with the help of her best friend Des, a former plastic surgeon barred from practice due to a drug addiction, she assists dying patients reach their final destination. This Canadian production tackles one of the biggest taboos of our time without relying on clichés. In this series, death is only the entry point from which the show tries to come to terms with our limitations as humans and as a civilization.

OFFICE KGDVS, BUREAU BAS SMETS, AND RICHARD VENLET
CREMATORIUM, 2019

Cremation, though a longstanding tradition in many cultures, has recently become a common funerary practice in much of the Western world. The Crematorium in Ostend, Belgium reframes the typical funerary space by making cremation a central and visible process for mourners. The single-storey building's inclined roof serves both a technical and symbolic function, with the cremators located at the highest point of the building. The public, administrative, and technical functions exist within lateral strips of space, while thin passages and auxillary spaces work to separate the reception and waiting areas from the ceremonial spaces within the building. Cremation has been integrated into the circulation and design of the space, and in doing so, the ritual of funerary practices has been redesigned.

View of the cremators, with roof lights and a double facade of glass and perforated metal connecting interior space to the landscape

DEATHLAB
CONSTELLATION PARK, 2015

Though grieving the deceased is an accepted reality, less accepted is visible grieving within the public sphere. Constellation Park is a network of suspended memorial shrines composed of illuminated vessels that uses the biomass of the deceased to generate light. Each vessel is a temporal "mourning light" that naturally begins to dim after a year to symbolically mark the transition from grieving to the acceptance of loss. These cloisters and shrines are woven together by public pathways and multi-level clearings that connect the memorial into the urban fabric. This iteration of Constellation Park is designed to be sited underneath the Manhattan Bridge, but the concept can be incorporated into a variety of public infrastructures. Underpinning this project is the reconceptualization of death from a finale to an encore, during which one's physical remains serve a new purpose—both for their loved ones and the public at large.

Constellation Park's multiple pedestrian levels offer numerous spaces to publicly grieve

DAN CHEN
END OF LIFE CARE MACHINE, 2012

As Baby Boomers are beginning to enter elderhood, healthcare systems are quickly requiring more care labourers. End of Life Care Machine is a speculative project that responds to the growing need for elderly care by contemplating how these tasks could be delegated to machines and robots. It questions the capacities of technology to replace human intimacy in the most vulnerable moments, offering a proposal for how robotic technology could be deployed to comfort and care for people who are nearing death. Composed of a padded robotic mechanism that strokes the patient's arm and a customizable recording that offers soothing words, the machine attempts to simulate comfort and care for those without human companionship in their final moments.

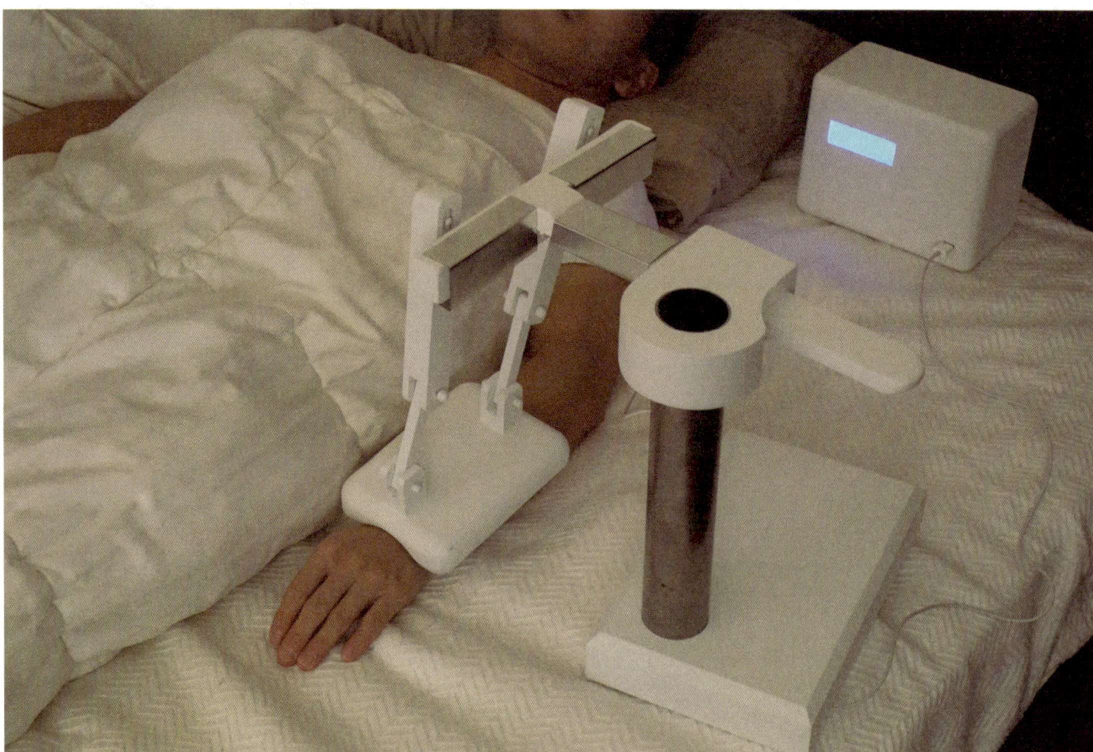

Hello, my friend.

I am the End of Life Care robot.
I have detected that you are at the end of your life,
but please don't worry.
We will ensure that you have the best possible experience.
I am here to help you and guide you through
your last moments on earth.
I am sorry that your family and friends are not able to
be here with you, but don't worry.
I will do my best to comfort you.
You are not alone, you have me by your side.
We hope you will have a pleasant afterlife.
Time of death: 11:45

Goodbye, my friend.

COMMON ACCOUNTS
CLOSER EACH DAY, 2016–2021

Decades of technological progress related to sanitation, disease control, and hygiene have separated the material business of death from everyday life, keeping it largely out of site in the contemporary city across continents and cultures. New technologies, however, present unique opportunities to derive material, ceremonial, social, and ecological value from death, while traditional means of human disposition are threatened by diminishing land availability, environmental

concerns, and the prospect of a digital afterlife. Closer Each Day is a speculative proposal for a network of ceremonial and technological protocols that reintegrate death into the urban environment. The Protocol Drawing depicts prototypes for housing anchored around the virtual afterlife, including memorial gardens fertilized by anatomy-centered chemistry, "transfer cases" that produce micro-ecologies and energetic outputs from human remains, and repositories for the personal effects of the urban dead. In addition to the identification of value, the proposal explores opportunities for public engagement beyond biological expiration, and a symbolic nearness to death that yields a productive civic proximity.

Karla Rothstein

A Space for Voluntary Euthanasia

A Space for Mortal Agency

Veiled Realities:
Though few of us regularly see or acknowledge it, death is intertwined with almost everything else in life. Human civilizations have historically built around and above the remains of their dead. Over time, especially in Western urban contexts, mortality has become increasingly socially and spatially marginalized. As the visible presence of dying and death has receded to distant graves or behind veiled processes, a psychic disconnect has widened, alienating us from a vital facet of our humanity and sense of collective responsibility that consciousness of mortality can offer.

How do subjective perceptions shape our sense of community and place?

Précis:
Cities are living, responsive organisms that reflect and react to the individuals, communities, and societies that inhabit them. Building infrastructures and systems that interact with and scaffold the fundamental needs of society is a powerful tool toward shaping our senses of place, belonging, and interdependence. The environment is ripe for public architectures to engage our shared mortal circumstances and support individual agency and collective responsibility amidst the fragility of existence. Death is integral to life, and places of death and remembrance should intertwine with the ebbs and flows of our days, bringing us together through deeper understandings of humanity and shared purpose.

When were you last with someone actively dying, or in a cemetery?

Re-evaluating norms:
Challenging persistent preconceptions and lingering taboos, social infrastructures can be reconceived to provide new forms of sanctuary. Scales from the urban to the intimate exist simultaneously and can be reframed to support ante- and post-mortem practices. New design ideas can facilitate the coexistence of energetic public life with intimate expressions of bereavement in spaces that synthesize and support spirited everyday joys, critical contemplation, and accommodate personal choice.

Imagining and working toward new possibilities requires belief in the prospect of change. In cities around the globe, the ways in which we live merit urgent and thoughtful reconsideration. Projects with profound social, creative, and political implications will reflect and catalyze a recalibration of values. Through design, public policy, and a critical understanding of past and present realities, we will proactively construct safe, intimate spaces to die, to mourn, and to memorialize the dead, that are guided by our shared humanity, acceptance of mortality, and celebrations of life.

How does architecture facilitate engagement with the scales and complexity of individual human lives and the city?

Dignity is personal:
In the nature of a palimpsests' serial temporality, urban architectures will artfully choreograph the shifting and simultaneity of diverse layers of time, program, and occupancy. Positive messaging shapes social norms, guides change in public behaviour, and engenders empathy. Culturally, the

West has come to frame death more as a health issue to be managed by medical personnel, diminishing the involvement of family and community. Professionalized "death systems" administer and mediate the process for millions of individuals and families every year. But this structure has limits, and standardizing concepts of agency inevitably excludes new understandings.

How much space does a single life occupy? And who decides for how long?

In the 1960s, counter-cultural "death reformers" highlighted concerns about rights and dignity for the dying, reframing dying as an affirming and positive transformational experience. Today's reformers continue to challenge rationalized and medicalized end-of-life systems toward establishing dignity in death and the spatial resources required for gentle transitions, contemplation, and remembrance. Broadly, we must advocate for honest, therapeutic, and even joyful experiences for the dying, their loved ones, and those managing deaths. An explicit ecological perspective has to be incorporated into how and why death practices should change, promoting more humanitarian and environmentally sustainable rituals.

Can we build bridges of agency between new spaces for managed death and new forms of remembrance?

Death is Political:
Our relationship to death is shifting. With increasing sophistication of biomedical devices and treatments comes ambiguity in defining legal, biological, and medical parameters of death. The urgency in advocating for the active management and engagement of one's situation and circumstance in their

death and disposition remains directly connected to respect for human dignity and personal agency. In exploring the spaces and processes of dying, disposition, and grief, we necessarily engage the contested politics of "acceptable" paradigms of dying and evolving definitions of mortality.

In the midst of the COVID-19 global health crisis, it is more evident than ever that we should each be thinking about and articulating end-of-life choices: instigating and participating in personal, national, and global discussions related to the complex realities of our time. Advance Directives should include conversations about life-support scenarios, personal definitions of quality of life, terms of death, disposition preferences, and duration or absence of memorial markers.

The city's relationship with death is being challenged and re-calibrated, to provide new scaffolds for civic-sacred public spaces where a covenant between humanity and the natural cycles of the planet is affirmed, and where death is accepted as an essential and natural part of life.

Which metrics of incapacity and quasi-living constitute a person's death or justify aid-in-dying?

Cultivation of Compassion:
While end-of-life ideologies and debates are not new, public discussions of dying, death, and grief have increased significantly in the past decade. The number of physician-assisted deaths performed around the world has also increased, and preferences around dying and death are discussed more freely and openly. Creating space to facilitate aid-in-dying establishes opportunities for families and friends to engage more intimately with mortal processes while fostering deeper human connections.

Mourners deserve spaces that are both uplifting and address non-binary views on religion and spirituality. Structures for shared experiences and new rituals that are consoling while also resilient enough to interweave the messy realities and complexities of our time must be built.

Can new spaces that support both human fellowship and mortal agency be envisioned?

Progress:
Embracing the coexistence of opposing ideas is crucial and comes from a place of strength and resilience. Caring for a loved one does not require holding on to them, regardless of pain and suffering. Grief often precedes a death. When a loved one is terminally ill or no longer able to meaningfully engage, loss is already palpable.

The idea of emotional closure is a myth. We need spaces and systems of care that support learning to live with the complex and personal realities of dying, death, loss, grief, and remembrance.

Human beings are capable of intentional adaptation. Ecologically positive and socially supportive solutions can respond to the protean needs and values of twenty-first-century urban residents, while enhancing public space and helping to restore intergenerational connections.

As understandings and rituals of death evolve, how are stories shared, transformed, and forgotten?

Title: Upload
Season/Episode: S01E01
Year: 2020
Network: Amazon Prime Video
Country: USA

What would happen if, just before dying, one had the possibility of uploading their consciousness into a sort of digital heaven—a heaven that takes on the form of a luxury resort? That's what Nathan chooses in *Upload*, a series produced by Amazon Prime, a streaming service that has changed the way we consume audiovisual content and perhaps even our digital consciousness. What if we've already all been unknowingly uploaded?

WILLIAMSON WILLIAMSON
GRANGE TRIPLE DOUBLE, 2016

As housing becomes more and more unaffordable, multi-generational living has developed into an unavoidable reality for many families, even in societies in which it is not a traditional mode of dwelling. Grange Triple Double caters to multi-generational living in a multi-unit Toronto residence. Behind the continuous exterior façade lies an interior that is fragmented to create spaces for the various members of an extended family: a unit for a nuclear family sits on top of a unit for an elderly couple, which is adjacent to a third unit that can be used to generate rental income or to one day house adult children before they have children of their own. This spatial layout grants a certain degree of autonomy to the members of each household, while the proximity of the units and the communal spaces located between them create a living arrangement conducive to mutual care: grandparents can easily look after their grandchildren and be cared for by their children when needed.

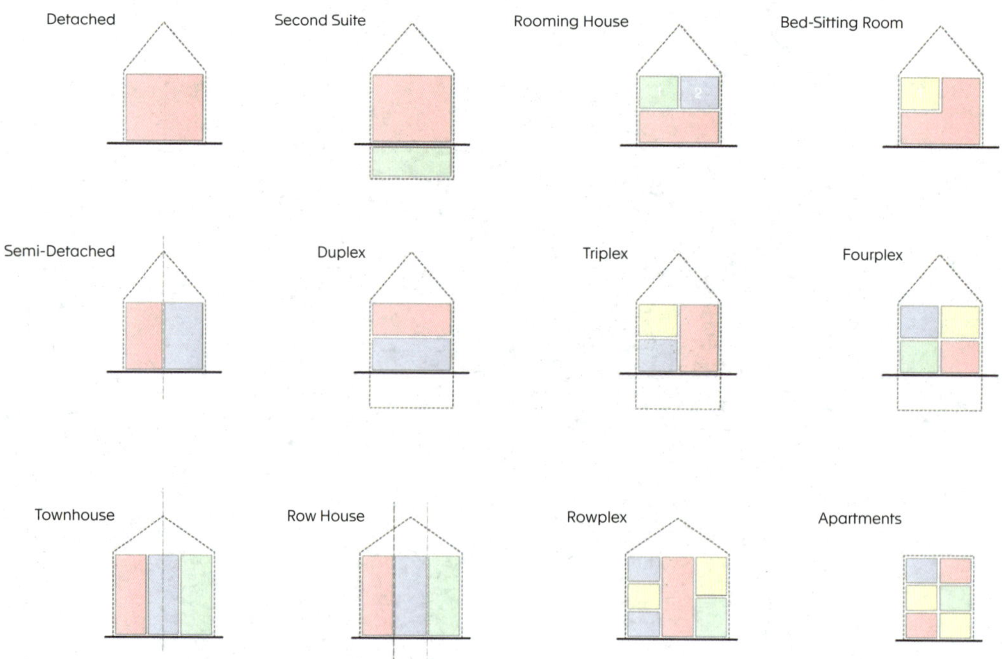

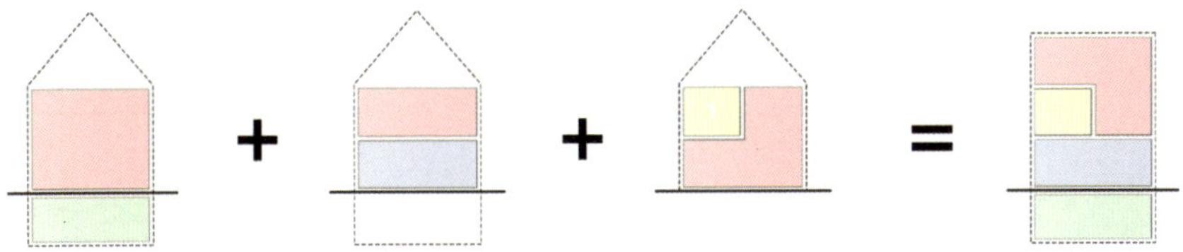

Massing showing family units and rentals stacked on the corner

GO HASEGAWA
HOUSE IN KAWASAKI, 2017

Living with one's parents later in life creates familial dynamics different from those in the normative nuclear family. House in Kawasaki subtly negotiates these dynamics in its housing of a young couple and an elderly parent. Located on a hillside, the house's design incorporates the topography into the building's program to give each of the tenants privacy: a steep incline runs through the house, separating the mother's home from the rest of the building, which is occupied by her daughter and son-in-law. The naturally-derived incline renders the couple's unit difficult to access for the aging parent, enabling a vertical division and creating privacy without the need for enclosing doors.

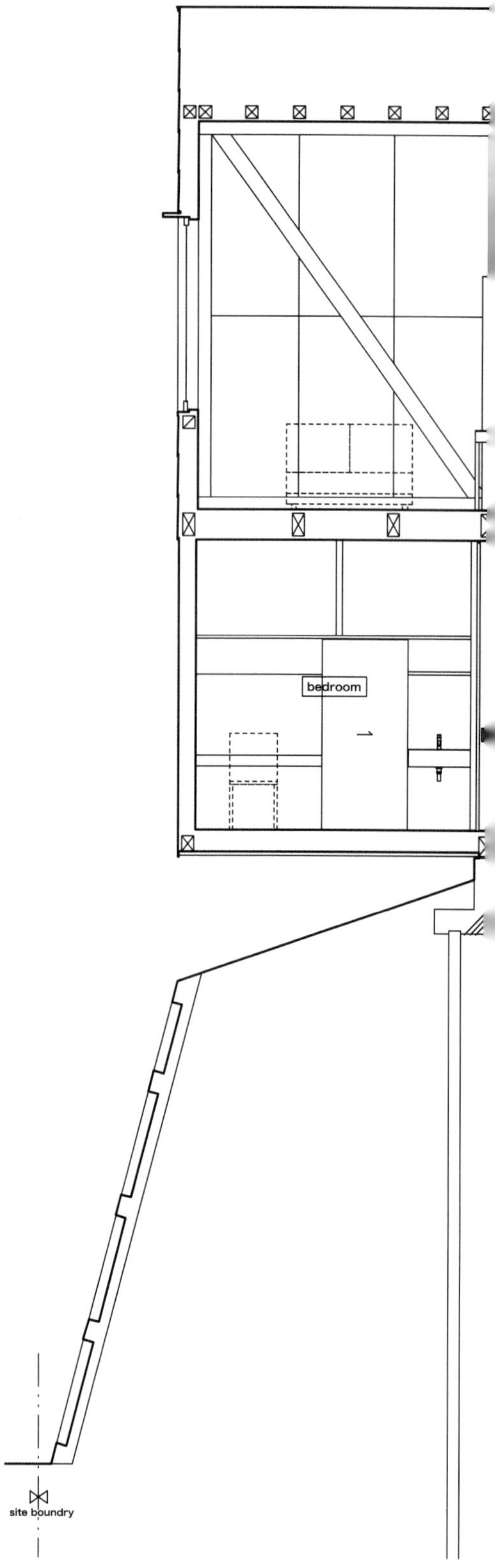

Building section of House in Kawasaki, showing the way the slope naturally separates living spaces

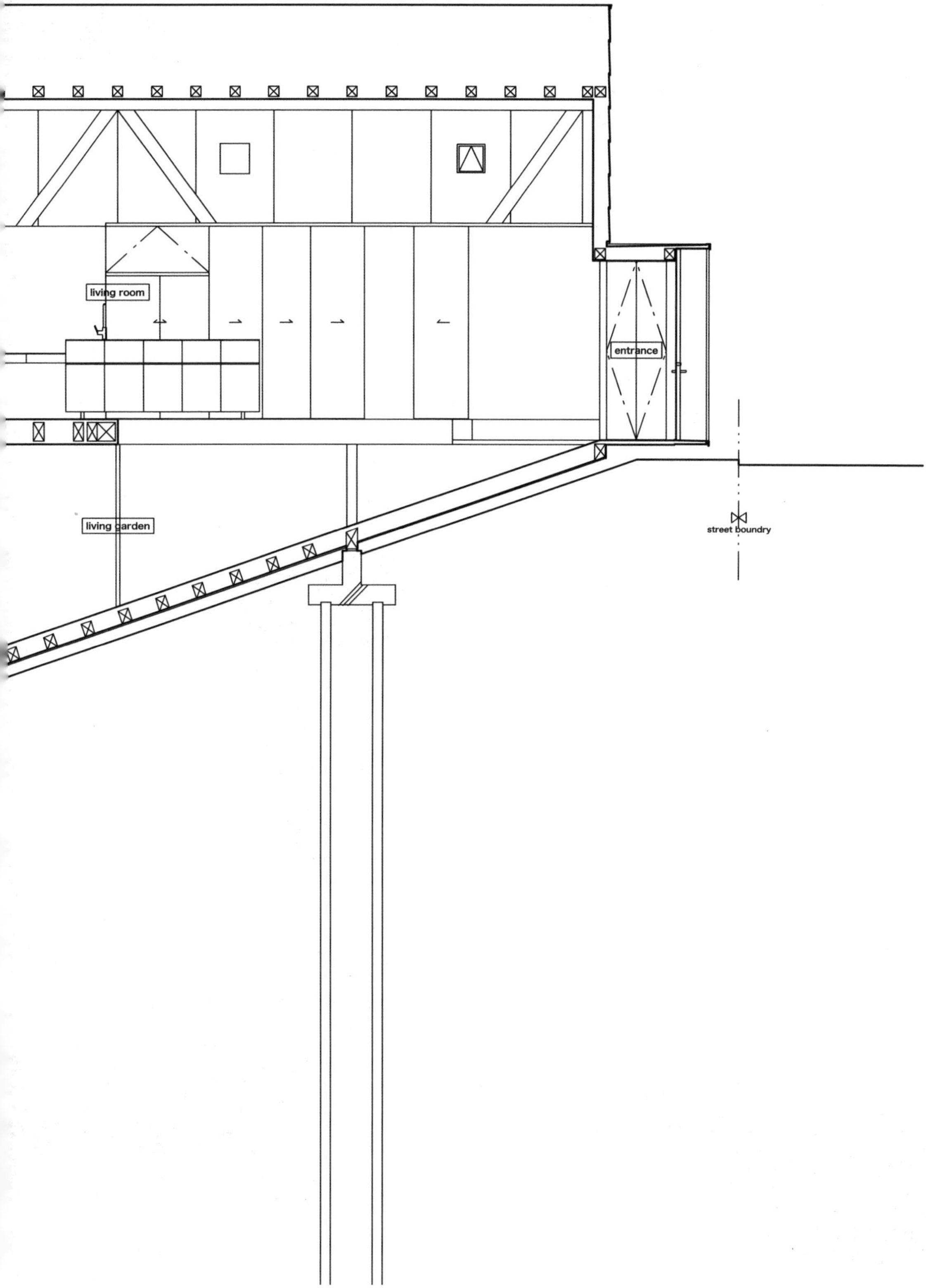
living room
entrance
living garden
street boundry

Elisabeth Ubbe, *Homebirth in Water*, 2020

Elisabeth Ubbe, *Homebirth in Water*, 2020

Elisabeth Ubbe, *Homebirth in Water*, 2020

Fertility clinics provide a multitude of services: testing and screening for early pregnancy, egg viability, hormonal levels, sperm potency, genetic diseases, coinciding for donor services, egg retrieval and storage for young women and for those who want to preserve their eggs before undergoing required treatments that would destroy them. Fertility clinics are transactional spaces—spaces in which money is exchanged for services that affect one's health and life.

While the fertility clinic requires its patrons to potentially commit to years of effort to become pregnant, once pregnancy is "achieved," the reproductive body frequents the clinic for eight weeks, at which point the expecting body no longer visits the clinic and returns to their obstetrician-gynecologist. Fertility clinics require short outpatient treatments, and not inpatient overnight stays. The nature of the clinic is as a space for clients with a high turnover rate, who typically require its services for only a matter of months, as opposed to the lifetimes spent with a family doctor or general practitioner, for instance. It follows that fertility clinics are less focused on creating and maintaining spaces for comfort because their aim is to have protracted relationships with their clientele rather than long-lasting ones. Emphasis is on service over comfort.

Seemingly, when it comes to fertility, the space of service in the clinic is engineered for efficiency so that does not necessarily require its own building or even its own formal type. The word fertility is a descriptive, an adjective qualifying the noun "clinic." Like its title, the fertility clinic exists as a hybrid form, not its own building, not identifiably separate from the set of other types that includes the office and the laboratory. The fertility clinic is frequently identifiable as such through a sign on the building's exterior and through wayfinding on its interior. A patron may arrive through a parking lot and building lobby or through a building lobby and elevator. There is typically a check-in desk with a security guard, as security is an underlying condition through the infertile experience. Most likely there is a bathroom and water fountain in proximity to the entrance. A vending machine with candy and chocolate is part of the as found, as are few tall plants that require little water to survive. Typically, these spaces are bleak and aesthetically somewhere between a hospital operating room, laboratory, and waiting room. Whatever the building's organization, individuals approach it with the expectation that they will be meeting others to assist them in the next steps of their healthcare—with the understanding that they are not alone.

While the idea of achieving fertility has resulted in a contemporary solution in the form of the fertility clinic, fertility is not and has never been about being alone in this singular pursuit. In fact, if fertility is looked at across cultures and throughout history, it is seldom understood as an autonomous subject and not exclusively thought of in relation to human bodies alone. There are innumerable deities dedicated to fertility, and many cultures and religions have more than one dedicated to the subject. In almost all instances, the deities responsible for fertility are also intimately linked to a rather wide range of other subjects and themes: from nature and agriculture to grains and maize, animals, love, life and death, wind and water, chocolate and rainbows, beauty and sexual power, art, healing, knowledge, and wisdom. In other words, fertility is about being connected to the elements and the world, and it is, by nature, connected to something larger and beyond any individual reproductive body. The current trend in fertility treatments, however, displaces all of these things by returning care of the reproductive body to the domestic realm, to the home, and to caring for oneself by oneself in private. As noted in a growing number of news articles, thousands suffer in silence, as society has not been openly accepting of disclosures or discussions of miscarriage and infertility. As fertility treatments increasingly tend not to require a space outside of the home for support, it returns the ill-reproductive body once again to isolation in the privacy of the home. The narrative is reconfigured by withdrawing into seclusion, and a removal from a larger social body. The question about when and where fertility should intersect the public is emerging as a crucial issue of our time.

While the clinic primarily supports the crucial care of individuals looking to have a child, it is also a representation of the respective positions of the healthy- and ill-reproductive bodies within society. The ability to receive treatments and care for infertility is already limitedly available to those who can afford the time and money necessary to alter their condition with the hopes of becoming pregnant and birthing a child. This presents a great challenge to the type as it is inclusive to some and exclusive to others. This fact makes the clinic a problematic type as it does not offer itself as a space to everyone. The question of whether there should even be a clinic dedicated to this issue is one to be considered. By propagating the clinic, is the implication that only those with privilege—with time and money—are worthy of fertility treatments, and sinisterly those worthy of reproducing? Based on how society builds and uses the fertility clinic, it seems so.

Why does there need to be a dedicated independent building or physical space outside of a hospital setting for fertility treatments? Why does the fertility clinic too often exist as a silo or seem to exist this way in the United States, despite regulatory agencies such as the Centers for Disease Control, Food and Drug Administration, and the Centers for Medicare and Medicaid Services all in place to review? The United Kingdom offers the best available practices for regulation. And why would the only other solution be to receive

these treatments at home? The answer to all these questions is, in part, because society continues to operate under outmoded adage that women "suffer in silence," which has turned into the contemporary understanding that suffering reproductive bodies should therefore, too, suffer in silence. The absorption of the fertility clinic into another larger infrastructure would, in theory, require less maintenance costs and offer services that reflect the needs of its users, from help with mental health concerns of depression to anxiety to dealing with the physical stress of treatments. This formulation serves to make treatments available to a wider group of people, and would reinforce a sense of societal belonging among people receiving treatments. This model would also create an opportunity to support the entire development of the pregnancy, including what quickly comes after birth, when one is typically left on their own to raise a child—at least in America. What would this setting look like? Being further absorbed into a complex, corporate, sterile setting would presumably not reduce stress or risk of illnesses such as COVID-19. That said, a retreat from the clinic to the home as the only other alternative space for care privileges few instead of many. Though it is difficult to argue against wanting to face a crisis and private matters within the comfort of one's home, the lack of interaction with untrained professionals and with other patients is a lost opportunity for both receiving compassion and sharing knowledge. How can there be equity in care from the very beginning of life? The paradox is that when fertility treatments are undertaken within the space of an institution, they affect the domestic. Even with the move to in-home testing and monitoring of some aspects of fertility, examinations by a medical professional still need to occur so that it seems as though a complete separation of treatment from the medical institution is not fully possible.
A reimagining of the fertility clinic begins by creating a new connection between mental and physical spaces, between domestic spaces and medical institutions, and between home and clinic.

JUNE14 MEYER-GROHBRÜGGE & CHERMAYEFF
TRIANGULAR BED, 2014–2015

As normative notions of family and cohabitation change, the shapes, dimensions, and proportions of domestic furniture become increasingly worthy of reconsideration. Irregularly shaped and large in size, the Triangular Bed encourages sleeping arrangements that are not considered conventional. The bed allows for collective and individual activities to take place on it simultaneously—whether it be sleeping, cuddling, reading, or working. Up to four people can use the bed, be they a polyamorous couple, a full nuclear family, a group of friends, or any other number of arrangements. The bed's triangular shape notably changes the usual relationship between bed and bedroom furniture, and creates different spaces within the room in which it is placed than a typical rectangular bed would. The Triangular Bed represents how expanded definitions of love, family, and intimacy might be designed for in the domestic realm.

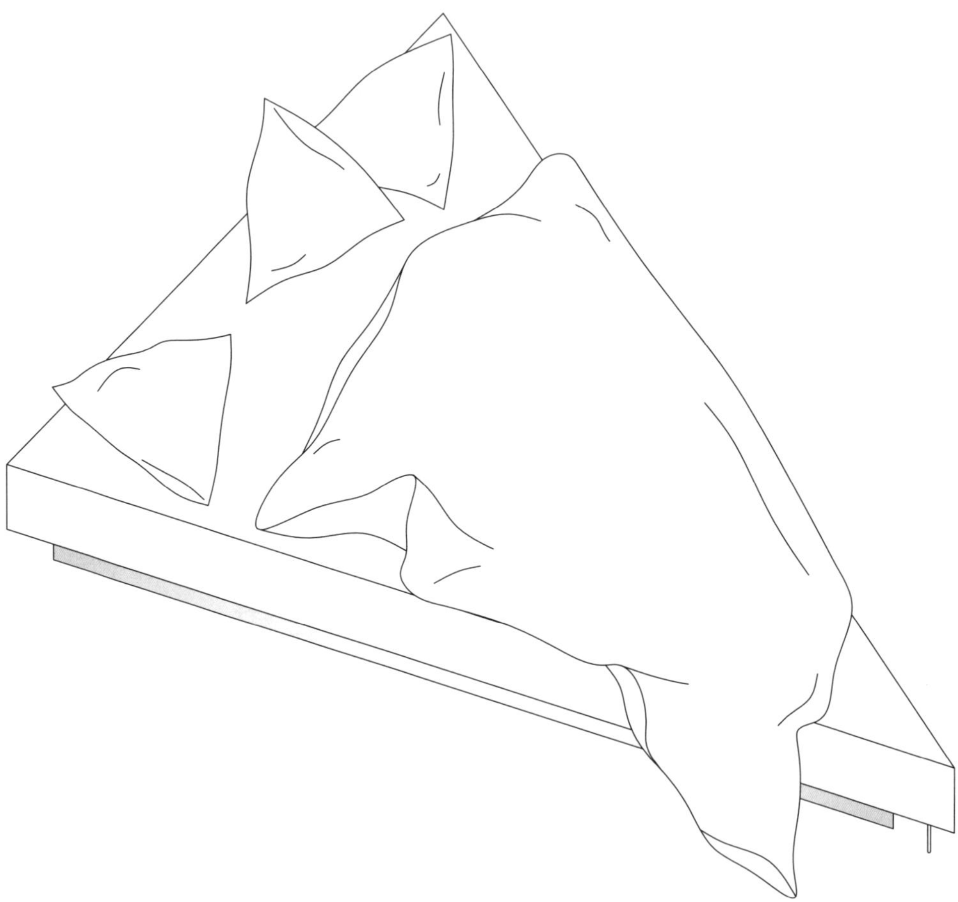

AI HASEGAWA
SHARED BABY, 2011–2019

Technological innovations continue to destabilize traditional notions of what constitutes a family. Shared Baby is a conceptual project that considers the possibilities of in vitro gametogenesis, a recent innovation that allows numerous embryos to be grown from minimal genetic material. The technique uses genome editing to allow the combination of genetic material for any desired number of donors in an embryo, meaning that it creates the possibility of having more than two biological parents. Shared Baby speculates on the social realities of this method and explores a parenting model that is analogous to the sharing economy—in which homes, cars, and other material goods are readily shared—in order to imagine what it would look like to share the responsibilities of raising and caring for children.

Title: The L Word
Season/Episode: S01E01
Year: 2004
Network: Showtime
Country: USA

The L Word is the first television series with an ensemble lesbian, bisexual, and transgender cast to be aired by an American broadcaster. The title refers to how the word "lesbian" had been relegated to the realm of the unmentionable, but the series reframes the word as a point of pride and as a means of belonging to a community. The show paved the way to present narratives about different forms of families on mainstream television, but was itself the product of the normalizing aesthetic of the early 2000s, which was conceived of for the male gaze (the show's protagonists are sex symbols), and its setting is in upper-class liberal spaces, with its specfic professions and cultural obsessions.

KAMILA RUDNICKA
WAY SELF-INSEMINATION KIT, 2019

With new forms of family now gaining visibility and people entering parenthood outside of heteronormative relationships, there is a growing demand for accessible and affordable fertility treatments. The Way self-insemination kit, which doubles as a sex toy, is designed for at-home intrauterine insemination—infusing pleasure into a typically clinical process. Specifically positioned as an intermediary method to try before committing to more costly and physically taxing procedures such as in vitro fertilization, the self-insemination kit allows those who wish to become pregnant and who have access to sperm with a means of incorporating pleasure into their insemination, outside of a clinical setting.

As online personas are imbued with more and more information—provided both by individuals and by technologies that track online behaviours—humans have become collections of objective data points. DigiD8 is a dating application that utilizes an algorithm to match users with one another not based on their online habits, but on their genetic compatibility. The company positions itself as allowing for "health-informed life planning" by screening potential partners for genetic mutations that could result in passing on genetic diseases to future offspring. The application raises questions about who gets to determine what diseases should not be passed on to future generations, and to what extent society is willing to let algorithms determine the future.

Eradicate barriers to health-informed life planning

digid8.com

Does your family fit into the standard single-family home? When was the last time you received a hug?

Elena Dorfman, *Still Lovers, Valentine 3*, 2002

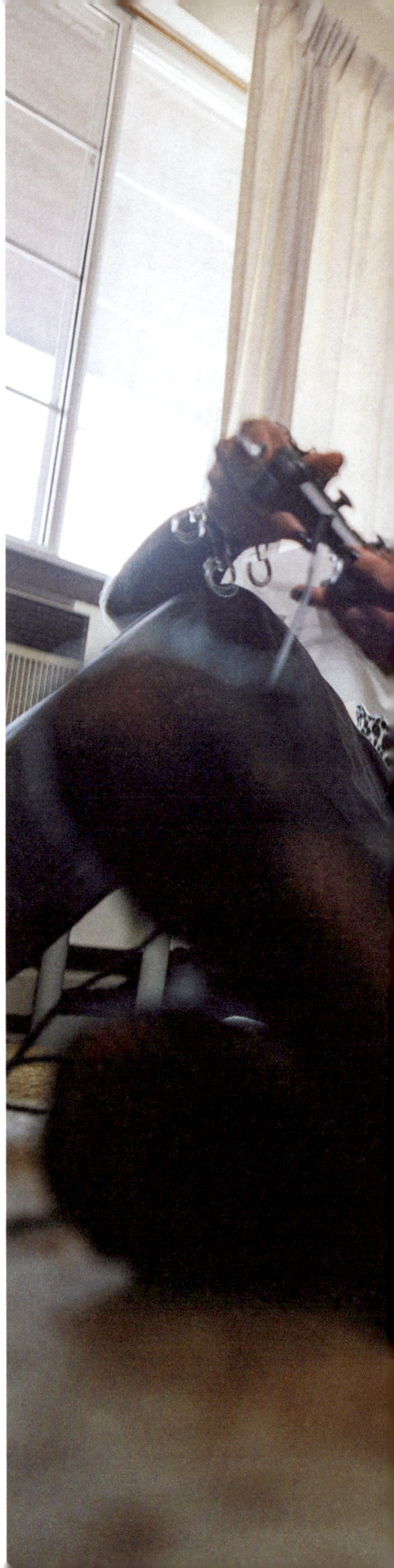

Elena Dorfman, *Still Lovers, Sidore 4*, 2001

FOR LIFE

Elena Dorfman, *Still Lovers, Galatea 4*, 2002

Title: Fleabag
Season/Episode: S01E01
Year: 2016
Network: BBC Three
Country: UK

Fleabag was adapted for television from a play by the show's writer and leading actor, Phoebe Waller-Bridge. With her simultaneously fragile and strong persona, Waller-Bridge has become an icon for a generation of single women. The show follows a soured version of Bridget Jones who is sarcastic and perfectly at ease with not feeling at ease about sex, love, her body, partners, family, and work. With the maturity and attitude of today's thirty-somethings (and perhaps even those who are slightly older) the show depicts the existential crisis faced by an entire generation and in doing so serves as a collective therapy session.

TAKAHASHI IPPEI
APARTMENT HOUSE IN TOKYO, 2016–2018

The twenty-first century has seen a global increase in people living alone, and the desires for living spaces have become more and more individual and specific. Apartment House in Tokyo indulges these new desires by creating distinct and highly personalized individual spaces. The house includes eight unique dwellings, each of which predominantly provide a specific function: a house for bathing, a house for working, and a house for cooking, among others. The traditional domestic space that included a full suite of functions has been subverted such that each mono-functional dwelling only exists for its resident at specific moments and for specific uses. Rather than going without the other functions typically provided in the domestic space, residents must use the city's infrastructures—restaurants, bath houses, etc.—giving those who live alone encouragement to leave the privacy of their homes and seek social interactions in the urban sphere.

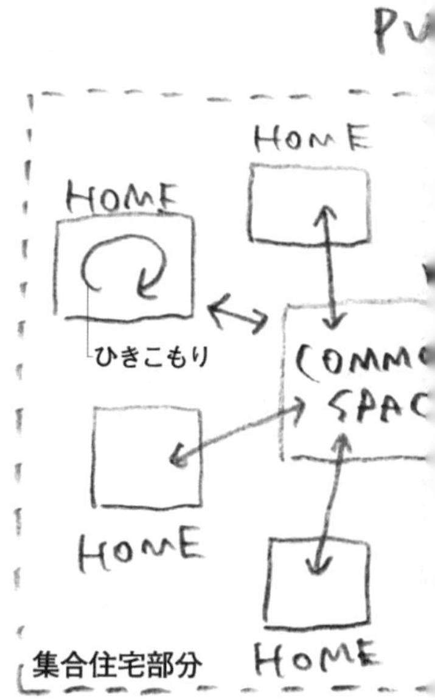

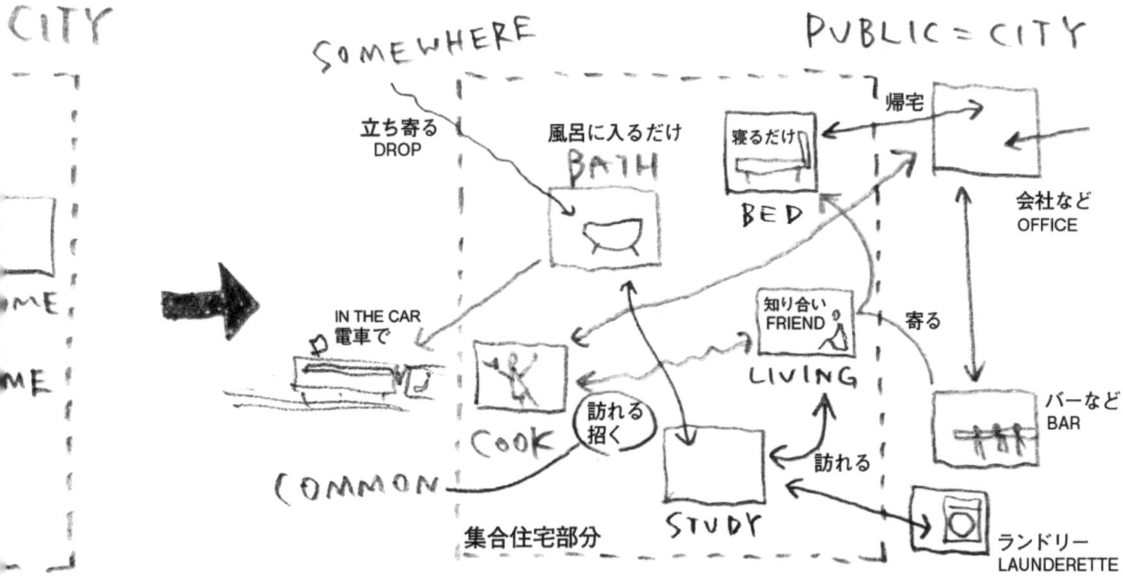
CITY
SOMEWHERE
PUBLIC = CITY
帰宅
立ち寄る
DROP
風呂に入るだけ
BATH
寝るだけ
BED
会社など
OFFICE
IN THE CAR
電車で
知り合い
FRIEND
寄る
LIVING
COOK
訪れる
招く
バーなど
BAR
訪れる
COMMON
STUDY
集合住宅部分
ランドリー
LAUNDERETTE

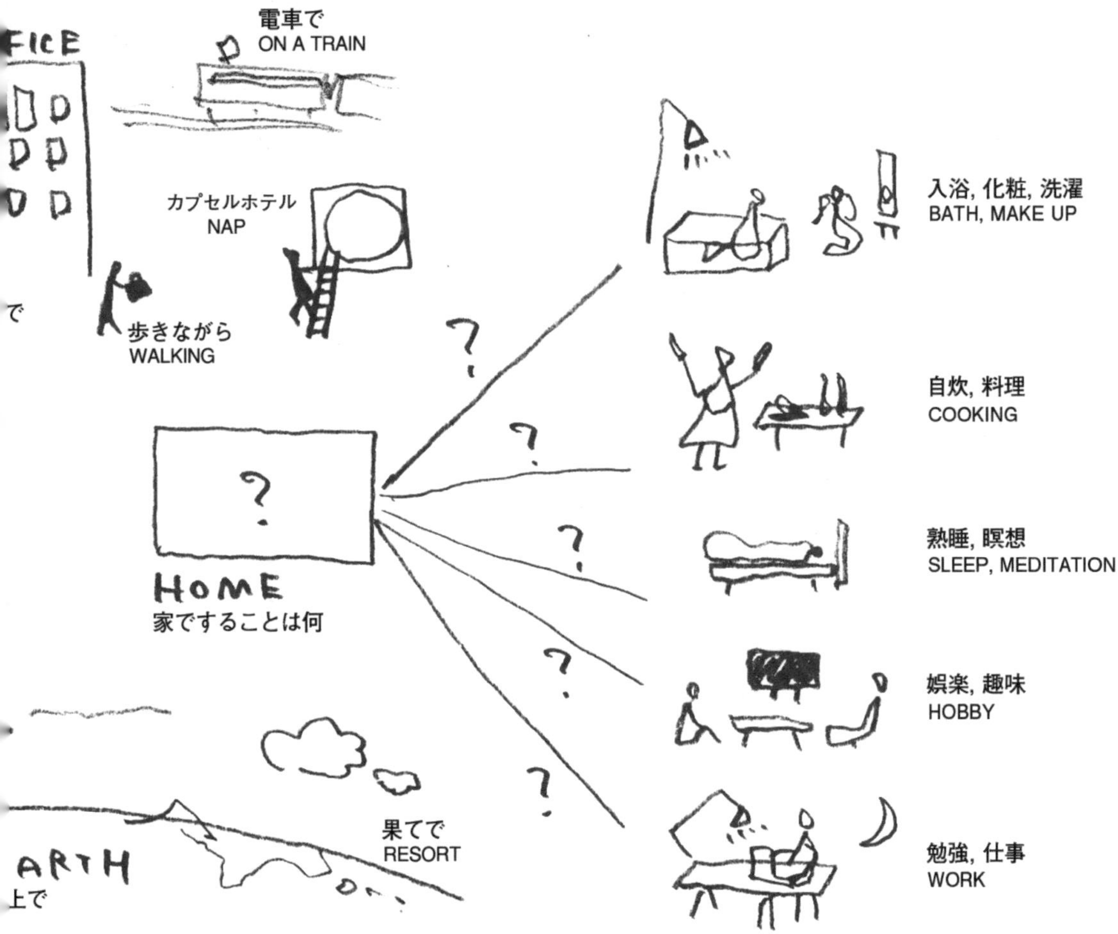
電車で
ON A TRAIN
カプセルホテル
NAP
歩きながら
WALKING
入浴, 化粧, 洗濯
BATH, MAKE UP
自炊, 料理
COOKING
HOME
家ですることは何
熟睡, 瞑想
SLEEP, MEDITATION
娯楽, 趣味
HOBBY
果てで
RESORT
勉強, 仕事
WORK
ARTH
上で

Collage in plan and section to illustrate the particular use of each space

KITCHEN TYPE
LIVING TYPE

Big spoon

Jamie Diamond, *Skin Hunger, Cuddle Party*, 2019

Receiving
For you/me
What you WANT
putting self 1st AND
respecting the givers limits
Doing OR Done to
will you...?
may I...?
REQUEST
Thank You!

Jamie Diamond, *Skin Hunger, Receiving and Giving*, 2019

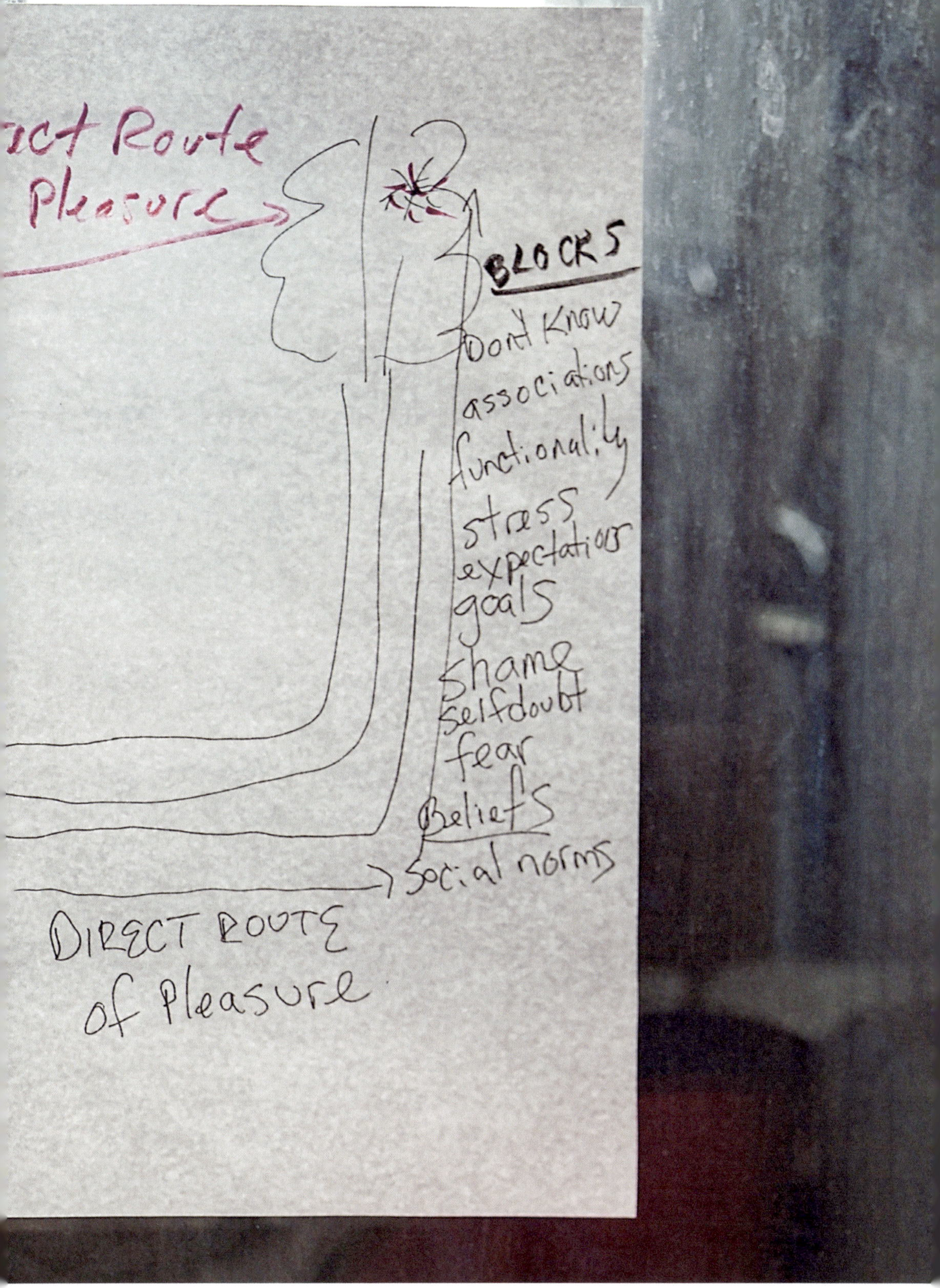

 Jamie Diamond, *Skin Hunger, Route to Pleasure*, 2019

LUCY MCRAE
COMPRESSION CARPET, 2019

As loneliness becomes increasingly pervasive in contemporary society, Compression Carpet positions the body as a site for intervention to remedy feelings of isolation, offering mechanical touch in place of a human hug. The machine is conceived to be operated by two people, one of whom gets wrapped in plush cushions reminiscent of various flesh tones, while the other turns a handle to increase the tightness of the machine's embrace. As human interactions take place more and more in the digital realm and physical selves become siloed off, Compression Carpet provides necessary feelings of intimacy, touch, and affection.

Photograph: Scottie Cameron

Title: One Day at a Time
Season/Episode: S01E01
Year: 2017
Network: Netflix
Country: United States

One Day at a Time is Netflix's remake of the very successful sitcom by the same name, which originally aired in the late 1970s and early 1980s. In keeping with the tried and true model of depicting contemporary forms of families on air, the 1970s show's protagonist is an Italian-American divorcée raising a teenage daughter and facing everyday problems with good cheer. Netflix's remake updates the synopsis to address issues of assimilation and cover current geopolitical horizons. In the remake, the protagonist, Penelope Alvarez, is an Army Nurse Corps veteran who lives with her Cuban mother and her

second-generation American children. Alvarez's family is multi-cultural and intergenerational, and these characteristics are the cause for all sorts of familial conflicts and confrontations that take place around the family room sofa.

KENT KIRKLAND AND MONICA MCGRATH
DUPLEX WITH "TRANSPORTER," 2011

In Canada, more than one third of separated or divorced adults share custody of their children. Not only does shared custody involve several logistical and economic challenges for guardians, but it can also be stressful for children who must frequently move between homes as per custody agreements. Nesting, or the post-separation living arrangement in which children reside in a single dwelling while guardians take turns living with them, offers a way to alleviate the burden caused by continual movement. This post-divorce duplex in Edmonton is purpose-built for a nesting arrangement: each guardian has an entirely separate unit, other than a shared hallway nicknamed "the transporter," where both of their children's rooms are located. There is a lockable door at each end of the hallway, each of which leads to a different unit. Every week, the children switch the door that they use to access domestic functions beyond the bedroom, leading them to a different parent's unit, while the other door remains locked.

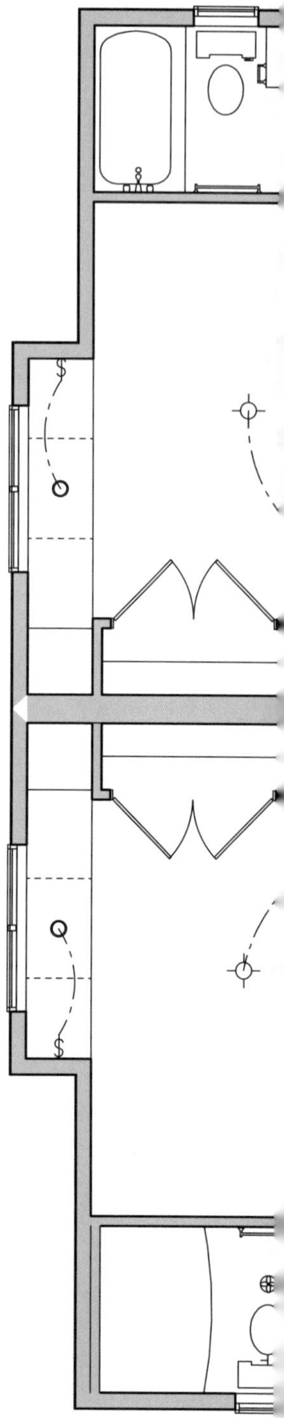

A central wall separates the residences of a divorced couple, while a "transporter" hallway allows their children to travel easily between the two separate homes

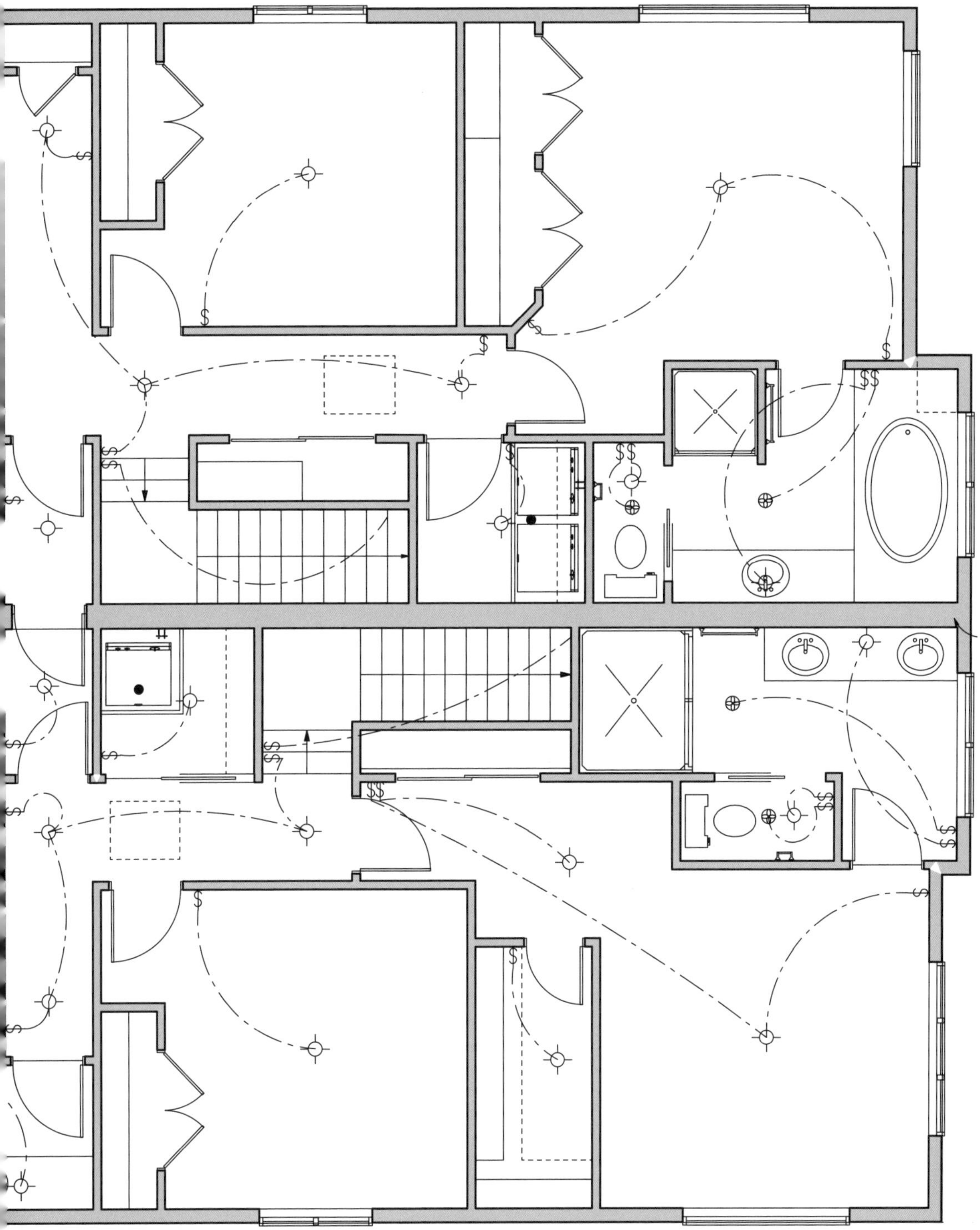

The rise of online dating websites and application that allow individuals to find partners with whom to share romantic relationships has inspired a new form of online service, one which facilitates intergenerational companionship and affordable housing. Nesterly, a website that pairs seniors who have spare rooms in their homes with college students looking for affordable housing options, introduces people to live with one another in intergenerational households. While those brought together by the app may in fact develop intergenerational friendships with one another, most app users are likely to remain in a contractual—albeit mutually beneficial—relationship.

YANGYING YE
HAPPILY EVER AFTER, 2019

Polyamory, open relationships, and individuals who intentionally remain single are all part of new romantic realities that challenge monogamy as a social norm, yet broad acceptance and the design of the built environment lag behind in their inclusion of this diversified scope of love. Happily Ever After embraces the many forms of romantic relationships that go beyond monogamy and marriage. Encouraging players to test a variety of romantic trajectories, the game was conceived of to question the default thinking around relationships and to design new forms of intimacy. Players must earn as many heart-shaped love points as possible throughout the game in order to achieve the "highest happiness level." As such, they may find themselves in yet another self-optimizing capitalist practice, not unlike Monopoly. Rather than challenging society's overarching paradigm, the game reframes economic maximization to the maximization of happiness, which has ramifications in even the most intimate of relationships.

ANAIS LANGLAIS-SCHMIDT
TRAUMHAUS ROYAL, 2021

Though the structure of the nuclear family is quickly ceasing to be the norm, much of the existing housing stock was designed to be occupied by such families. A group of young professionals purchased a semi-detached house, originally built with this family structure in mind, to accommodate nine adults, one toddler, and the constellation of relationships between them. From the basement to the attic, each of the house's spaces have been reconceptualized to host the variety of intimate and professional relationships within this close group of friends. Though all of the walls are left intact and no new walls were erected, a simple redefinition of spaces and a negotiation of domestic, social, and romantic roles renders this single-family home a testing ground for a new way to define and live as a family.

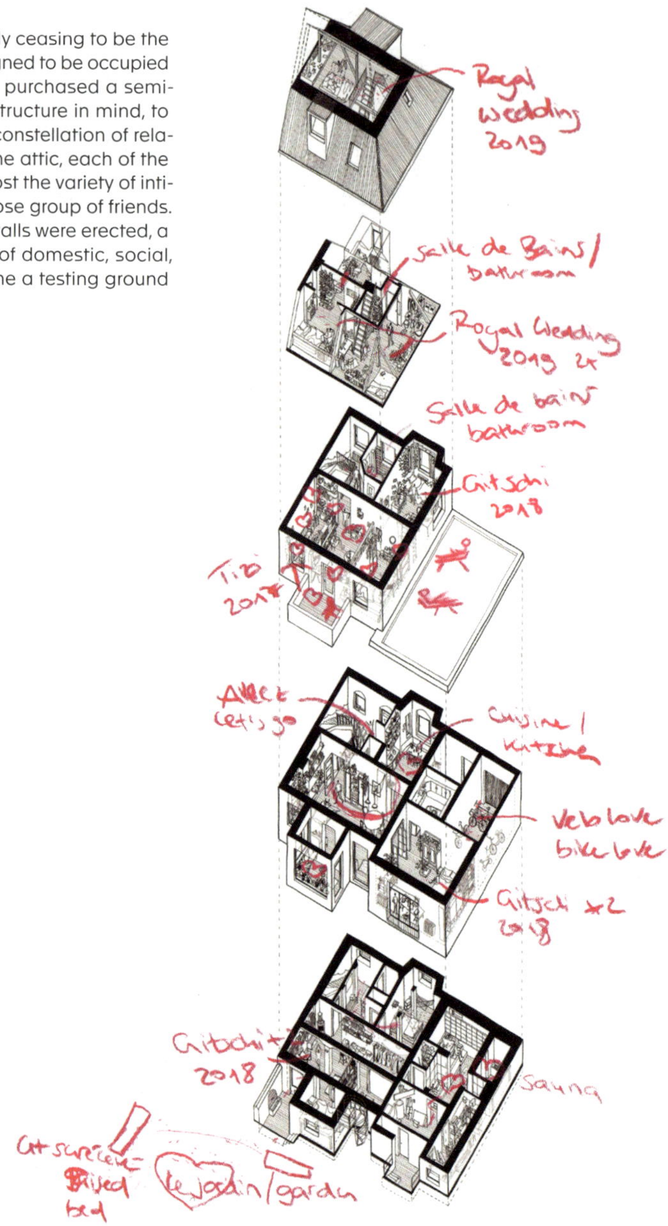

Left: Function of each room
Centre: Personal use of each room
Right: Personal association of each room

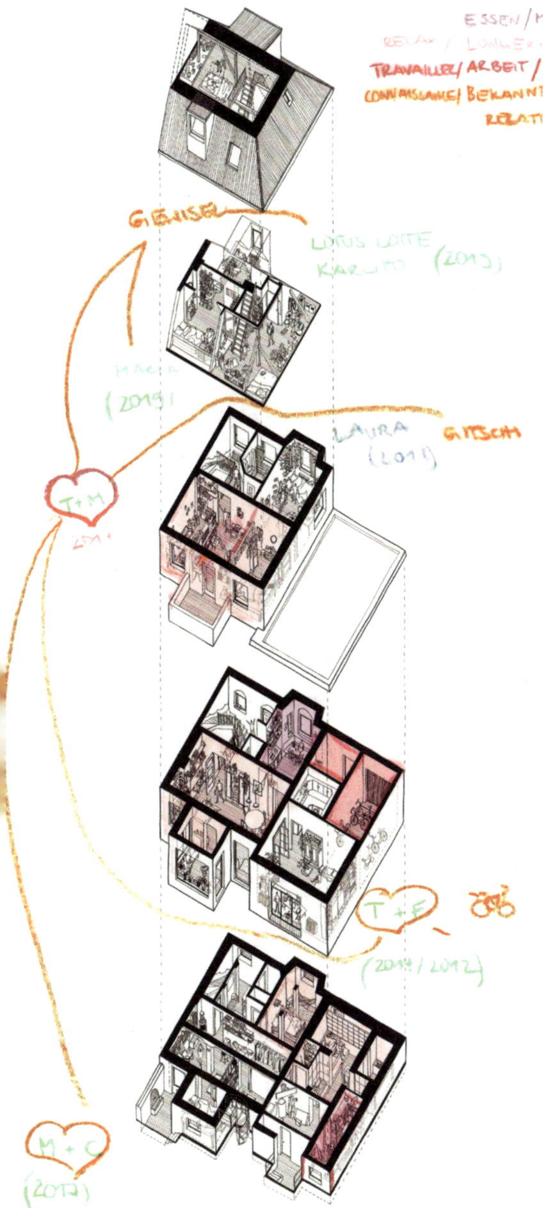
ESSEN/
TRAVAILLER/ ARBEIT/
CONNAISSANCE/ BEKANNT
LAURA
(2011)
T+M
T+F
(2014/2012)
M+C
(2017)

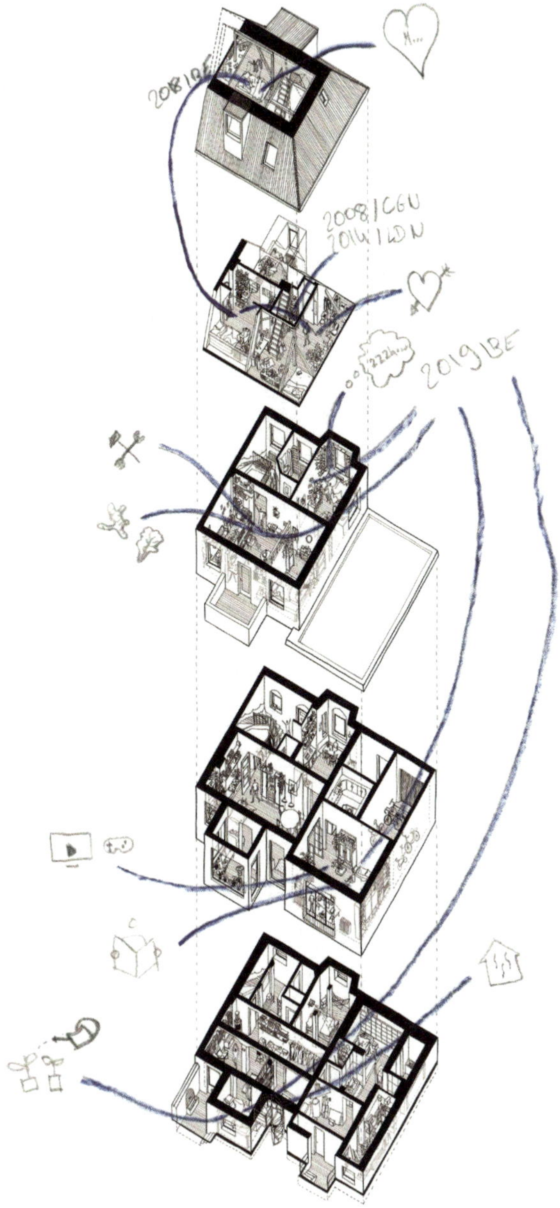
2018/BE
2008/CGU
2014/LDN
2019/BE

What comes first: the home or the family? Does the home serve our idea of the family? Or is our idea of family simply a function of the way in which homes are designed and built?

The design of the typical family home is most often derived from a generic template driven by market interests. It makes many assumptions about the nature of the "family" that it might contain. Living rooms, kitchens, smaller bedrooms, and a single master bedroom—a name that is in and of itself enough to forewarn us that its idea of family is a very particular one, one that reinforces a patriarchal structure by means of the language of real estate listings. The formula that is used to create this kind of home is shared and transmitted like meme, as if it were a naturally occurring fact of life. Those involved in large-scale housebuilding—including architects—act as if they have little agency in its authorship and as though they are instead obliged to ritualistically recite its logics. They behave as if "architecture" is simply the physical container for a fixed idea of family, rather than recognizing that the real design project is the family itself.

The typical family home arranges a set of spaces as a series of thresholds: the spaces with more public functions are usually found on the ground floor and the more private ones are found upstairs, where the bedrooms are arranged such that the master bedroom has the most privacy of all—possibly with an en suite bathroom of its own. This quasi-ceremonial sequence positions the marital bed as a sacred space, offspring as being overseen within its own cells, and the ground level as a semi-public agora that mediates between the family and the street beyond.

The subtext of the family home can be read in its particular arrangements of sex, love, and power—arrangements that are often motivated by shame and control. This is made clear by how frequently the design of the home is employed as a moralizing device, imposed from above to "improve" the behaviours of its inhabitants.

This generic solution, first developed in the West as a derivation of historical forms of living arrangements and codified at various historical moments (including but not only in Georgian and Victorian homes, early twentieth-century suburbs, postwar developments, and mass-housing projects built from the 1980s onwards), has become a global template, exported first through colonial forces and later through the hegemony of global banking. In other words, this typical house has its own family tree, and its branching off often coincides with societal changes: the rise of a middle class, technological innovation, the introduction of social welfare, and models of development economics, for instance. But just because the form has a lineage does not necessarily mean that it is in any way functional. The home (in this generic form) imposes its bastardized and ideological pattern onto the reality of what a family might actually be—part of the solution might even involve putting the generic home on a couch and asking it about its mother.

The generic home's idea of the family is singular, more specifically, it's nuclear: the model of a Western married heterosexual couple with two kids. The possibility of a family is, however, far more diverse and fluid than this retrograde model. It may or may not include a couple, a thrupple, or a single parent; it may or may not include children, the number of whom may or may not remain constant from day to day; it may or may not include the parents of parents or the children of children for reasons of culture or care.

If we were to frame the question of the home as an architectural one (rather than say, an economic one, which is of course related to the notion of the home as often being conceived of as a financial instrument rather than a spatial or functional entity), and if we were to frame the question optimistically, i.e. operating under the assumption that the generic model of the home can escape its own orbit, then, perhaps, answering the question of the home would require an understanding of the spatiality of the family itself. How can a home manage all of the intimate thresholds between bodies, love and sex, care, and togetherness and apartness? How can the fixed material of architecture accommodate change over time, whether changes occur day to day or over the course of lifetimes? Custody arrangements, hookups, breakups, ageing, and other familial narratives require accommodations that allow them to unfold within the framework of the home.

What might domestic thresholds look like if they negotiated a wider spectrum of relationships and conditions? While working through this question may mean breaking apart the fixed notions of domestic spatial units of halls, corridors, and bedrooms, the abolition of spatial difference in, say, the conception of the open plan can reliably resolve these issues. Following this abolition, we will have to engage with questions of bodies and civility, as well as the many possibilities of sex—possibilities that may or may not include long-term partners, naked strangers, and teenage experimentation. Sex may indeed prove to be the ultimate problem of the family home.

We cannot assume that the history and culture of the home is irrelevant. After all, there are many models of domesticity that precede this generic home that might prove useful (or at least suggestive) in rethinking it—even those that this current model has borrowed from directly. History can be radically inspiring, even if only because it reveals other worlds that are (or were once) possible.[1]

The home is architecture in its most revealed form, exposed as a project at the fault line between intimacy, fantasy, dreams, and fear on the one side and collectivity, society, and politics on the other. Resolving the question of the contemporary home should first require understanding the spatiality of the modern family and its various component bodies in space, and their shifting roles and relationships over time. Architecture's role in making the spaces of contemporary domesticity might also mean confronting its own house. That is to say, we must recognize that architecture is not a neutral, benign, or objective problem-solving activity. Architecture is a product of the same history that produced the typical family home in question. Perhaps any attempt to design a home for contemporary domesticity should first interrogate its own internal organization of issues of power, gender, and sex before it sets out any plans for the home.

1 Note here, for example that even something as fundamentally and apparently self-evident as the bedroom is a relatively modern invention.

Title: The New Normal
Season/Episode: S01E01
Year: 2012
Network: NBC
Country: USA

With their series *The New Normal*, Ryan Murphy and Ali Adler have radically and critically reconsidered the entire relational imaginary of the American sitcom—from its high schools (such as those seen in *Popular* and *Glee*) to its nuclear family (as in *American Horror Story*). The new normal in the show is that of a homosexual couple who, looking to start a family, ask a young woman who gave birth to her own daughter as a teenager (and who herself has a conservative mother) to act as a surrogate mother. The show is a stinging and ironic response to the politically correct portrayals of new families in recent series such as *Modern Family*.

CHRISTOPH WAGNER
LOVO LEBENSORT, 2019

Though some societies are gradually becoming more accepting of people with non-normative gender identities and sexual preferences, many continue to be discriminated against by housing providers. Lovo Lebensort is a housing project located in central Berlin and run by the Schwulenberatung counselling service that provides housing for individuals of all ages and socioeconomic statuses who identify as queer. Rather than shared apartments, the project is organized by shared floors that each have private rooms and a number of communal spaces. The building also includes an apartment that houses seven elderly individuals, and three maisonettes that are rented out at market rates and that subsidize the rental costs of other units. The building's design reflects the intention to integrate the individuals it houses into the neighbourhood, while still catering to their individual needs.

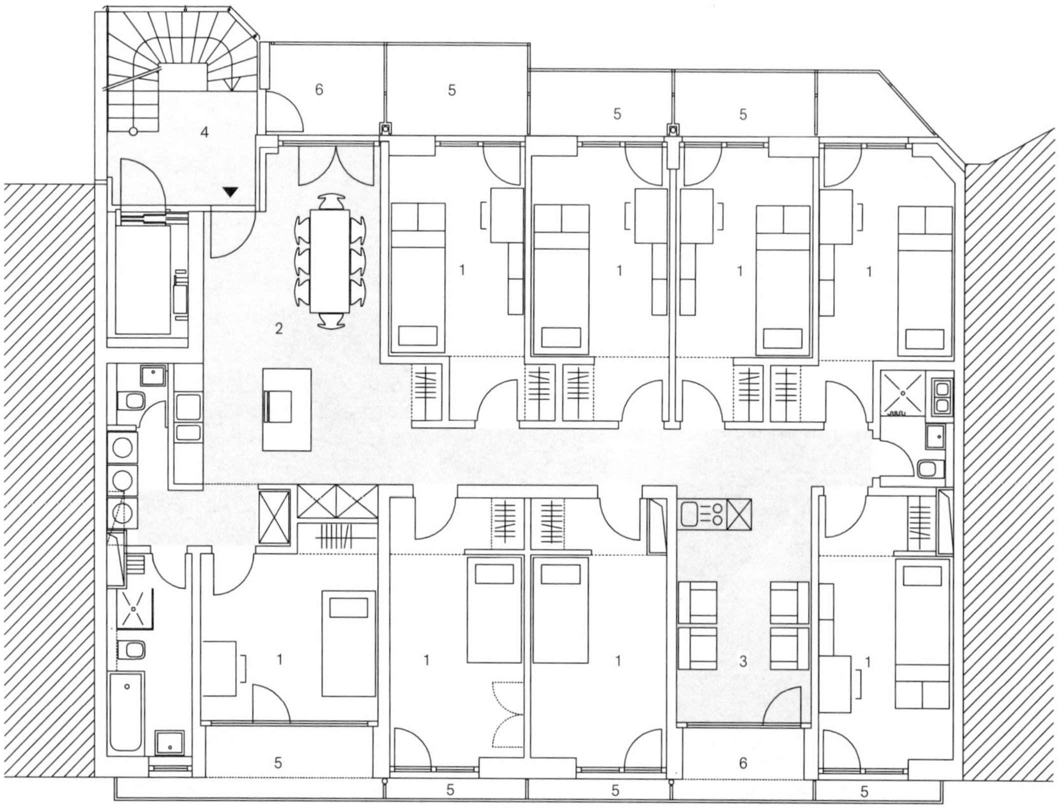

1 apartment
2 common kitchen
3 lounge
4 open staircase
5 private balcony
6 common balcony

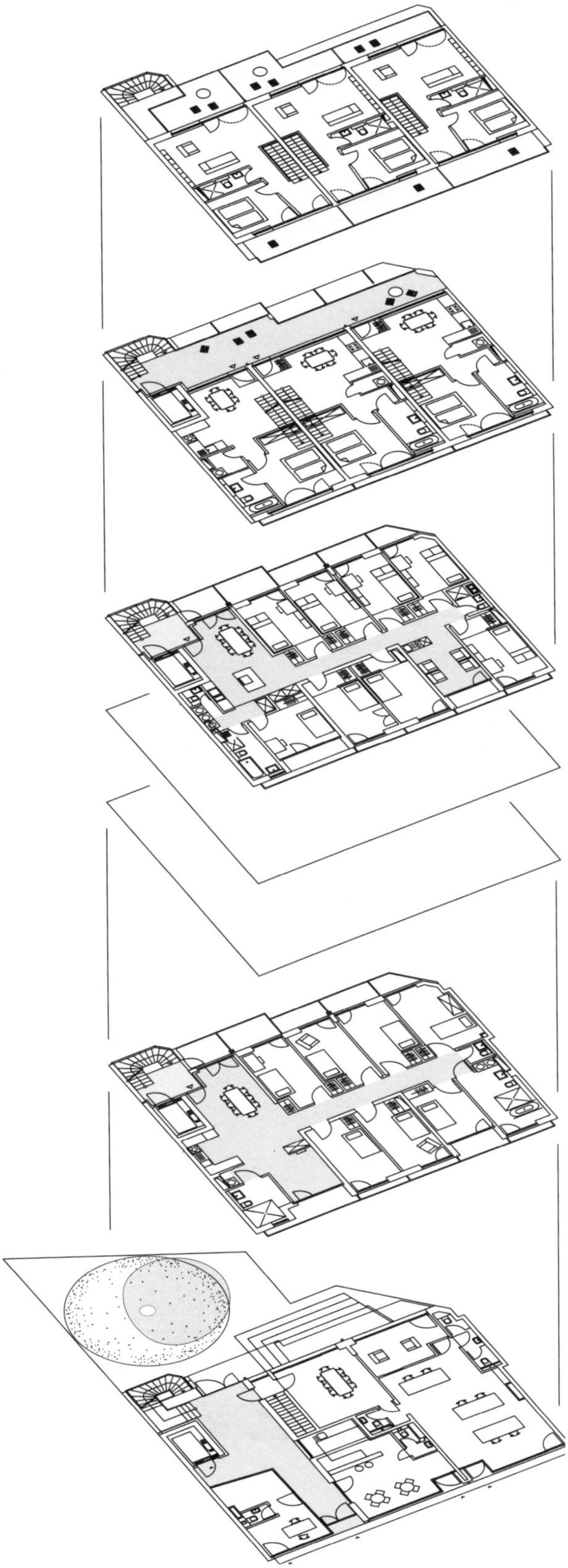

07 3 maisonette apartments for 2–3 locals

06

05 3 shared apartments for 8 refugees + students

04
1 common kitchen
2 lounge/living space
3 bathroom toilet
4 access balcony "laubengang"

03

02 nursing apartment for 7 elderly people in need of care

01 common space

5 office and help desk
6 info-cafe
7 steps to lower courtyard
8 common garden and playground
9 commercial space

EXPANDED DESIGN
WUNSCHMASCHINE WOHNANLAGE,
2014–2016

As land prices in urban areas remain at an all-time high, many architects are urgently considering ways to densify cities. Wunschmaschine Wohnanlage imagines a densification and diversification strategy for Vienna's modernist social housing stock. The project dismantles the spatial rigidity of these estates by introducing flexible spaces called *Typ X* that accommodate the changing and fluid spatial needs of households. These spaces can be rented on long-term or short-term bases and as extensions to individual apartments—accommodating aging parents, new partners, long-term guests, or work needs. This adaptability aims to create housing in an inner-city neighbourhood that caters to more diverse types of households and living arrangements.

TYP A — 1 room apartment, 34.4 m^2
TYP C — 3 room apartment, 73.5 m^2
TYP X — 1 room apartment, 20.0 m^2
TYP G — 1 room apartment, 43.0 m^2
TYP B — 2 room apartment, 54.8 m^2

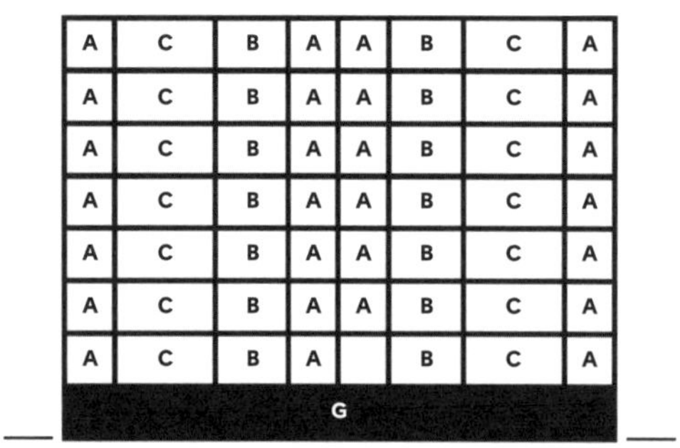

☐ Private
■ Communal

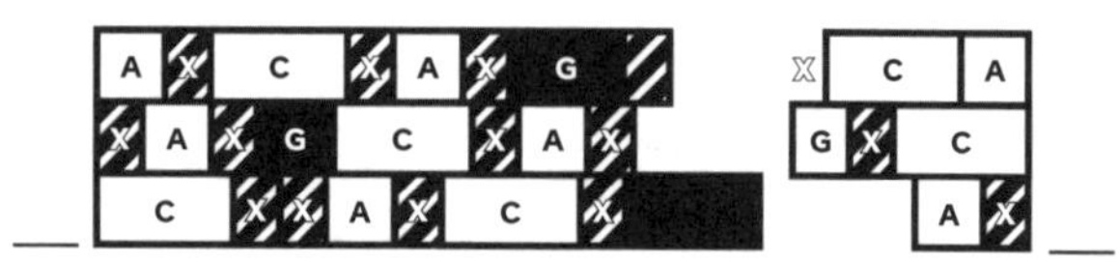

☐ Private
■ Communal

Collage, "Wunschmaschine Wohnanlage" ("Dream Machine residential complex")

Axonometric drawing, "Wunschmaschine Wohnanlage" ("Dream Machine residential complex")

SOMETHING FANTASTIC
CONSTELLATION HOUSE, 2021

Though people's lives are made up of cycles that evolve over time and in response to changes in circumstances and conditions, typical apartment unit floor plans are entirely static. Constellation House aims to align the places of living with the rhythms of daily life by proposing a new high-density residential model that breaks apartments up into rooms for day and night on different floors. Circadian rhythms determine the layout of the building, which allows for certain spaces that cater to being alone (the night rooms) and others that support collectivity (the day rooms). The design also addresses time on a longer-term and more communal scale: children grow up, parents age, and relationships dissolve, all of which can result in vacancies within conventional housing types. The day and night rooms can thus be rented either to or from neighbours as needed, while the communal floors function as larger gathering spaces. By dividing the building into day and night rooms, changes in household structures and members can more easily be accommodated.

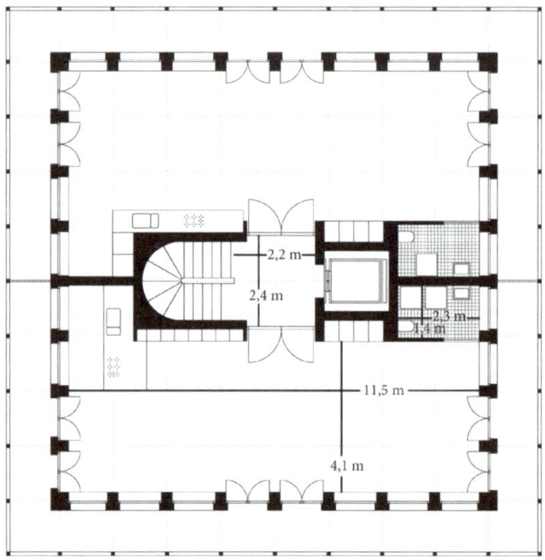

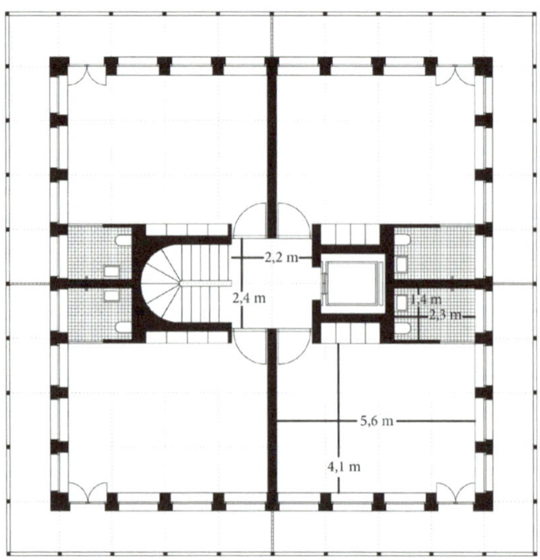

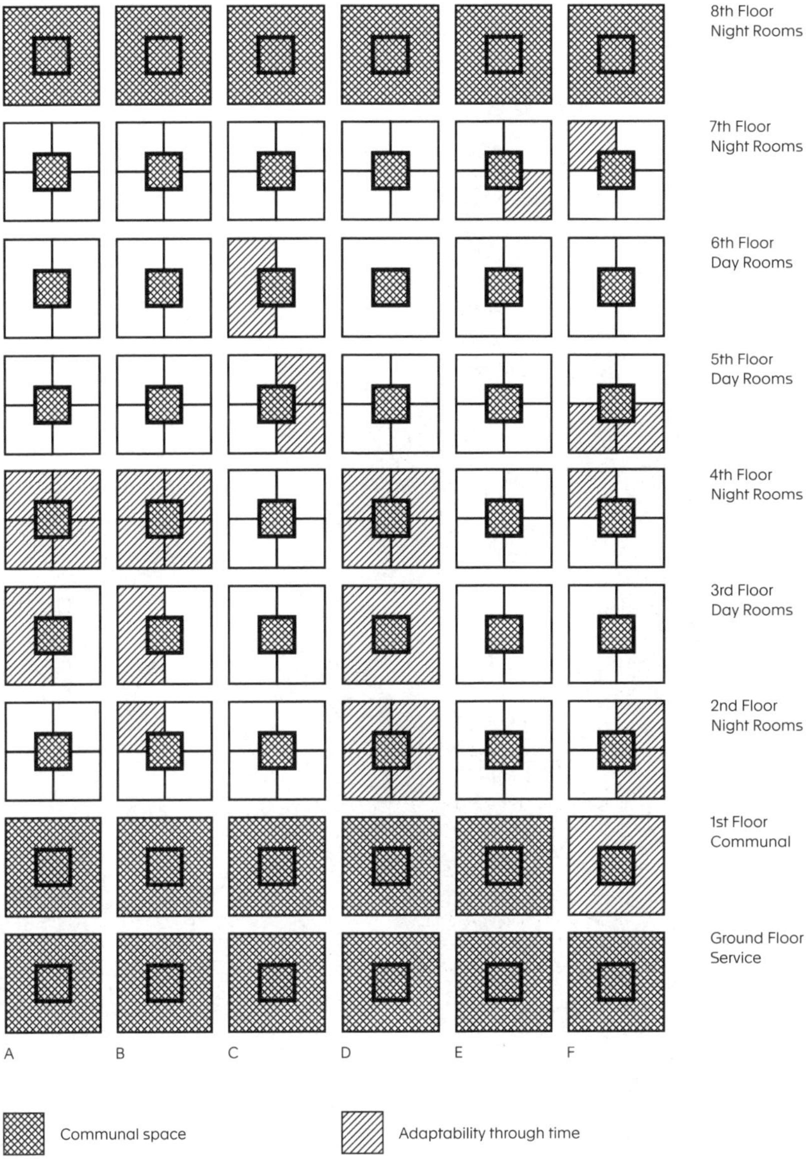

Floor plan usage constellations

A
The initial apartment features one day room and four independent night rooms connected through the communal staircase.

B
If the spatial needs of a resident grow, they may rent additional independent night rooms from one of the other residents.

C
If their spatial needs become less, they can rent out some of their independent night rooms, either to a neighbour or to external persons on a day-to-day basis.

D
If two parties decide to use their day rooms together, they can do so without compromising on their night privacy.

E
If the house decides to have a communal guest room, this is possible without any further modification of the structure.

F
If in later years the spatial needs of the residents shrink, one of the communal floors could be used as a lobby for a guest house, that rents out all the night rooms no longer needed on a day-to-day basis. The possibility of using these night rooms when family members return is kept open.

Aubrey Wade, *No Stranger Place*, 2015

Aubrey Wade, *No Stranger Place*, 2017

Aubrey Wade, *No Stranger Place*, 2016

Aubrey Wade, *No Stranger Place*, 2016

9: © Dafydd Jones from *Screen Time* published by Circa Press

10: © Peter Titmuss/Alamy Stock Photo

13: © Jamie Diamond

17: © Samantha Friend

20: © OMMX

21: © Degelo Architekten

24: © Common Accounts

28: © Vincent Fournier

31: © Terra0

42-47: © Alice Proujansky

49: © Bob Daemmrich/ Alamy Stock Photo

50, 51: © Samantha Ingalina, Benson Chien

52: © Mariah Tauger, Los Angeles Times/Getty Images

53: © 2050+ and -orama

54, 55: © Jesse LeCavalier

56: © Comedy Central

72: © Sveriges Television SVT

78: © Certain Measures

79: © Stephan Bogner, Philipp Schmitt, and Jonas Voight

80: © Joel Eden Photography/Kiva Systems

82: © StrongArm Technologies Inc. All rights reserved

88: Pods (from L to R): © Phonebooths Inc. All rights reserved © BUSYPOD. All rights reserved © Office Pods by Getawayer Canada Inc. All rights reserved © Orangebox Limited. All rights reserved

89: © Nemo Miller. All rights reserved. Photo © Janelle Hanson

90–95: © Michael Schmelling

99: © N H D M

105: © CCA

106: © Endemol. Photo Getty Images

118–123: © Michelle Groskopf

124: © JesseDStreams

125: © CCA

126: © Monkeypaw Productions

138–143: © Paul Graham

148: © Edwin Bruining/HIG Traffic Systems. All Rights Reserved

149: © Klemens Schillinger. Photo © Leonard Hilzensauer

152–157: © Lucas Foglia

158, 159: © UNSense

160, 161, 163: © CCA

162: © The Future Market

164: © Broadway Video

170–175: © Bryan Thomas

176: © Bloomberg/Getty Images

177: © CCA

179, 180: © Estudio Teddy Cruz + Fonna Forman

182: © 40 Acres and a Mule. Photo David Lee/Courtesy Everett Collection/Alamy Stock Photo

188: © BIPOC Studios

202: © USA Network. Image: Getty Images

204: © Coop Himmelb(l)au. Photo © Markus Pillhofer

205: © CCA

212–217: © Brittany M. Powell

219: © Podshare

220, 221: © Edouard Francois

222, 223: © Jack Self

224–227: © Dogma + NEW Academy

229: © CCA

230: © Assemble

232: © Big Talk Productions

234, 235: © Sam Chermayeff Office

236–239: © June14 Meyer-Grohbrügge & Chermayeff

240, 241: © Other Architects

244–249: © Nadia Sablin

250–253: © Pollard Thomas Edwards

254: © Skydance Television. Image: Alamy Stock Photo

268: © Cameron Pictures

270: © OFFICE Kersten Geers David Van Severen

272: © LATENT Productions (@latentnyc) and Columbia GSAPP DeathLAB (@gsappDeathLAB)

274: © Dan Kun yi Chen

276: © Common Accounts

284: © Amazon Studios

286, 287: © Williamson Williamson

288: © Go Hasegawa + Associates

290–295: © Elisabeth Ubbe

300: © June14 Meyer-Grohbrügge & Chermayeff

301: © Ai Hasegawa

302: © Showtime Networks Inc.

304: © Kamila Rudnicka

308–313: © Elena Dorfman

314: © Two Brothers Pictures

316–319: © Takahashi Ippei Office

320–325: © Jamie Diamond

326: © Lucy McRae. Photo Scottie Cameron

328: © Sony Pictures Television

330: © Kent Kirkland and Monica McGrath

333: © Yangying Ye

334, 335: © Anais Langlais-Schmidt

340: © Twentieth Century Fox. Image AF archive/ Alamy Stock Photo

342, 343: © Christoph Wagner Architekten

344, 345: © Expanded Design

346, 347: © Something Fantastic

348–355: © Aubrey Wade

2050+ and -orama
Christopher Anderson
Nicolas Asfouri, Assemble Studio
Center for Spatial Technologies
Certain Measures
Dan Chen
Sam Chermayeff Office
Benson Chien and Samantha Ingallina
Aaron M. Cohen
Thaddé Comar
Common Accounts
Coop Himmelb(l)au
Degelo Architekten and Gamperle AG
Cynthia Deng and Arta Perezic
Jamie Diamond
Dogma + NEW Academy
Elena Dorfman
Republic of Estonia
Estudio Teddy Cruz+Fonna Forman and Kotti+Co
Expanded Design
Lucas Foglia
Maison Édouard François
The Future Market
Salwan Georges
Ginger Design Studio
Paul Graham
Michelle Groskopf
Max Hampshire, Paul Kolling, and Paul Seidler
Ai Hasegawa
Go Hasegawa+Associates
Het Nieuwe Instituut
HOME-OFFICE
Taikan Hoshino
Dafydd Jones
June14 Meyer-Grohbrügge & Chermayeff
Anaïs Langlais-Schmidt
LATENT Productions and Columbia University GSAPP
DeathLAB
Jesse LeCavalier
Stefan Marx
Valérian Mazataud
Marisa Morán Jahn and Rafi Segal
Mueller Sigrist Architekten
Christinne Muschi
N H D M
Ewa Nowak
OFFICE Kersten Geers David Van Severen
Other Architects
Pollard Thomas Edwards
Brittany M. Powell
Alice Proujansky
Anna Puigjaner MAIO
rework
Kamila Rudnicka
Nadia Sablin
Klemens Schillinger
Michael Schmelling
Jack Self
Space Popular
Something Fantastic
Giulia Spadafora
Special Projects
Marie-Claire Springham
StrongArm Technologies
Takahashi Ippei Office
Teple Misto
terra0
Bryan Thomas
Elisabeth Ubbe
UNSense
Jonas Voigt, Philipp Schmitt, and Stephan Bogner
Aubrey Wade
Christoph Wagner Architekten
Nick Waplington
Williamson Williamson
Hardy Wilson
Yangying Ye

COLOPHON

A SECTION OF NOW:
SOCIAL NORMS AND RITUALS AS SITES FOR
ARCHITECTURAL INTERVENTION

This volume is published by the Canadian Centre for Architecture (CCA) and Spector Books in conjunction with the exhibition *A Section Of Now: Social Norms And Rituals As Sites For Architectural Intervention*, organized by and presented at the CCA from 13 November 2021 to 1 May 2022.

Publication:
Editor: Giovanna Borasi
Editors-in-charge: Ushma Thakrar with Alexandra Pereira-Edwards
Project texts: Hannah Strothmann, Matthew de Santis, Megan Marin, Ushma Thakrar, Alexandra Pereira-Edwards
Editorial assistance: Matthew Kalil
Photography consultant: Melissa Harris
TV consultant: Andrea Bellavita
Translation from Italian: Art Apart, GmbH (Steven Piccolo)
Proofing: Katie Moore and Alexandra Pereira-Edwards
Rights and reproductions: Stéphane Aleixandre
Graphic design: Folder Studio, Los Angeles
Graphic design assistance: Jack Burnside
Printing and binding: die Keure

Exhibition:
Curator: Giovanna Borasi
Curatorial team: Francesco Garutti, Megan Marin, Hannah Strothmann, Ushma Thakrar
Research: Matthew de Santis, Iro Kalargyrou, and Laura Aparicio Llorente
Photography consultant: Melissa Harris
TV consultant: Andrea Bellavita
Exhibition design: Sam Chermayeff Office, Berlin & New York
Graphic design: Folder Studio, Los Angeles
Design development: Sébastien Larivière and Anh Truong, with Jasmine Graham

The Canadian Centre for Architecture is an international research centre and museum founded by Phyllis Lambert in 1979 on the conviction that architecture is a public concern. Through its collection, exhibitions, public programs, publications, and research opportunities the CCA advances knowledge, promotes public understanding, and widens thought and debate on architecture, its history, theory, practice, and its role in society today.

CCA Board of Trustees:
Phyllis Lambert, Founding Director Emeritus
Bruce Kuwabara, Chair
Pierre-André Themens, Vice-Chair
Guido Beltramini
Giovanna Borasi
Stephen R. Bronfman
Barry Campbell
Michael Conforti
Timur Galen
Sylvia Lavin
Frederick Lowy
Greg Lynn
Gerald Sheff
Serge Joyal, Honourary Member
Warren Simpson, Honourary Member

The CCA gratefully acknowledges the support of la Ville de Montréal, le ministère de la Culture et des Communications, the Canada Council for the Arts, and the Conseil des arts de Montréal.

COLOPHON

© 2021 Canadian Centre for Architecture, Montréal
All rights reserved under international copyright conventions.

No part of this book may be reproduced or utilized in any form or by any means, electronic or mechanical, including photocopying, recording, or any information storage and retrieval system, without permission in writing from the publisher, or in Canada, a license from the Canadian Copyright Licensing Agency. For a copyright license, please visit www.accesscopyright.ca or call (800) 893-5777.

Legal deposit: 2021
Printed and bound in the European Union
First edition

978-1-927071-77-9
Canadian Centre for Architecture
1920 rue Baile
Montréal, Québec
Canada H3H 2S6
www.cca.qc.ca

978-3-95905-507-9
Spector Books OHG
Harkortstraße 10
04107 Leipzig
Germany
www.spectorbooks.com

Bibliothèque et Archives nationales du Québec and Library and Archives Canada cataloguing in publication

Title: A Section of Now: Social Norms and Rituals as Sites for Architectural Intervention/editor, Giovanna Borasi; authors, Ann Neumann, Helen Hester, Nina Power, Jen Schradie, Joanne McNeil.
Names: Borasi, Giovanna, 1971– editor. | Neumann, Ann (Author), author. | Hester, Helen, 1983– author. | Power, Nina, author. | Schradie, Jen, author. | McNeil, Joanne, author. | Centre canadien d'architecture, issuing body.

Description: Issued also in French under title: Une portion du présent : les normes et rituels sociaux comme sites d'intervention architecturale. | Co-published by Spector Books OHG.
Identifiers: Canadiana 20210050233 | ISBN 9781927071779 (softcover)

Subjects: LCSH: Architecture and society. | LCSH: Social norms.
Classification: LCC NA2543.S6 S43 2021 | DDC 720.1/03—dc23

Distribution:
Germany, Austria: GVA, Gemeinsame Verlagsauslieferung Göttingen GmbH&Co. KG, www.gva-verlage.de
Switzerland: AVA Verlagsauslieferung AG, www.ava.ch
France, Belgium: Interart Paris, www.interart.fr
UK: Central Books Ltd, www.centralbooks.com
USA, Canada, Central and South America, Africa: ARTBOOK/ D.A.P., www.artbook.com
South Korea: The Book Society, www.thebooksociety.org
Japan: twelvebooks, www.twelve-books.com
Australia, New Zealand: Perimeter Distribution, www.perimeterdistribution.com